GOD SAVE THE FAN

GOD SAVE THE FAN

HOW PREENING SPORTSCASTERS, ATHLETES WHO SPEAK IN THE THIRD PERSON, AND THE OCCASIONAL CONVICTED QUARTERBACK HAVE TAKEN THE FUN OUT OF SPORTS (AND HOW WE CAN GET IT BACK)

Will Leitch

WITH ILLUSTRATIONS BY JIM COOKE

HARPER

An Imprint of HarperCollinsPublishers
www.harpercollins.com

HarperCollins books may be purchased for educational, business, or sales promotional use. For information, please write: Special Markets Department, Harper-Collins Publishers, 10 East 53rd Street, New York, NY 10022.

Grateful acknowledgment is made to the following for permission to reprint illustrations: Lou Cabron/10ZenMonkeys.com, page 126; Jim Cooke: pages viii, 8, 84, 132, 224, 286; Jim Cooke/The Black Table, page 272; A. J. Daulerio/The Black Table, page 196; Deadspin: page 33; Aileen Gallagher/The Black Table, pages 56, 57, 58, 61; Matthew Johnson/289 Studios, page 289; Will Leitch, page 172; John Price/Deadspin.com, page 147; Brett Shebish/Deadspin.com, page 35; Scott Shelley/Deadspin.com, page 162.

FIRST EDITION

Illustrations by Jim Cooke

Library of Congress Cataloging-in-Publication Data is available upon request.

ISBN: 978-0-06-135178-5

08 09 10 11 12   WBC/RRD   10 9 8 7 6 5 4 3 2 1

For the three people who turned me on to sports:
Bryan Leitch, Mary Dooley, and Willie McGee

CONTENTS

INTRODUCTION

In which your intrepid narrator attempts to use Michael Vick as a metaphor for a new age of sports journalism while spending only fifty words on that whole dogfighting business. Includes the phrase "Feed the donkey."

In April 2005, The Smoking Gun—the investigative journalism Web site devoted to uncovering public documents that get lost in our nation's labyrinthine legal system—posted a complaint from a woman named Sonya Elliot. A twenty-six-year-old health care worker with difficulties keeping her own health care in order, Elliot had sued a man for giving her herpes simplex 2. (That's the herpes that, according to our friends at Wikipedia, is characterized by lesions "on the shaft of the penis, in the genital region, on the inner thigh, buttocks, or anus." So you know.) She confronted the man at his Georgia home, telling him, "I've got something to tell you. I've got it."

The man, as any man in his position might have done, lay before her and begged for forgiveness. Elliot claimed "[the man] had not known how to tell her about his condition, and that it was not something that he liked to talk about." (Understandable.) The man, worried about his standing in the public eye, asked her not to reveal his condition but made no offer to make amends, financially or otherwise. She researched the matter and learned that, to protect himself, he had undergone herpes "testing and treatment" under a fake name. His choice of moniker: "Ron Mexico." This is one of those pseudonyms that is funny for an abundance of reasons, almost all of which are impossible to quantify. (Though it does conjure up images of sombreros, wispy mustaches, and, perhaps, a burro.) Had this man taken care of the woman to whom he had given herpes from the beginning, she would have never filed a lawsuit—and the name "Ron Mexico" would have never reached the public consciousness. And that, friends, would be a tragedy.

As just about everybody now knows, "Ron Mexico" is Atlanta Falcons quarterback Michael Vick. In 2008, Vick is known as the perpetually embattled former phenom who flips his home fans the (nonfoam) middle finger, carries marijuana onto airplanes, and enjoys watching dogs kill each other.

We could talk for hours about Vick's dogfighting conviction, and what it meant in a cultural sense, but I'm going to claim the Nancy Grace Sports Rule on this one: The minute a sports story becomes fodder for cable talk shows—see *Lacrosse, Duke* and *Bonds, Barry*—it transforms into something that's not the slightest bit of fun for real sports fans to talk about. We're gonna focus on the pre-dogfighting Vick, the one who once seemed like the most exciting football player we'd ever seen, even though he was electrocuting puppies at the time.

Actually, now he's pretty much *just* known for killing the dogs himself. Which is the type of "do it yourself" attitude we admire in our athletes. But in 2005, Vick was the face of the NFL, the most marketable athlete in the U.S.A.'s most marketable sport. He was young, charismatic, and blessed with extraordinary talent. He was a primary endorser of Nike and Gatorade. A commercial at the time featured Michael Vick: The Ride, in which a fan, at an amusement park, straps into a seat and is rocketed across a football field as if he is Vick. He darts to and fro, flips about, and just misses landing in a group of large men with long hair before a final end-zone gyration. Four months before the lawsuit, Vick had signed a ten-year, $130 million contract, the richest deal in NFL history. Michael Vick was the face of the NFL, the sport America reveres and obsesses over more than any other. He very well might have been on his way to becoming the most popular athlete on earth.

And here he was, accused of giving a woman herpes and attempting to hide it by using the most ridiculous alias imaginable. (I have tried to come up with one that's more amusing. The best I could do was "Harvey Guam." It doesn't come close.) The whole incident was a matter of public record.

I read The Smoking Gun with jaw agape. Vick had been an untouchable and smiling corporate beacon who could do no wrong. He stood as the future of athletics, the man who would be football's version of Michael Jordan, only with braids. And now *this*. I eagerly awaited the public reaction. Would he be mocked on ESPN talk shows? What would the *New York Post* headline be? ("MEXICO'S PROBLEMS SOUTH OF THE BORDER" was my guess.) How would his coaches handle the news? Would it cost him his endorsement possibilities? (I couldn't imagine Gatorade would like its spokesperson to gulp its beverage while sporting a lip sore.) Would his wide receivers suddenly be afraid to catch his passes? Would they wear an extra pair of gloves? I couldn't wait for the fallout.

I zipped over to ESPN.com, the Web site I checked twenty times a day and used as the alpha and omega of sports coverage, and found . . . nothing. Not a single mention. I went back and checked the date on The Smoking Gun story; it was actually three days old. Perhaps, however unlikely, I'd missed the story on ESPN? I headed back into the archive, on the Falcons team page, on Vick's personal page. As Ron himself might say, *Nada*. This simply could not be. Surely, ESPN, the arbiter of all that affected the world of sports, hadn't missed the whole story? Vick news had anchored half the SportsCenters of the previous year, and he'd been featured on the cover of the network's magazine twice in the last six months. (Impressive, considering it comes out every two weeks.) Obviously, *somebody* over there had to have known. Right?

Two weeks later, my copy of *Sports Illustrated* arrived. Though the magazine had become conspicuously thinner in recent years, it was still all I used to parse a week's worth of sports news and to gain some perspective. I'd read *Sports Illustrated* since I was a boy; my first masturbatory experience was to its swimsuit issue. (At least I *hope* it was the swimsuit issue.) *SI* was the Mount Everest of American sportswriting, the magazine of record. With much joy, I noticed this particular week's issue had Michael Vick on the cover! At last: Someone had finally tackled the story I'd been trying in vain to talk to my friends about for the last fortnight.

I ripped open the magazine and flipped directly to the Vick story. It opened with an anecdote about Vick coming *this* close to reaching the Super Bowl, and rehashed all his teammates' tales of wonder at his amazing athleticism. The Falcons had a new coach that year, and insisted that Atlanta run the West Coast Offense, a system that would appear to be antithetical to Vick's particular skill set. The story detailed all the issues in Falcons minicamp, how Vick was working with his coach and trying to make the system work for him. This was all information I already had; *when were they going to mention Ron Mexico?*

And then I finished the story. There was nothing. I kept looking to see if I'd missed a section where the story jumped, or if I'd accidentally glossed over the Mexico mention. I reread this story three times. Michael Vick—the representative of all that is supposedly right about the world of sports, a man being sued for giving a woman herpes and using a bizarre name to hide the story—was on the cover of a national magazine . . . and the herpes business wasn't once mentioned. This was *the cover story*. And nothing. *Nada.*

This was *precisely* the type of story sports fans eat up, and the two major sports media outlets had entirely ignored it. If they weren't going to talk about it, who would?

I found this all a bit odd.

LATER, after I'd started Deadspin, an independent sports blog I founded to discuss and ferret out stories like the Ron Mexico one, stories that real sports fans actually talk about, I asked one of my sources at ESPN why they had ignored the Mexico story. His response was telling:

"Will, there's no way ESPN is gonna touch that story with a ten-foot pole. You know how much money the NFL pays ESPN? You know how much money they have invested in Michael Vick? The minute we ran with that story, we'd have NFL PR jumping down our throats within a matter of seconds. They'd kill us, and we knew it."

To this day, if you do a search for "Ron Mexico" on ESPN.com, the only results that show up are fans' fantasy team names. And yet, I understood ESPN's position. When you are the only game in town, and your business is staying in the good graces of the leagues that provide you with access, you can't exactly start raining firebombs on those leagues' sacred cows. But, I wondered, if ESPN isn't going to report that story, and *SI* wasn't going to report that story, who was? It was then that I decided to start Deadspin. The world has herpes to blame.

The notion of Deadspin was to speak to the average sports fan, the guy (or lady) who plunks down $40 for a game and wants to shoot the shit with his/her buddies in the upper deck. An easy populist position, I grant you—but that was the plan. I had the advantage of having once worked as a sports reporter and realizing that it's a soul-crushing job that sucks all the fun out of sports. I had seen the sunken eyes of those who once dreamed of a career in sports and later realized that "career" meant sitting in a cramped box with bitter middle-aged bald men trained not to react with joy to the sports they once revered. When you cover sports on a regular basis, you don't cheer for something revelatory to happen; you root for the game to be over quickly so you can get back to the hotel. Sports becomes a *job*. And sports should never be a job. I had no desire to work for ESPN, or as a full-time sports reporter, so doing Deadspin—which had no connection to any team, league, or sports organization—allowed me to stand aside and observe the world of sports the way a fan does; that is, the way a normal person does. I wanted fans to be involved in the sports world, to shape their own experience of the games. I wanted to write about sports the way we talk about sports. And I wanted Deadspin to be about all of us, to be a place where sports fans could talk to one another without the barricade that decades of sports coverage has placed in our way.

I've been fortunate enough to see that happen; it was clear that sports fans had been hungering for a place to congregate without all the clutter that had weighed them down for years. I take no particular credit for this. I never wanted the site to be some sort of "Hey, everybody, I'm Will, here are my opinions on sports, now react to me" site, the way most mainstream sports media corporations had patterned their new media endeavors. I never felt that Deadspin sparked a movement because of my wit and wisdom. What makes Deadspin fun, and what makes every day I work on it better than the last, is that everyone takes part. It's not my site; it belongs to the readers who contribute and comment as a means to take some time away from their day jobs. No longer would a story be kept from us fans because it was financially advantageous for someone to do so. We could take charge and write our own script for the sports world. They're our games, after all.

Years of major media inertia has fomented a culture of complacent hero worship, bland game recaps, and stale "up with people" soft focus features that are meant to humanize the athletes—but in fact only reinforces the Athletes Are Different from You and Me maxim that has defined sports coverage for decades. But that's not why we, the fans, watch sports. We watch sports to be entertained. Life is hard, man; every day, we are faced with the crippling challenges of daily life. We worry about our job, our family, our friends, our careers, our mortgages. We worry that if we don't keep constant vigilance, it will all come crashing down on us. We worry that we'll always be at war; we worry that someone's gonna show up at the mall with a dirty bomb and destroy everyone. We just try to stay on top of it all. And we need something to take our minds off all this shit that keeps us up at night. We need sports. Sports are what we watch when we just can't look at another spreadsheet. They're what we use when we need to get away from our lives for a little bit. Every human needs the escape, and sports provides this splendidly.

By definition, anyone who works in the world of sports, whether as a player, a coach, a broadcaster, a reporter, the guy who rubs Kobe Bryant's calves after every game, whoever . . . by definition, they all believe sports are more important than they actually are. Why wouldn't they? *Sports are their lives.* When you take sports so seriously, when your very livelihood depends on it, you by definition cannot relate to the way that the average sports fan connects to sports. Sports are what we fans invest ourselves in to get *away* from life; when it is your entire life, you end up writing stories only for those who also write, broadcasting only for those who also broadcast.

It is natural that those whose entire lives revolve around sports would be threatened by fan empowerment; after all, we're the ones who pay for all this. If we all realized that, hey, we don't need to listen to these idiots on television screaming at us . . . they'd be out of a job. But it's vital for sports fans to realize that we *don't* need them, that we can choose what we want now.

We just have to take charge and realize our power. Hopefully this book will help with that. And if it doesn't, hopefully it will at least be funny. Because if we cannot laugh at the ridiculous world of sports, we truly cannot laugh at anything.

So strap in, put on your protective gloves, and let's catch some Ron Mexico passes. Put on the sombrero, grow the mustache, feed the donkey. There's a whole new world out there: Let's go.

PLEASE, GOD, NO, NOT ANOTHER ESSAY ABOUT STEROIDS

Let's just say, hypothetically speaking, that you are not an accountant, a systems analyst, or one who lays pipe for a living in a nonsexual way. Let's say, instead of whatever it is that you do, you are an inventor—a chemist, even.

Let's say that during your rigorous studies in the field of chemistry (with a little biology thrown in, you know, for the *ladies*), you come across an amazing compound. This compound, accidentally discovered while searching for an even *more* effective way to give your grandfather an erection, has regenerative powers beyond the realm of human comprehension. When you test this compound on lab rats, they not only recover from strenuous activity quicker—whatever strenuous activity lab rats might need to recover from—they actually grow muscle mass *without any physical activity at all.* That is to say this compound makes the rats stronger, faster, and smarter . . . it turns them into superrats.

You are amazed by this discovery but are concerned about the rats. Would they become overly aggressive? Would they suffer from reduced genital size—a serious problem, though, hey, it happens to lots of rats!—or perhaps some sort of heart ailment? You run them through every test you can find, and nothing appears to be wrong with them. All the compound did was turn them into muscle-bound, physically and mentally superior rats, with no side effects whatsoever. Full of fevered dreams of a Nobel Prize (and all the cascading fountains of poon that come with it), you decide not to worry about a test group of human subjects; you skip that step and just distill it into liquid form—you call it, oh, Jesus Juice or something—and drink it down yourself.

You notice the effect within seconds. You are instantly bench-pressing twice your body weight, running a mile in six minutes, and able to solve sudoku puzzles in a matter of seconds. You're perhaps most dumbfounded by your hand-eye coordination; when you accidentally knock over a bottle of your magic beverage, you are stunned that you instinctively grab it before it hits the floor. After about six hours, the effects wear off, so you drink some more, and it all comes back. You immediately submit the juice to the Food and Drug Administration, and after years of testing, they officially announce that the juice (since dubbed "Jack Sauce," after your four-year-old son who can now juggle cars) has nothing but positive effects on human beings. No long-term negative effects, no added stress on the body, no problems whatsoever. It's all good. *Nothing is wrong with Jack Sauce at all.*

A statue of you is erected in your hometown, and you spend the rest of your life wearing suits of thousand-dollar bills and having a series of initially thrilling threesomes that provide diminishing returns but are still worth the trouble. You sail into your golden years as the most beloved and famous human being on the planet. Congratulations!

Okay. Now, legitimate question: If this Jack Sauce existed, and it truly had no side effects and only brought joy and health to humans, would it be okay for athletes to use it before games? Could they drink down a good batch before taking the field? If they were feeling worn down in the seventh inning, could they do a few shots between innings?

Or would that be cheating? Immoral?

How you feel about that question can be instructive to consider when weighing in on the issue of steroids. For all the column inches and broadcast minutes devoted to the concept, it's difficult to find a single side to the "debate" that makes much sense. And it's something we better figure out pretty soon, because if you think performance enhancers are bad now, just wait. Science is a crazy thing; Jack Sauce will be here before you know it.

HEADING into the 2006 National League Championship Series, the St. Louis Cardinals were extremely concerned about third baseman Scott Rolen. Rolen had struggled with injuries throughout his career, but by Game 3 of the NLCS he was as banged up as he had ever been. His shoulder hurt, his knee hurt, he even had a sticky film on him that just wouldn't rinse away. He was an absolute mess, but his shoulder was the biggest sore spot; he couldn't generate any bat speed and was slumping when the Cardinals needed him most.

Rolen—a tough midwestern guy whose face looks like he's more suited for riding a combine and complaining about how the Dixie Chicks are gettin' too goddamned liberal—had been feuding with manager Tony LaRussa about the extent of his injury. In a last-ditch effort to bump Rolen up somewhere near 100 percent, LaRussa went to Cardinals trainer Barry Weinberg (See? There are Jews in sports! They're the trainers!) and requested a cortisone shot. The cortisone shot is a staple in sports, used to provide temporary relief for lingering pain in trouble spots.

The cortisone shot is also a—gasp!—steroid. Cortisone is produced naturally by the body, released automatically when a person is under stress. Injectable cortisone is produced in a lab but is rather close to what the body produces on its own. It is, by definition, a performance enhancer, and it's even an *injection*. If something hurts, you can inject it with cortisone, and the pain will go away. It is a far more effective and immediate performance enhancer than human growth hormone or

Decadrol or whatever else players are always trying to sneak past the censors (that is, if said censors happen to exist).

The thing about cortisone is that it has no side effects. It doesn't do anything but make a person feel better.

So, Rolen took his shot and, lo and behold, within a matter of hours he started hitting the ball again. His reinvigorated bat, along with the Bugs Bunny curveball of closer Adam Wainwright and the power that Jeff Suppan derived from his hatred of stem cells, led the Cardinals to a series victory and, ultimately, a World Series title. (Woo!) Suddenly, Rolen and Tony LaRussa weren't fighting anymore, and no one remembered his earlier slump. He was a hero.

And nobody gave a damn about his cortisone shot. In fact, fans, if they knew about the cortisone shot at all, were ecstatic about it—anything to get him to start driving the ball to right-center again. And why wouldn't the fans be happy? Science helped an athlete best utilize his natural abilities through a synthetic compound that artificially tricked his body into thinking it was healing itself. That's exactly what a steroid does. This one just happened to not have any downside to it. And someday, no steroids will.

Meanwhile, Mark McGwire, Barry Bonds, Jose Canseco, and Rafael Palmeiro have put up the most historic of numbers during an age of baseball when every aspect of the game is focused on the home run—a.k.a. the "Look How Big *My* Cock Is" period—and they're the pariahs we flagellate for all the sins of an era. These men's heads grew to Rosie O'Donnell size while their testicles shriveled to the size of, oh, Rosie O'Donnell's, and their back looks like your face did when all you could think of was your algebra teacher while masturbating into a sock. (And by "when" I mean "Tuesday.") These players, while they (mostly) deny it, bore the signs of serious steroid users, but they were hardly the only ones, doing it during a time when there were no rules against it and probably facing pitchers just as roided up as they were. None of those players will likely make the Hall of Fame—Bonds has the best chance—and they will forever have the word "steroids" attached to their name. If there's a day that McGwire walks down the street and isn't serenaded with "Hey, Mark, I'd ask you how your day is going, but I'm not here to talk about the past," that will be a day that McGwire decided not to walk down the street. It's over for him, and all of them.

But we love the cortisone shots. If anything, McGwire and company are being punished for bad science; they were unfortunate to play in an age when the steroids were crude and could actually cause long-term damage. They are labeled cheaters, as if there were a time before them that the game was "pure," like there will ever be a time like that in the future. We scream at these guys because it's easy to.

I should hesitate to use the term "we," though, because most fans, deep down, don't really care about steroids that much. Most fans, as much as they might like to throw plastic syringes at Bonds and boo McGwire during the rare times that he pops his head out of his mole hole, are much more pure about sports than paid sportswriters. We don't fool ourselves into harboring illusions. We'd really rather not know, but if we do have to know, we'd prefer that our team just win. If McGwire had led the Cardinals to a World Series title, Cardinals fans wouldn't have minded if he had scored the winning run while in the throes of an ether binge. This is not an instance of fans sticking their collective heads in the sand, as many sportswriters would like to perceive it. It's a matter of keeping our sports in perspective.

Baseball suffers the brunt of the steroids controversy, because baseball is the sport that most writers care the most about, and—more important—probably once played and believed, in their heart of hearts, that they could have actually thrived at, if that damned high school coach had just believed in them. (I am 100 percent guilty of this; if Mark Jackley had recognized my brilliance at pitch calling and blocking balls in the dirt for the

1993 Mattoon Green Wave, I'm convinced I'd be backing up Yadier Molina right now. And I'd give a damned good quote and be extra special double plus nice to the groupies too.) Baseball is seen as the game that normal people can play—this is the only reason why John Kruk was so popular; it is astounding that he's now making a living by *talking*—so when superhuman players dominate the game, it destroys the fantasy that baseball is the people's game. Thus, everyone comes down harder on the baseball players. Nobody cares that everyone's doping in cycling and track and field. Who plays those sports anyway? Can you even call those sports?

And don't kid yourself: Everyone's doping. NFL commissioner Roger Goodell must pray to his Ditka every night that baseball takes all the steroid hits for his league. Two years ago, it came out that four Carolina Panthers players actually bought and used steroids *the week before the Super Bowl*. Can you imagine if it had been proven that Bonds did that before the World Series in 2002? People would *still* be anal-raping that guy. But with football no one seemed to notice. People were just surprised that one of the users was the punter.

Then, two years ago, San Diego Chargers linebacker Shawne Merriman, one of the top defensive players in the game, tested positive for an injectable steroid (typically, he said it was accidentally ingested from an over-the-counter supplement, which is like saying you "accidentally" had sex with your secretary) and was suspended for four games. Was there outrage and betrayal? Was the sports world finally convinced of the NFL's epic steroid menace? Well, let's compare the reactions to Merriman's positive test to Rafael Palmeiro's just more than a year earlier.

Michael Wilbon on Palmeiro (*Washington Post*, August 3, 2005)

"Oh yes, baseball is facing a crisis. In this current climate of suspicion, is it fair to start looking at any pitcher with biceps with increased skepticism, too? Well, maybe it isn't fair. But that won't stop anyone. And where, exactly, is the commissioner of baseball while such an obvious crisis breaks out? Apparently hiding under his desk."

John Clayton on Merriman (ESPN, October 23, 2006)

"The four-game steroid suspension of Chargers linebacker Shawne Merriman really comes at a horrible time for the team. Linebacker Shaun Phillips is expected to be out four to six weeks with a calf injury. They've lost linebacker Steve Foley for the season. The only outside linebacker of note is Marques Harris or Nick Speegle, which might force the Chargers to move Tim Dobbins or Donnie Edwards to the outside."

NOW that's some hand-wringing! (During the 2007 season, Merriman never got his own Nike ad.) Those who defend the NFL stance on steroids say that NFL fans are just more honest than baseball fans; they already assumed that most of the NFL was roiding up and therefore just pout if one of the guys on their fantasy team gets caught and misses a few games. It is generous to call this a "defense"; still, the average fan has more important questions to attend to than "Is the game on the level?" Because, it isn't.

This is hardly just a sports thing. Show me an industry in which the vital players don't try to take every opportunity to give themselves even the slightest competitive edge, and I'll show you an industry that isn't around anymore. The NFL can't afford to be entirely honest about the raw number of its players who use performance-enhancing drugs, but we fans know the score. And we don't mind.

But this doesn't stop the *tsk-tsk*ing of the average sportswriter, most of whom gleefully ignored the steroid "problem" of the '90s because they were too busy giving McGwire and Sosa prose back rubs. But that's the thing: There really isn't a steroid problem. There's just a perception problem. You can't fine or suspend scientists, and you'll never discover a test that will detect everything. And, all told, we'd rather you not discover one anyway. If Scott Rolen needs a steroid to win games for the Cardinals, legal or otherwise, as long as he wins them, I don't care. Just don't tell me. Being a sports fan mostly involves blissful ignorance of the outside world, and that is just *fine*. That is, after all, why we watch sports in the first place.

And if you think we don't mind now, wait until the Jack Sauce is invented. Frankly, I'd like to type an extra twenty words a minute. I might even figure out a way to rid myself of all those dangling modifiers and extraneous adverbs, which I have a tendency to overdeploy, extensively. Please don't test my urine.

WHY GILBERT ARENAS MATTERS MORE THAN LEBRON JAMES

During the 2007 NBA playoffs, when the Cavaliers were making their run to the finals, I noticed something odd among my fellow sports fans: Everyone was rooting against LeBron James. Anytime I'd watch a game with someone, or I'd mention LeBron on Deadspin, the instant reaction was mild (with the exception of that semifinals Game 5 vs. Detroit).

This is the opposite of what one would expect. Since the age of fifteen, LeBron has been groomed for the role of NBA supernova. He was on the cover of *Sports Illustrated* at the age of seventeen, he signed a $90 million deal with Nike before he'd played his first game, he had a ready-made entourage (that included Jay-Z!) on the day the Cavaliers won the right to draft him. Everyone was initially concerned that a teenager wouldn't be able to handle all the attention, but LeBron never seemed all that fazed by it. He averaged 20.9 points, 5.9 assists and 5.5 rebounds during his rookie year at the age of eighteen, becoming only the third rookie ever (Michael Jordan and Oscar Robertson are the other two) to reach those plateaus. He also did it all in the way we allegedly like our players to do it: He played unselfishly, dishing the ball around, making his teammates better while remaining unafraid to take the big shot at the end. He never gets arrested—he leaves that to his mother, who was once *maced* after a DUI arrest—and he's a smiling pitchman for the countless sponsors who have signed up for Team LeBron. He's everything we have always claimed to want in a superstar.

Yet no one, outside of Cavs fans, seems to truly *love* him. Not in the way, say, that they loved—or loved to hate, the way Knicks and Pistons fans loved to hate—Michael Jordan, the guy he (and everybody else) has obviously patterned his career after. He's done everything Jordan has done, and perhaps even a little more; sure, he doesn't quite have the slit-your-throat-to-win-a-$5-bet competitiveness of Jordan, but he also doesn't seem quite as fake as MJ. Jordan wants you to believe he not only is the best basketball player in history, but is also casual enough to hang out with Kevin Bacon in his underwear.

But LeBron's dominance—and he's asserted about as much dominance as a player can assert without winning a title (yet, anyway)—has not made him as universally beloved as you (or his sponsors) might expect. Sure, he's succeeded in his goal of becoming the global brand, the guy even people in China know the name of. But I never get the sense that he *inspires* people. Rooting for LeBron James is like rooting for Nike in a way that rooting for Michael Jordan never was.

I think the reason for this is Gilbert Arenas.

Arenas couldn't have had a more different introduction to the NBA than LeBron. Considered something between a shooting guard and a point guard, he was undrafted in the first round in 2001 and ended up at Golden State. He immediately became an unheralded crowd favorite—LeBron was five times as famous as Gilbert was at Arizona in 2001, and he was seventeen years old—and, most dramatically, improved his game to an unprecedented level. He was a guy who had grown into himself without the hype. He became a human, one of us. And this is why he is the opposite of LeBron James, and why his existence illuminates all the flaws in LeBron's plan for world domination.

The stories of Arenas's accessibility are legendary at this point. A personal favorite involves a guy who ran into Arenas at a bowling alley. (Can you imagine running into LeBron at a bowling alley? They would have shut the place down and made it a private party the minute they heard he was coming. It somehow seems perfect that Arenas would spend a random evening just bowling.) The guy, noticing Gilbert, walked over to him, introduced himself, and told him he's great. Gilbert smiled and asked if he wanted to join the game. Stunned, the guy did, and they spent hours together. Afterward, Gilbert invited him to go back to his place with his friends to play video games all night. *So they did.* This is beyond any rational comprehension of what we expect of our athletes. To say that Gilbert is Just Like Us is oversimplifying it; Gilbert is only himself, and therefore all of us. His lack of pretense makes him human. And we know, now, that athletes are human. We were too jaded to ever believe otherwise.

LeBron's ideal shoe commercial involves him doing something amazing and all of us shuddering in its wake. Gilbert's? Well, just ask him.

> You know how I always throw my jersey into the stands after a game? In Washington, they just go crazy for it. So in this commercial, that's what I'm gonna do with my shoes. I've just hit a game winner, and I throw these shoes. Everyone starts to react, and you see everything in slow motion. Everyone's pushing, shoving, doing whatever it takes to try to get to these shoes. People from the 400 level, they're jumping off the ledge, they're missing the pile, hitting nothing but chairs, and you can just see in people's faces like, Ooooh, that hurt. While all this stuff's going on, one of the shoes pops out of the crowd, and a little girl gets it and she takes off. A couple of people see she has it, and they start chasing her, and she's

looking back running—and then she gets clotheslined by a kid
in a wheelchair. So he picks the shoe up and says—he's gonna
have the only line in there—"They said I couldn't get it. Heh.
Impossible is nothing." And then he rolls off.

This, friends, is batshit nutty of the highest order, in the most
likable way possible. You couldn't get a team of comedy writers
to come up with something half as bonkers as what Gilbert
rattled off the top of his head. Here are some more Gilbert
highlights:

- He sponsors a professional Halo video-gaming team.
- He once took a shower in full uniform for no reason. "I
  don't know why I did it," he said.
- He boasts of staying in the hotel during road trips, watch-
  ing infomercials and "buying colon cleanser."
- He gleefully admitted to trying to vote himself into the
  All-Star Game.
- When asked how well he played after one victory, he said,
  "My swag was phenomenal."
- He claims his favorite nickname is "Agent Zero," which was
  given to him by the Dada-esque Web site Wizznutzz.

Oh, and Gilbert has his own blog, where he once "wrote":

> I did something bad yesterday. It wasn't bad, but it was either
> me or her . . . I dropped my daughter. I had my daughter in my
> arms and I was ready to go put her to bed because she was
> sleeping. But I was just outside first because I forgot to put my
> brakes on in my car. So it was wet outside and I only had on
> my house slippers and they were wet when I came back in the
> house. When we got to the stairs I slipped, and you know, my
> left leg can't bend. So it was either both of us stumble down
> the stairs, or drop her. So I had to drop her. She's okay. She
> dropped on her butt first.

Can you imagine *LeBron* admitting something like that? No, wait, imagine *Jordan* doing that. Gilbert Arenas is constitutionally unable to be anything other than Gilbert Arenas, and this is why he's so much more successful at being all things to all people than LeBron—who desperately wants to be—ever will be. LeBron thinks that by his saying nothing, we will fill up the empty vessel with our hopes and dreams. But we know better than to do this anymore. The athletes we've worshipped have disappointed us; they've turned out to be human beings like the rest of us—flawed, vain, confused. But they will never admit it. *Here's who I am,* says Arenas. *I don't have the heart or energy to be anything else.* This is not how athletes are supposed to carry themselves. But it's how they should. This is when we love our athletes—when the myth goes away and we believe they're handling themselves the way *we* would handle ourselves, if we were so blessed to be professional athletes.

In one breathtaking post, Gilbert laid out what it meant to be a fan, and a player, and how they tie together:

> When we step inside that court and people come into those arenas and sit down, it's not about what they did that day, it's not about their rent, their jobs, how bad their day is going. It's about, "I'm going to forget about it for two hours."

Never has the essence of what sports means been summed up so well by someone who exists smack in the center of it. The reason LeBron James will never truly capture our hearts is because he thinks we want another Michael Jordan. We don't. We want someone who isn't faking it, who recognizes that the price you pay to be a Michael Jordan is not worth the toll it takes on your soul. He just has to be himself, an original thinker, someone who we feel is being straight with us. Michael Jordan never was this, and LeBron James never will be. We see through it now. *We don't believe him.*

Gilbert Arenas will never be the player LeBron James is, but his existence is in direct contradistinction to what LeBron James, and most athletes, really, have devoted their entire careers to. This is why, in twenty years, when we think of LeBron James, we will think of Gatorade, and when we think of Gilbert Arenas, we will smile and think of ourselves.

YOU'RE MORE INTERESTING THAN AN ATHLETE. REALLY!

In college, I once wrote a piece for the *Daily Illini* about a night I spent out at a campus bar with then–Illini basketball star Kiwane Garris. It is a measure of the limited success of the Illini at the time that Garris was the closest thing we had to Elvis; these days, he's bouncing around the development league and wondering if they need undersized point guards in Spain. I'd like to say that my story idea was founded on the altruistic ideals of participatory journalism, a desire to get in the head of a star athlete by witnessing him in his social environment. I certainly pitched it this way, but, mainly, I was just hoping I'd have a chance at a couple of his cast-off girls. *If we can't have Kiwane, how about the floppy-haired dork with the notebook and the Nirvana T-shirt at the table with him?* It was at a midwestern public university, and I wasn't in a fraternity; I needed all the help I could get.

The enterprise could hardly be considered a success. Kiwane met me at the bar and spent most of the evening avoiding me; to be polite, he humored me with a game of darts and a pint of beer. Then he vanished into a tight semicircle of people that I was unable to penetrate. He wasn't rude. He just had better freaking things to do than waste a Saturday evening having a stupid kid with bottles of Wite-Out in his pocket following him around. (My attempts to persuade him that the Wite-Out could get him high proved ineffective. Wite-Out won't get you high, by the way, and drugs are bad for you anyway.) I didn't have much of a story and, appropriately chastened, I finished up the rest of my beer and headed home to drink Mad Dog, play Sega hockey, and masturbate. It was a typical college night. I ultimately wrote a column in which I had an imaginary conversation with the ghost of Lou Henson, even though Lou Henson was alive and not terribly difficult to get on the phone. I was not the best college journalist.

The mind-set behind my column, though, was sound. Even in college, I was much more of a sports fan than I was a sportswriter, and if you really twisted my arm about it, I'd have to admit I really just wanted to tell my friends and family that I'd gone out drinking with an Illinois basketball player, because I was cool that way.

Sports fans love to tell stories about running into athletes in the regular world. On Deadspin, we even once ran a series of reader-submitted stories called "Athlete Run-Ins," in which people sent in their favorite athlete sightings. A few of these were brilliant—one guy who had worked as a ballboy at the Australian Open wrote about Andy Roddick being scared into shock by the sight of a man in a rabbit costume while having brunch; tennis players are absolutely underrated in the realm of total weirdos. A few tales were scary but most pretty much went like this:

> *Fan:* Hey, [Name of Athlete, or, more likely, Unflattering Nickname]! You SUCK! The team I root for is vastly superior to yours. You cost me money! You make too much money! You are not as tough as you think you are and I suspect I could best you in a battle of physical supremacy.
> *Player:* Hey, man, that's not very cool.
> *Fan:* You are correct, and I apologize. May I buy you an alcoholic beverage? Here we have a common bar napkin.

Could you grace it with your signature?
Player: Sure. (exits, stage left)

Inevitably, these stories would end with "Yeah, so, cool guy!" even though the entire interaction probably took no longer than forty-five seconds. I stopped running them after a couple of months, mostly because I no longer believed them and you can't exactly start throwing unsubstantiated stories on the Internet, because that would cause the series of tubes to collapse, forcing our economic structure to implode on itself. And that would severely diminish our capacity for easy access to pornography. But that was the pattern: Meet athlete, insult athlete, be surprised that the athlete is another breathing, walking human being who can form words in the same (or similar, anyway) language as the fan, immediate apology, and devolution into blatant hero worship. The process is sped up or slowed down by the insertion of alcohol, depending on whether the poison is ether or light beer.

This is bizarre. The interactions we have with the athletes we obsess over are mostly limited to the virtual; they are muscular stat machines that in no way relate to our lives as walking humans. When they cross over into everyday existence, we have to stop and wonder. Are they heroes? Are they regular people? Are they names on our fantasy teams who just happen to have a pulse?

Years ago, back when the primary ethos of sportswriting was the creation of larger-than-life titans, the fact that Joe Namath could (occasionally) throw a tight spiral was more than enough to classify him as someone who should be emulated and adored. Many of the sports leagues that employed these "heroes" were not near the popularity level that they are today. Everyone was on the lookout for a smiling face to stand in front of the corporate conglomeration and be loved not just by sports fans, but also by normal people who go to the supermarket, worry about their dress size, and only watch one football game a year. Each league was graced with their big star; it was Namath (or maybe O. J. Simpson) in the NFL, Mickey Mantle (or Pete Rose) in baseball, Michael Jordan (or Magic Johnson) in the NBA. It wasn't enough for the hero to excel athletically; he had to stand out as the model of modern masculinity. Everyone contributed to this, and everyone benefited. If Jim Palmer could throw a nasty curveball, well, jeez, why *wouldn't* he know what kind of underwear I should be wearing? (If you've seen Palmer's old Jockey advertisements, it's now painfully clear that he, in fact, had no fucking idea what kind of underwear I should be wearing.)

But we can buy all of this for only so long. Advertising has evolved to the point where a celebrity spokesperson isn't enough anymore; in fact, we're all a little confused as to why Michael Jordan and Kevin Bacon are hanging out together in their underpants. Sure, athletes still have endless endorsements, but they don't have the same effect anymore, because we don't treat our athletes like we used to. Just because Peyton Manning has an impressive passing rating and can flap his arms like a deranged falcon doesn't mean that we want to be like him. And thank God for that.

Fact is, the world is larger now, and that has made it smaller for athletes. As teams and leagues and PR people and personal handlers work harder to bring the athletes closer into our lives, we see them more for what they really are: just advanced versions of every smaller athlete we've known in our lives. That is to say: Each one seems to be a bit of a dolt.

Think about every athlete you've known in your life. (If you are an athlete, congratulations on having someone buy a book for you, and even more congratulations for actually opening it.) Were you friends with them? Or were you one of the adoring masses forever on the outside looking in? Hell, maybe they gave you a wedgie.

Take that small disconnect between normal people and an overblown high school or college athlete, and multiply it by

45,000, and you have the modern professional athlete. Realize
that there is no real motivation for professional athletes to care
about anything other than their chosen sport. From the moment their talent is discovered—and this is happening earlier
and earlier—they are immediately displaced from the rest of
humanity and directed to concentrate solely on their perceived
marketable skill. It's almost not their fault that they exist in a
self-aggrandizing bubble; what else are they ever encouraged to
concentrate on but themselves? They're essentially antisocial
piano prodigies who can jump. By the time they make it to the
professional level, their relation to the regular world is nonexis-
tent. Even when an athlete is praised for being "well-spoken" or
"thoughtful," it's almost always in a public relations construct.
Perhaps the smartest athlete in the NBA is Washington Wizards center Etan Thomas, and he can't stop punching his teammate Brendan Haywood. (Brendan is constantly pulling out
Thomas's dreadlocks.) Athletes are not connected to the world
around them because they do not have to be. If you didn't have
to be, you probably wouldn't be either.

The modern athlete has zero connection to any of our lives
whatsoever, and if you met any one of them in real life, and you
got to know him, and he got to know you . . . you probably
would not be able to stand each other. No matter how much Jim
Edmonds might mean to me as a Cardinals fan, no matter how
many times I've screamed his name while leaping into the air,
if I knew the guy on a personal level, I'm rather certain we
wouldn't be able to find a single common reference point. I
think I'd probably hate him. And I highly doubt he'd be particularly fond of my collection of Woody Allen movies either.
Does that somehow mean that I care less about him? No. It just
means that I treat him for what he is: a player on a team I root
for, a guy who makes me happy and disappoints me only on a
completely superficial level. In this way, our bond is unbreak-
able.

The Web has helped shrink athletes down to our level. The

days of Red Smith weaving tales of brilliance and assigning godlike qualities to the players are over. Athletes really are just like us, and they're entirely not like us. By bringing them closer, they are pushed farther from us. And we wouldn't have it any either way.

Not that I wouldn't buy Kiwane Garris a beer if I saw him today. Heck, I probably can afford one more than he can. Bet he still gets more girls, though.

BEN ROETHLISBERGER
DRINKS LIKE A CHAMPION

In February 2006, Deadspin was only a few months old, and I was still trying to find my footing. I have few firm rules as one who allegedly "covers" sports, but one of them is no press passes. My dislike of the press box is well documented, but I still wanted to have something special for that year's Super Bowl between the Steelers and the Panthers in Detroit. (Future generations will never believe that a Super Bowl was held in Detroit. I don't quite believe it, and I watched it.)

My first thought was to simply jump in a rental car and drive to Michigan, crash on a friend's floor, and throw myself into the experience full-bore. I firmly believe that the *real* story of any of sports' Big Events is found *outside* the arena, where the wretched excess of America's corporate sports culture is on glorious display. I didn't need a press pass to cover the Super Bowl; I didn't even need tickets.

That said, doing Deadspin is a full-time job, from 7 A.M. to 6 P.M. every day, and I knew the notorious Super Bowl week nightlife would certainly take its toll. Super Bowl week is basically Woodstock for sports reporters. It's the one event every major media figure shows up for, and they all play grab-ass all week. Through Deadspin, I've cultivated countless anonymous media sources—you can never overestimate people's desire to bitch about their jobs—and every single one of them asked me if I was going to Detroit. "We should meet up, man, have a drink!" This very much solidified my desire not to go. When you are too caught up in the coverage of sports, you can't tell what's going on anymore; if I started writing just for sports reporters, not actual fans—you know, *normal people*—I'd be just like everybody else. If I can, I will avoid other people who write about sports.

That said, *somebody* probably needed to go, so I called on my old Black Table colleague A. J. Daulerio to serve as tackling dummy. His job was to try to break into parties, talk to crazed fans, and basically document all the lunacy. I felt more comfortable having the bird's-eye view; the last thing I wanted was to be stuck covering the expected stories—"Oh, no! One player on one team is not displaying the proper reverence to a player on the other team! SCANDAL!" Sportswriters are so bored during Super Bowl week.

A.J. had fun in Detroit, but four days before the big game, I felt a gnawing dissatisfaction with the Super Bowl in general. There was an element of joylessness among fans; it was, essentially, the same shit.

And then, one Tuesday evening, I received an e-mail from a man I'd never heard from before: "Thought you might enjoy these . . . our boy big ben slammin' it home."

Attached were six photographs of Pittsburgh Steelers quarterback Ben Roethlisberger—considered at the time the golden boy representing all that is great about Sport—off-his-face drunk, wearing a T-shirt that said "Drink Like a Champion." One photo included a shot of Big Ben pouring a bottle of tequila down the throat of a lovely young lass.

That's my favorite one.

Seriously, being an athlete is so much more fun than being pretty much anything else. (Unless you're bouncing your head off concrete . . . but that's another story.)

These photos are consistently satisfying, not because they make Roethlisberger look like some bad guy, but because they make him look like a normal human being. The week of the Super Bowl, Roethlisberger was a supposedly handsome twenty-three-year-old millionaire having the time of his life. There is absolutely nothing wrong with that. But he had been stage-managed into this "hero" role, because there was money to be made off of a clean image. Nothing is "dirty" about Roethlisberger drinking; it's just real. It doesn't make fans dislike him; it makes him *more relatable.*

The photos are also funny, and that's why I ran them.

The reaction was instantaneous and enormous—briefly, anyway. A Pittsburgh television station ran a story on the photos, and the Web version of the story was linked off the Drudge Report. Reporters stuck in the dumb Media Day circus contacted me for stories they were working on. It became the biggest day in my site's young history.

But why? I think it's obvious: Even though the Super Bowl is the biggest sporting event on the calendar, everything besides the game is mostly a dull, joyless affair. Golden Boy Ben Roethlisberger pouring tequila down a woman's throat was plain *interesting;* sure as hell more compelling than another Joey Porter interview in which he lets us know, again, that he feels disrespected. It was, finally, some *news,* something fans could actually talk about.

Not that the fans ever found out about it. According to a reporter who told me about it months later, the Steelers (with the backing of the NFL) sent out a bulletin to media folk in Detroit saying that Roethlisberger could not be asked about the photos and, in fact, anyone who wrote a story about them would be in danger of losing press credentials. The Pittsburgh television station, WTAE, that did the story about the photos? They took them off the Web within two hours. I called the man who had interviewed me about them. A role-reversal had occurred: suddenly *I* was the investigative reporter.

Gus Rosendale, the reporter, said, "Turns out they decided not to run it. Thanks for all your help, anyway." Since I had seen the story, I knew this wasn't true, so I pushed further, contacting news editor Bob Longo, who said it was an "editorial decision" not to run the story. Again, I knew this wasn't true, so I sent him the Google news cache page of the WTAE story, and we had the following exchange:

> Me: So the thing is, it certainly seems like you DID decide to run it . . . until people actually started seeing it, at which time you took it down, for whatever reason. Would that be an accurate statement?
> Him: That is accurate.

Later that day, another Pittsburgh reporter called me: "We got shut down by management because of that story. Apparently, there's concern that our [elderly] owner may frown on our quarterback slugging tequila with bar whores while brandishing the face of a Don Martin cartoon."

Now listen: This is hardly the end of the world. I suspect America's sports fans can survive without some drunk athlete photos. But I learned an important lesson about the insular nature of the sports media world: Sometimes if the people in charge don't want a story to get out, it simply won't.

They didn't want it out then. But now? Pittsburgh sports clothing stores carry Roethlisberger's "Drink Like a Champion" T-shirt.

Information wants to be free. And so do drunk quarterback pictures.

YOU KNOW HOW I KNOW YOU'RE NOT GAY? YOU'RE AN ATHLETE

There are hundreds of thousands of different reasons that a professional sports locker room is dramatically different from your office—to start, smacking a coworker on the ass after a successful PowerPoint presentation is likely to result in derision, and perhaps even litigation, though I suppose you never know until you try—but one of my personal favorite examples involves former Pittsburgh Steelers quarterback Kordell Stewart.

For those of you with short memories, or who had Stewart in a keeper fantasy league and still haven't woken from the blackout, he was a notoriously fickle performer, blessed with otherworldly talent but a brain that seemed wired for just about any profession *but* football. (In boxing, they'd say he had a million-dollar right hook but a ten-cent head; in my hometown of Mattoon, Illinois, he'd be referred to as "all hat and no cattle," even though I don't know anyone who owned any cows and the only guys who wore cowboy hats were ones who'd only recently recovered from Garth Brooks's Chris Gaines phase.) The torment he brought to coach Bill Cowher, and Steelers fans in general, is legendary; this is a guy who was so inconsistent as a starter that *Tommy freaking Maddox* was welcomed as a savior when he replaced him. And Tommy Maddox is the type of guy who was almost certainly born "Tommy" and was never once referred to as "Thomas," or even "Tom."

Worse than Kordell's constant interceptions, fumbles, and tendency to wear his helmet backward, though, was his inability to be a leader. A football team is constructed in a way that makes every individual both irrelevant and irreplaceable; on three-quarters of the plays, whatever you do makes no difference, and on the other fourth, you're the only person who matters. The only exception to this is the quarterback. Not only is he the sole man to touch the ball every play—other than the center, of course, and his job is simply to snap the ball, throw up his hands, and try not to giggle when he's being tickled—he's also the one all action revolves around. When the team is exhausted and vomiting, it's the quarterback they look to. He must be calm and not, you know, *crying.* The most famous example of What a Quarterback Should Be is Joe Montana. The story most often used to illustrate the genius of Montana involves Super Bowl XXIII, when the 49ers were driving late to score the winning touchdown over the Cincinnati Bengals. Montana, with his team frantic in the huddle around him, supposedly noticed the late actor John Candy leaving his seat in the stands and said, "Hey, guys, look, John Candy's here, and he's leaving." This, apparently, loosened the team up, forcing them to break into laughter, because football players are extremely easy to amuse. (I always imagine football players e-mailing each other Monica Lewinsky jokes. Still.) They then scored the winning touchdown. I have never believed this story, not because it would be impossible for Montana to have noticed Candy (he was, after all, rather rotund), but because it's tough to imagine somebody giving John Candy tickets to the Super Bowl. I mean, jeez, he's Canadian.

Regardless. Montana was unflappable under pressure, which, along with the Bill Walsh–Jerry Rice offense that made Montana look like a master technician, is why Joe Montana is Joe

Montana and, say, Jake Plummer is known primarily for growing facial hair. Whatever *it* is, Montana had it.

Kordell Stewart did not. There were technical reasons for
this—his oft-aimless "scrambling" tended to wear down his
linemen, for one—but the perception was that he was not a
Leader of Men. He was erratic, shy, and complex. He was also
sensitive and, now that you mention it, had a bit of a lisp.

After another season of struggle, the whispers were impossible
to ignore. Rumor had it that Kordell Stewart was, gasp, *gay*. And
by "gay," I mean, "has sex with men." And by "has sex with men,"
that is to say, he "enjoyed anal sex, touching the penis of fellow
humans who possess the Y chromosome, and occasional fisting."

Of all the crimes Stewart could have committed—beating his
wife in the off-season, for example, or raping a coed—this was
without question the worst. Because there is no greater offense
in the world of sports than being gay. Playing in Pittsburgh
didn't help; surely there are steelworkers who enjoy the company of men, but they're likely quiet about it, or at least try not
to listen to Coldplay too loud. Kordell had taken a beating from
every writer and fan in the greater western Pennsylvanian area,
he had been shoved face-first into the turf of every stadium in
the AFC, he had even been hanged in effigy, a difficult thing to
accomplish these days. (First off, Pittsburgh doesn't have many
trees.) But this was unacceptable. This tag would not do.

Kordell, for all his faults, recognized this immediately and,
before the 1999 season started, he called a private team meeting.
Players only, no coaches, no media, no training staff. Just Kordell
and his troops, clearing the air.

How'd the meeting go? What'd they talk about? I'll let
Sports Illustrated's account tell the tale:

> *Stewart's sensitivity and his low profile off the field made*
> *him seem distant to teammates during his difficult*
> *periods. Moreover, some Steelers admit they were fazed*

> *by rumors that Stewart was gay, until he called a meeting*
> *before the 1999 season and issued a denial that included*
> *graphic descriptions of heterosexual acts he enjoys. "I*
> *could see the humor in the situation," Stewart says, "so I*
> *decided to have some fun with it. At one point I said,*
> *'You'd better not leave your girlfriends around me,*
> *because I'm out to prove a point.' A couple of guys said,*
> *'Fuck you, Kordell,' and we all cracked up."*

This is without question one of the most amazing paragraphs a major sports publication has ever printed. It packs unparalleled beauty into every word, and the more layers you peel back, the more it reveals. It wouldn't surprise me if the whole paragraph turned out to be a palindrome.

Let's make sure we have this straight. To prove to skeptical teammates that he was not gay, Kordell Stewart:

1. Called a team meeting where he proclaimed he was not gay.
2. Illustrated his point by describing the various sexual acts he particularly enjoyed.
3. Warned his teammates that he was willing to bugger their girlfriends to make it clear as possible that he was capable of such acts.

This really happened. I did not make it up. I mean, can you *imagine*?

"Yeah, guys, I love sex with women. I mean, *love* sex with women. I love, say, blow jobs. Blow jobs are the best. Also great? Anal sex. Man, I just love to pound a girl's ass. Let's see ... what else ... oh, rim jobs! Some good salad tossing! Don't you guys love that? Also great? Boobs in my face! Who doesn't love boobs, right? Am I right? Who's with me?! Right? Big boobs rule! You know what I don't love? Cock! Cock is totally not what I'm into. I like the vagina! Mmm, vagina! Yeah! So, you know, let's go play some football!"

Sweet heavens a-mighty. I'd give up my parents for an audio-tape of that meeting. Hey, careful: He's out to prove a point!

Kordell Stewart is no longer in football and, as far as I know, is not openly gay. But that's not really the point; he could wave that freak flag all he wanted, and it wouldn't make much difference. What matters is not that Kordell called the meeting to disprove rumors that he was gay so his teammates would believe in him again; what matters is that this strategy *worked*.

I CAN'T think of a profession, or any part of our cultural landscape, really, that remains as backward about homosexuality as sports is. Sure, discrimination because of one's sexual orientation is prevalent everywhere, particularly in the tragically closeted world of musical theater. But everyone, from the most rock-jawed marine staff sergeant to the youth minister down the street, at least admits they've *met* a gay person. They might not agree with the lifestyle, they might be terrified that their son will bring home a huge black man, they might even think that only heterosexuals should partake in the undeniably perfect institution that is marriage. But they publicly admit that there are gay people, and that the act of being gay involves having sex with someone who is of the same gender.

Though I've yet to have the experience of knowing another man in the biblical sense—but hey, the night's young!—I have seen several other men naked. Not once have I feared that one of them was going to have sex with me. This was the source of a particularly amusing conversation with my father. At an old job, I worked in Chelsea, the traditionally gay section of Manhattan. I went to the gym there in the mornings, and when I mentioned this to my father, he, half-jokingly (I think), said, "You better watch your back in there." I laughed. "Dad, you clearly have never seen the gay men in Chelsea. I'm in horrible shape, and I'm the fattest guy in there. If a man actually hit on me there, he would immediately be ostracized by the gay community and would never have sex again." I don't think this comforted my father.

That is to say: The main justification the athletes unfortunate enough to have their antigay sentiments caught on record give is that they spend so much time naked with their teammates, and that would be "weird." But there has to be something else there. Perhaps the story of former San Francisco 49ers running back Garrison Hearst is illustrative.

Hearst, after the coming-out of anonymous (and retired) defensive tackle Esera Tuaolo, told the *Fresno Bee:* "I don't want any faggots on my team. I know this might not be what people want to hear, but that's a punk. I don't want any faggots in this locker room."

As you might suspect, these comments didn't go over particularly well in the city of San Francisco, and Hearst apologized the next day. (The comments were considered a bit more palatable in the football community; ESPN "analyst" Sterling Sharpe, when asked about Tuaolo and Hearst's comments, said, "[Tuaolo] would have been eaten alive and he would have been hated for it. Had he come out on a Monday, with Wednesday, Thursday, Friday practices, he'd have never gotten to the other team." All the more reason to save your gay thoughts for the weekend!) But few considered Hearst's apology sincere, and he was not fined or suspended by the NFL for the comments, unlike baseball's John Rocker a few years earlier.

But what revealed the real culture of NFL locker rooms was not Hearst's comments, but what the 49ers did afterward.

At the time, the 49ers' director of communications was a man named Kirk Reynolds, who was considered an inventive and up-and-coming star by the classy world of sports information directors. (I don't want to get into too much detail here, but I imagine every sports information director in the country coming home after a day's work and staring into a mirror for an hour, splashing his face with water and whispering, "They pay

me six figures for this . . . they pay me six figures for this.")
Reynolds was responsible for setting up Hearst's "apology" and
dealing with the public aftershock. The lesson he took from this
was: You can't change the attitudes of the players, but you can
tell them not to be so stupid to announce their feelings.

Reynolds came up with a way to explain to the 49ers players
why some people in the Bay community might take offense at
the word "faggot." Rather than stick them in a boring meeting
with platitudes of "sensitivity training" and "proper community relations," he made a video.

The half-hour video features Reynolds playing San Francisco mayor Gavin Newsom (who actually allowed the team to
film in his office, a move he later regretted, immensely). It has
the production values of a particularly amateur porn film, shot
with shaky handheld cam. This was likely not a stylistic decision; Reynolds, who comes across as a well-meaning fellow, has
little future in the world of cinema.

The "film" has eight segments. We meet Reynolds, playing
the "mayor," and he offers to take the team on a tour of the
great city of San Francisco. He comes across as a grossly ste-
reotypical Asian man—"My name is Suk! My whole name is
Suks!" In a send-up of Newsom's gay marriage initiative, he
pretends to preside over a marriage of two lesbians. This ends
with the two women making out and ripping each other's
clothes off. (Reynolds concludes the segment with a cheerful
"Embrace diversity!") My personal favorite bit occurs when
Reynolds gives advice on what players should do if they happened to, say, get arrested. Reynolds gives more helpful advice
than "Don't drop the soap," but he does make sure to include
that, too.

The message of the video was surely helpful to the players:
Don't call people "faggots." Don't get arrested. Remember that
when you hire two hookers and someone finds out about it, it
will make the newspaper. What really mattered, though, was
how Reynolds framed the message. Reynolds is a smart man,

but he knew a training video for football players had to be base and simple. Want to get football players to listen to what you're saying? *Give them some lesbians.* Want them to laugh at your jokes? *Make fun of an Asian.* It's basic football math.

No players ever commented on the video publicly—they learned Reynolds's lesson well!—but it stands to reason that they paid closer attention to what Reynolds was saying than they would have had he handed out a pamphlet. He realized he was dealing with alpha males with little desire for an opening of their worldview, so he made the video as crude as possible. It seems to have worked; no 49ers have made any Hearst-esque statements since watching the video, though their attitudes likely haven't changed a lick.

Reynolds was not so fortunate; the video leaked to the *San Francisco Chronicle,* which didn't take too kindly to the racial stereotyping and naked lesbians making out in the mayor's office. Reynolds was fired immediately (he now works for a gambling Web site in the Bay Area), the victim of a stunt that might have worked among the jockstraps, but doesn't play in a town like San Francisco.

Reynolds knew you couldn't change attitudes; you could just hope nobody outside the locker room found out. And this is why we have never seen a gay athlete come out while he's still playing. Despite Sterling Sharpe's charming dissertation, it's unlikely a gay player would ever be murdered. But his career would be over.

Remember Mike Piazza's famous press conference in New York, when he was forced to tell a crowd of reporters that he was no friend of Dorothy's? (Piazza's bleached blond hair did him no favors in this regard.) The hubbub began when Page Six ran a blind item about an "area-catcher" who was involved with an "area-weatherman," an item that went unnoticed only by those who had never heard of baseball. Piazza took great pains to emphasize that he had no problem with gay people, but made sure everyone knew he wasn't. Whether Piazza is gay or not is beside the point here; what was fascinating was how tense Piazza looked during the press conference. It was a direct battle between his obligations as a professional athlete and his obligations as a human being. He seemed to know it was ridiculous that he should hold a press conference just to explain that he wasn't gay . . . but he knew it was necessary nonetheless.

Many have speculated on when the first active athlete will come out—John Amaechi doesn't count—and who it will be. Considering the number of professional athletes, pretending there aren't any gay ones is unrealistic, though it does stand to reason that the percentage is lower than in interior design or, say, accounting. The mainstream sports media, having missed not only the boat on steroids, but also the water, the ocean, and the earth, considers this its final big scoop. I've always thought of the Internet as the most likely facilitator; inevitably, an athlete's going to be caught, Travolta-style, smooching with another hairy fellow. The picture will leak to the Web, the player's publicity team will congregate, and, boom, suddenly there's a story of pride and bravery. There's no way that player doesn't end up on *Oprah*. In the initial media firestorm that will result, the player's teammates will say it doesn't matter, they just want to concentrate on this week's game. All will seem well. Sports is a welcoming environment!

And then the players will grow tired of talking about it, the team will lose a tough game, there will be whispers of the "clubhouse distraction," and next thing you know, it's not so cool to be gay anymore. And no one else will come out mid-career.

Why are sports able to get away with this? (Only the military comes close in the public arena, and they have the advantage of carrying weapons.) Because in your conference room meetings, where the boundaries of winning and losing are not so clearly differentiated, you can get away with being a distraction to your "team." A "positive work environment" actually matters in the office; nobody really cares about a positive work environment in sports. Just win, and look manly doing it. Being gay in sports means being something that alters from the norm; and that's the real crime.

Oh, and everyone's naked all the time. That makes a huge difference.

THE BALLAD OF
LUCIOUS PUSEY

Lucious Pusey is a linebacker at Eastern Illinois University, a liberal arts college in Charleston, Illinois, just a few miles from my hometown of Mattoon. This automatically places him in high standing in my book, along with John Malkovich, who went to EIU for a while before dropping out to open a personality distillation business.

Lucious Pusey is unlucky, because, well, his name is Lucious Pusey. I'm not one to labor over double entendres (really!), but that's an epic name right there. That's the type of name that'll affect a man's soul.

Apparently, anyway. Pusey, clearly tired after years of dealing with jerks like me, officially applied to change his name to "Seymour," marking him the first human in recorded history to *desire* the name "Seymour." I wrote about his name change on Deadspin, and a few months later, I received this e-mail:

> ooo so yall mother fuckers dont have shit else to say bout me
> huh . . . damn you know the funny thing is that mother fuckers
> like yall wont have the balls and say it to my face . . . when i
> make it to the league i willshoot a middle finger at yall and say

fuck all my haters . . . i am the realest, and my name is Lucious
Seymour get it right!!

I wrote him back and told him I was from Mattoon, and that we
should be friends. I did not hear back. He's listed in the 2007
EIU media guide as "Lucious Seymour," but we all know,
Lucious . . . we all know.

MY UNHEALTHY MAN
CRUSH ON RICK ANKIEL

I don't collect sports memorabilia, and I don't think it's normal for a grown man to wear a piece of athletic clothing just because another (richer) man wears the same thing and inevitably looks considerably better in it. I don't understand why people feel that if they own a jersey, or a game-used resin bag, or whatever, they are somehow closer to the games they watch. To cradle these objects only further reveals the distance.

That said, I own a Rick Ankiel No. 66 Cardinals jersey, and on top of my television I keep an Ankiel Staring Lineup figurine from the year he was named Rookie of the Year. (I like to think of this little toy sitting atop my cable box as my personal V-chip; its presence assures that no sexual indecency will take place at my apartment, because its presence assures there will be no women at my apartment.) These are the only two objects I own that can be classified as "collectibles." I doubt they're worth much, but they're among my most prized possessions: Rick Ankiel might be my favorite athlete of the last twenty years.

This may seem odd to you considering that Ankiel's contribution to the St. Louis Cardinals fan landscape has been one of almost unceasing pain. (And just when you thought the pain was over . . . more pain. But we'll get to that in a moment.) Ankiel broke into the majors at the age of twenty as the most storied Cardinals pitching prospect since Bob Gibson. (Okay, Steve Carlton.) An acrobatic lefty, Ankiel possessed a ninety-plus-mile-per-hour fastball and a devastating yo-yo, Bugs Bunny curveball that made you wonder if Ankiel had filled the ball with some sort of inert gas. He was also composed on the mound; a humble, likable kid, he seemed entirely unaware of the preternatural gift bestowed upon him. In interviews, he came across the way any of us would expect ourselves to behave if we were suddenly in the major leagues before we could drink. He once asked Mark McGwire for his autograph. But there was something odd there—a soulful fragility you could see in his eyes. From the beginning, you watched him the way you'd watch a small child play with a balloon—ennobling, even spiritual to watch, but you couldn't help but cringe in anticipation of the *pop*.

Even at twenty, Ankiel had some history. His father had served time for dealing drugs and, estranged from Ankiel for years, was notorious for showing up outside the players entrance or sneaking past unsuspecting guards. (His brother also had trouble with the law.) This is hardly unusual in the world of sports, of course; some might call this "the NBA." But Ankiel's reaction whenever he was asked about his father was troubling; he would look off into the distance as if he had briefly forgotten he was being interviewed at all, and then apologize for not wanting to get into it. Eventually, St. Louis reporters learned not to bother him, allowing the man-child to tiptoe his own way.

That was never going to last, though, because Ankiel was just too good. God, that curveball! His first full season, 2000, was the breakthrough not just for him, but for his team. Thanks largely to Ankiel and his mentor in the rotation, Darryl Kile, the Cardinals reached the playoffs for the first time in four seasons. In the first round, they faced the Atlanta Braves.

Something odd happened the last week of the season. Ankiel's pinpoint control betrayed him. He walked several hitters and even threw a couple of wild pitches. It was a late-season, mostly meaningless game, and no one seemed too disturbed by it. And then came the game against the Braves.

A friend who was in attendance at the Ankiel-Braves game—when everything suddenly went very wrong—described his experience to me:

"I went to the game with my boss, so I offered to grab hot dogs and beer while he found our seats. I was waiting in line—they didn't have televisions above the concessions, so I couldn't tell what was going on—and I listened as everyone geared up for the first pitch.

"And then: The strangest sound, one I've never heard fifty thousand people make. The crowd, every ten seconds, would make this anguished *uhhhhhmph* sounds, entirely in unison. It wasn't a boo, it wasn't a cheer, it wasn't anything I'd ever heard at the ballpark before. It sounded like an entire stadium full of people watching a dog unexpectedly devour a particularly cute rabbit. And it happened *five times*. Still in line, I couldn't fathom what was possibly going on out there. I was afraid someone was having a heart attack."

As we all now know, the crowd was watching a young man fall apart. Ankiel's collapse culminated during a moment against the eventual National League champion Mets in the NLCS. The cascade of wild pitches made me want to hide under my couch. Ankiel's humiliation was compounded by the serpentine New York media. The Cardinals lost the series, and even though we all held out hope, it was clear the Rick Ankiel we knew was gone.

But boy, did we ever hold out hope. After Ankiel's mental issues wiped out his 2001 season, elbow surgery wiped out 2002 . . . and 2003. With any other guy, we would have long ago written him off and forgotten him, or at least tried to. But Ankiel's talent and mysterious story kept us rapt. He became St. Louis fans' wayward but beloved nephew whom you kept close to your heart no matter how much harm he did to himself, and to you.

Then came 2004. Ankiel showed up to spring training healthy and . . . throwing strikes! To ease his mind and keep his head straight, the Cardinals sent him to the lowest levels of the minor leagues and encouraged him to have fun. It worked; free of whatever mental barriers that stood in his way, he just enjoyed himself and showed all his old talents. By this point, Cardinals fans were afraid to speak his name, lest it cause him to shatter again.

By September, it was time for Ankiel to make his return to Busch Stadium. And then came my proudest moment as a sports fan.

Imagine if Ankiel had played for either New York team, or, gasp, *Philadelphia*. After a public meltdown like Ankiel's, booing would have been the *best* of it. There'd be nothing left of him but a few strands of hair. But when Ankiel returned to pitch at Busch Stadium, playing on one of the best Cardinals teams in anyone's lifetime, he received the most deafening cheer of the season. The Cardinals fans didn't need him to pitch well that year; they just wanted to see him and let him know they still cared about him. Ankiel pitched beautifully.

Because this is Rick Ankiel, the story doesn't end there; there was much, much more to come. During Spring Training in 2005, Ankiel—who the Cardinals had been quietly hoping could join the rotation that year—had yet *another* wild pitch streak/ meltdown/implosion. The yips had returned, and Ankiel was finished with pitching. So he decided he would become a minor-league hitter. It was insane. It was sad, sure, a last-ditch effort by a man-boy with no other options. But still: we watched, and we hoped.

And then, well, you know what happened then. Ankiel returned to the major leagues—I was at Busch for his first four games—and started bashing home runs at a Pujols-ian rate. (Better, actually.) He brought the Cardinals back into the pennant chase briefly and, more important, captured the hearts of baseball fans everywhere. The story we Cardinals fans thought only we cared about suddenly became everyone's story. Rick Ankiel was everyone's hero.

For about a week.

Then I learned the latest—leaving my girlfriend's apartment on a Friday morning. I picked up the New York *Daily News* like I do every morning I take the subway; it's the perfect size, and makes me feel like I'm a plumber who grew up in Bensonhurst rather than a yokel from southern Illinois. And there, on the front page, was Rick Ankiel. Human growth hormone cheat. Scam artist. *Bad guy.* I closed my eyes, and when I opened them was amazed to find that the image was still there. The story continued.

YOU have to realize that Rick Ankiel has always stood for hope. There was always an innocence to the hope; against all rational thought, we believed in Rick Ankiel, because if we could believe in him we could believe in anything. It was through our support, we believed, that Ankiel could frame his various comebacks. Our support, our patience, came from the very best part of us. We were so proud of ourselves. That morning, though, that innocence was replaced with something else.

I immediately tried to rationalize the HGH story. In 2004, the year Ankiel received the HGH, he was still a pitcher, recovering from Tommy John surgery and rehabbing in Memphis. (As the Web magazine *Slate* pointed out, HGH is hardly a "performance enhancer"; steroids are like doing heroin, whereas HGH is more like smoking weed.) Ankiel was a guy who had gone through so much, and he was just trying to return to some semblance of who he once was—by using a substance that was not banned by baseball at the time. Oh, and hey: Who cares about steroids anyway?

But I was kidding myself. I was giving leeway to Ankiel that I'd never given Barry Bonds.

Certain people like me will defend Ankiel no matter what, and others will think of him as a juicer until the end of time. The truth lies somewhere in the middle. The Ankiel HGH story is not really about HGH, it's not about the Cardinals, and it's not even about Rick Ankiel. Before the *Daily News* story, Rick Ankiel stood for all we love about sports, for his story existed in the black-white world we demand of our games. His story was pure; it was impossible not to be happy for him.

But as much as we might all try to believe otherwise—and, boy, do we try—the sports world is gray. Ankiel is not a monster or The Bad Guy now that we know he accepted HGH in 2004. But he's not, as we all believed, the Guy in the White Hat Here to Save Our Games, either. His story is a human one. His story is gray. And it always was.

At eight A.M. that morning, picking up my newspaper and stepping on the subway, I came to the realization that the world was entirely different than it had been ten minutes before, yet, of course, it was also exactly the same.

But I still believe in Rick Ankiel. Because if we can believe in Rick Ankiel, we can believe in anything. Still.

THE SAD SAGA OF THE
RETIRED ATHLETE

In January 2007, SpikeTV—desperate for promotion—invited me to play flag football at New York City's Grand Central Station against Kordell Stewart and Andre Rison. That's one of the more bizarre sentences I've ever typed, and I haven't even told you what happened yet.

Kordell and Bad Moon were participants in the *Pros vs. Joes* reality show on Spike, which pits retired athletes against normal people (if you can even classify anyone who would want to appear on a reality show as "normal"). The point of the program is to remind us, once again, that the athletes we watch on a daily basis operate on such a higher plane of achievement that, even after their prime has long since passed, they can still easily dominate even the most physically accomplished citizen. Because the show is on basic cable, the promotional event involved the two former football "stars" taking on various passersby in the Vanderbilt Room at 7:30 on a Wednesday morning. And Spike invited me, along with Deadspin columnist (and mustachioed madman) A. J. Daulerio, to compete. This put me at a distinct disadvantage; not only is 7:30 way too early for a blogger to be out in public, but, well, classifying me as a "physically accomplished citizen" is probably pushing it.

That said, A.J. and I were ready, mapping out plays while

our friend Aileen, on hand to digitally capture the proceedings, mocked us for wearing gym shorts and knee pads. We were prepared to dominate. Check out our game faces:

Before the first play, the PR guy who set up the event took us aside. I assumed he would try to explain why a national cable network would choose a tiny blog to help promote a television program, but he looked too depressed to even bring that up. (I did not push the issue.)

"No tackling," he said as if this was possibly going to be an issue. (My main goal was to walk on the "field" without falling over.) A.J. and I laughed it off, but the PR guy's face fell serious: "No, seriously; these guys both plan comebacks."

On the first play, A.J. covered Rison while I stayed in and made googly eyes at Kordell in an attempt to determine whether he's really gay or not. (Results were inconclusive.)

Kordell threw downfield—while I stood there wondering if he'd let me have a drink of his water—and Rison easily burned A.J. for a touchdown. Because it doesn't do much for promotion if a whole "event" lasts only ten seconds, they gave us another set of downs, this time with me guarding Rison. I played football my freshman year of high school, as a particularly weak strong safety—I had to quit the team halfway through the season because I was getting a D in biology (my grade due entirely to a severe fear of wasps: I think it's morally wrong to make a fourteen-year-old kid try to capture a wasp in the name of science for a bug collection). So it's safe to say, my Cover 2 experience was limited. Still, I stuck with Bad Moon, and Kordell, as Kordell tends to do, overthrew him, and we had our first stop. I gave A.J. a fist pound, and, doggone it, we were downright fired up. Rison and Kordell put their heads together, and, on the next play, Rison broke across the middle. For whatever reason, Spike had placed pylons in the middle of the field, and Rison's pattern sent me running right into it. It was not a graceful fall.

Rison caught the easy touchdown, and he and Kordell did a little dance. Actually, Kordell did a bit more than that; he jumped up and down, *whoop!*ed, and began screaming to the heavens. You had to be proud of them both; they had successfully scored a touchdown on a couple of out-of-shape thirtysomethings who hadn't played an organized football game in a decade and were up about three hours earlier than they were used to.

As we walked off the field, slightly proud but mostly bewildered, I turned to A.J.

"You know, he purposely ran a pattern that would send me into the pylon."

"I know."

"That seems unnecessary."

We looked back at Kordell and Rison, who were both still celebrating, and it occurred to me that there's nothing sadder than recently retired athletes. Even though their physical abilities, even in retirement, dramatically dwarfed both mine and A.J.'s, they still felt the need to resort to trickery to defeat us. I do not believe this is because they felt threatened by us. I believe it was all because an athlete is trained to win, in any way possible, regardless of the opponent. We could have been two NFL-level defensive backs, and Rison still would have tried to run me into that pylon. (I would hope an NFL-level defensive back would not be so easily duped.) Even though their NFL careers are over, they still have that instinct to scratch and claw for any possible advantage.

And this made me incredibly sad. Because at the end of the day, I was able to go home and go back to work, to hopefully improve my abilities, to continue plying my trade. But Kordell Stewart and Andre Rison . . . these freakish exhibitions provide them with their only opportunity to do the sole thing they've been trained to do.

Look at Kordell. He is thirty-five years old. Can you imagine being that age and knowing that your best years are behind you, that no one wants you to do the one thing you've ever had any skill at doing? It's little wonder they sign up for these shows. It's a reminder that they are special, that life isn't over. I might be living a frivolous life, but at least I have years left to turn it around and do something worthwhile. (Maybe.) What does Kordell Stewart do now? Learn to type?

This happens to even the most storied athletes. Look at the way Jerry Rice and Emmitt Smith, just a year or two after retirement, took to their appearances on *Dancing with the Stars*. They devoted themselves to the "competition," training with the vigor they once saved for the practice field. Smith took it so seriously that he actually won it; his joy upon taking first place wasn't even the slightest bit diminished by the fact that he was wearing gold tassels.

And Emmitt was the lucky one; typically, athletes don't even have a dopey dancing show to satisfy their competitive jones. Just look at Michael Jordan, whose legendary competitiveness drove him to make an ill-conceived comeback that has led him into a rather serious gambling problem. (Gambling is a typical post-athletic career affliction.) Studies have shown that, particularly in the NFL, athletes tend to suffer from depression and occasional alcoholism when the game they have been programmed to play is taken away from them. And this all on top of the financial difficulties athletes often face after retirement (or forced retirement); sure, we know Brett Favre will be fine when he finally (finally!) hangs up his spikes, but that backup Packers offensive lineman, the guy who played two years at two hundred grand a year before blowing out a knee at twenty-four and being pushed out of the game forever, what's he supposed to do now? He has little education and zero training to do anything but play sports, and now he has a lifelong medical problem. As much as it might be fun to joke about the desperate grasps at attention and victory that Emmitt Smith and Jerry Rice might put themselves through, at least people still recognize their names and care about them. The vast majority of retired athletes have no such good fortune, and sports does little to train them for the outside world.

In a way, even Stewart and Rison are lucky. They might not have the same celestial renown as Rice and Emmitt, but at least they were big enough names to be invited on a national cable show to embarrass themselves and feel somewhat important. Kordell might look like a fool, deliriously celebrating a sad little victory over two Internet dorks in a tiny room in Grand Central Station at 7:30 A.M. on a Wednesday, but that's still a victory he gets to have. Most are not so fortunate, and they wander through life remembering the cheers they'll never have the opportunity to bask in again. They have to realize that, at age twenty-six, the only part of their lives that will ever matter is over with. It's no wonder they're depressed; I'd be depressed, too.

Heck, it's enough to make you want to give one of those guys a hug.

A FEW MOMENTS WITH
JOHN ROCKER

I will confess to a long-standing fascination with John Rocker. I think it's because he never got a second chance. That is not to imply he deserved one; I don't consider myself qualified to decide who, in the fickle church of public opinion, is allowed to be forgiven and who isn't. Once he made his famous comments about "queers with AIDS on the 7 train" to reporter Jeff Pearlman in *Sports Illustrated,* well, John Rocker was the Most Racist Man on Earth, and that's all there was to it.

Not that he did himself any favors. Flipping off Busch Stadium fans, screaming at any reporter in sight, starting a promotional campaign called "Speak English" ... Rocker had a funny way of making matters worse for himself every time he opened his mouth. This could be because he's an idiot, of course, but still: We are Americans, and we love it when someone pays for his past crimes and redeems himself. Off the top of my head, the only people I can think of who never got a second act in America are O. J. Simpson, John Rocker, and maybe Gary Condit. (The jury's still out on Steve Bartman, but he'll probably require a Cubs World Series victory, so you can guess how that will turn out.) Rocker never dug himself out of his hole.

It's always been my theory that Rocker was stuck in the Racist Sarlaac Pit because demonizing him as The Racist to

End All Racists allowed us to all feel better about our own, subtler prejudices. No matter what might quietly reside in our own hearts, we can all pat ourselves on the backs and say, "Hey, at least we're not *that* guy." Racism is a larger part of our sports than we want to admit, though, and it's considerably more nuanced than queers with AIDS on the 7 train.

During another promotional event for *Pros vs. Joes* event back in 2006, I showed up and batted against Rocker during a freezing March morning. He struck me out on three pitches, and in my report of the event on Deadspin, I espoused a similar theory. Shortly after the piece ran, I received an e-mail from Debi Curzio, who, years before, had quit her job at a Brooklyn public relations firm to help out Rocker with his image problem. I found her story fascinating—there can't be many more difficult PR jobs on earth than having to constantly clean up Rocker's messes—and I wrote a brief story about Curzio for *New York* magazine. Curzio became the only PR person I ever dealt with for Deadspin, mainly because she didn't seem like a PR person: She seemed like the guy who cleans up after the elephants at the circus.

Anyway, shortly after Michael Richards made his famous fork-up-your-ass remarks, briefly grasping the mantle of America's Racist, Curzio asked me if I'd be interested in interviewing Rocker while he was sweeping through town. I gently questioned why Rocker was visiting the Sodom of New York City, and she said he was visiting his girlfriend. His girlfriend? Alicia Marie, an African-American fitness model who has to be a foot taller than I.

We met at one of my favorite bars on the Lower East Side of Manhattan, the three of us, and I was armed with nothing but an iPod recorder, a pack of cigarettes, and a couple of twenties to buy drinks. (It turned out not to be enough cash.) The interview was wide-ranging, fascinating, and batshit insane.

This is the only section of this book that is reproduced from Deadspin, but I've edited it and added footnotes so you don't feel like you are somehow being cheated. I'm including it because it's one of the favorite interviews I've ever been a part of, because I think it says something about celebrity, public perception, and the way athletes casually live their lives, and because I want to prove to you that sometimes bloggers go out and talk to people. Well, John Rocker, anyway. Enjoy.

Where you having Thanksgiving?*
At her parents' place. (points to Alicia Marie)
Really? Uh, have you met her parents before?
Yeah. I've met the younger sister, and both parents. I've met her mom once, her dad twice, and her younger sister went to dinner with us three weeks ago.
Uh . . . do they like you?
Alicia: I was initially worried about my dad.
I can imagine.
Alicia: But my dad, like, loves him.
Rocker: Yeah, we all went out to dinner and had a great time.
Really?
Rocker: Yeah. They really like me. They're really nice people.
Alicia: I grew up in Connecticut. They're the only black Republicans on earth.
Did you two really meet when John was pitching against me in Herald Square Bryant Park? I'm really pissed you struck me out, by the way. My excuse is that it was really cold outside.†

---

* The interview took place just a few days before Thanksgiving. Rocker was actually spending Thanksgiving with his black girlfriend and her family in Connecticut. You know how, in movies, Thanksgiving is always when families' buried secrets and resentments all come out? This seems like a perfect premise for a movie: Nationally known racist visits his girlfriend's upper-class, Republican black family. Wacky hijinks ensue!
† It was freezing, but this is of course a bullshit excuse. What I found amazing about batting against Rocker is that, after I swung and missed at two fastballs, he struck me out on a nasty, winding breaking ball. Rocker could have flipped the ball behind his back, caught it, and then set it on a tee, and I still would have struck out. Yet he felt compelled to bring out the junk.

Rocker: Well, when it warms up, let's try it again. Yeah, you were wearing the Rick Ankiel jersey, right?* Sorry about that. I don't know what happened to that kid. The first game he disintegrated was against us, actually, back in 2000. They ended up winning that game, though in the first three innings he had, like, eight walks. The media got on him so bad. After they beat us, they kept showing the highlights over and over. I guess he probably watched all the press about himself, and when he came back in spring training, that's all they could talk about.†

Anyway, yeah, we met there. I haven't actually picked up a ball since that day.

Really? You haven't pitched once? Not even in your back-yard or something? Do you miss it?

I miss parts of it. When I watch the playoffs I miss it, but when I watch Game 146 in the middle of August, I'm glad to be out at the beach instead. There's part you miss and parts you're happy are gone.‡

What's your schedule a lot like now? You seem to be in New York a lot, with Alicia around.

I'm here at least twice a month. She's my main business up here, but I'm meeting with my literary agent.§ I think I found an editor we feel comfortable with editing. I do a lot of work with a venture capital guy here too, and I'm always doing radio interviews and whatnot.

---

* As established, my Rick Ankiel jersey is without question my favorite piece of clothing. Women love it.
† Hearing John Rocker deconstruct one of my favorite players of all time is an emotionally unsettling experience, particularly when he's right.
‡ I find this honesty refreshing, yet I wonder if it's the real reason Rocker doesn't play baseball anymore. The life of an athlete requires such single-minded focus that an admission that it might be more fun sometimes to hang around at the beach than pick your nose in the bullpen for three hours while wearing long pants in 110-degree heat seems like an admission of failure. We all talk about how much we'd love to be athletes, and how We'd Love to Be There, but Rocker's offhand discussion of how miserable it can sometimes be to be a baseball player is likely much closer to the truth.
§ John Rocker has a literary agent.

And you two met when she was interviewing you? Because I want to make it clear that I'm not hitting on either one of you.

Yeah, all of her questions were, "Do you have a girlfriend?" "Would you like my number?" I just looked down her shirt, saw what I needed to see, and moved on (laughs).* I took a leap of faith, because she had a long coat on, and she could have had big birthin' hips or something.†

I see.

But I found her, and here we are. The hips are fine.‡

Yes. Want another drink?

Yes please.§

Okay. Let's talk about the 7 train story, of course. What I find amazing about the aftermath of the story, and this is what I wrote in the Deadspin piece, was that Americans love second acts. No matter what a celebrity does, if they say they're sorry for it, and seem legitimately apologetic, we tend to root for them to recover, at least until they screw up again. But that never happened with you. You gave that interview, and from every day since then, you were The Racist. You never got a second act. I'm not saying you necessarily deserved one, but people usually don't deserve one. Why do you think that interview just set it all in stone like that? Did you ever try to resalvage your reputation? Are you still trying? Is that what the book is for?¶

Naw, I don't think the book will help with that, and I don't care. The book is more conservative Republican rantings. The Bill

---

* It should probably be mentioned at this point that Rocker had already had a couple of drinks. My interviewing tactic mostly involves plying my subject with alcohol. Don't laugh: This is exactly how Seymour Hersh does it.

† True story: I named a fantasy baseball team "Big Birthin' Hips" after this interview.

‡ They are.

§ Rocker drinks Absolut Mandrin and Red Bulls the way Bill Clinton (and I) drinks Diet Cokes. I know I'm under the age of forty, so technically I'm not supposed to feel this way, but I think Red Bull is the most disgusting fucking thing I've ever tasted. I was not surprised that Rocker enjoyed it so.

¶ The original version of this question took about fifteen minutes to ask and required me to wake up both Rocker and Alicia.

O'Reillys of the world, they will appreciate it, the Rush Limbaughs of the world will appreciate it, but, unfortunately, most members of the media—well, I don't know what you are politically.

*I'm an agnostic. Politics terrify me.**

Well, anyway, those liberal media people, they'll appreciate some things, but I am a Republican. I'm not Republican in everything—I mean, look at my girlfriend[†]—and I'm not a huge pro-lifer, but I think 95 percent–plus of the media is liberal, and they see me as the Antichrist of liberal views.[‡] It's much easier for them to just keep piling on than to look closer and realize that, hey, we might have been wrong about this guy.[§]

It seemed that people felt like you were an outlet for their own sublimated racism. They were like, "Well, we must not be too bad, because we're not nearly as bad as this guy."

It was much easier to label me than sit down like you're doing and actually talk to me. It's a lot easier to label and move on. There are two or three hot-button issues in this country that people feel like they need to eradicate, and racism is one of them. So when you have someone like me who has said something, or has betrayed themselves to be such, if you can label them as The Racist, well, Katie bar the door, because we're going after him.[¶] Liberal America, which is probably 90 percent to plus of the media, that is their end-all, be-all of expressing themselves as liberals. They're all "happy, everybody get along, everybody

---

*This is not true. I just had little desire for a lengthy political conversation with John Rocker.

†This is one of my favorite statements about race relations and politics in America I have ever heard. You have to admire a Republican who says he's not *entirely* a Republican and, to prove it, points out that he does not hate black people. Hell, he even has sex with them!

‡We might have a small case of hubris here. I think this distinction is mostly held by Dick Cheney, or Joe Lieberman.

§I actually think Rocker is right here, but not for the reason he thinks. Nobody took a closer look at him after his 7 train comments, but if they had, I am not sure they would have changed their minds. Though, to be fair, he does have sex with a black woman now.

¶I am not from the South—central Illinois doesn't count—so I have no idea what "Katie bar the door" means.

mesh into one big happy union."* When these comments were made years and years ago, it became easier to label than to sit down and wonder, "Okay, what is really going on in this guy's head." That's what a huge purpose for this book is going to be. Yeah, these things were said, but these were the 45 minutes' worth of context that surrounded those things that were said. You can make anything look bad when you just strip it out.

To be fair, you are promoting a campaign called "Speak English."† That's hardly the type of thing that's going to change your image. You did choose that. That wasn't a misquote.

I'm not looking to pop any bubbles about myself; people are gonna think what they're gonna think. I came to that realization about a year and a half ago. I was doing *Hannity & Colmes,*‡ and because of that *SI* interview, I had been tiptoeing around every interview I did just to make sure I didn't say the wrong thing. I did that throughout that whole interview, and on the way home, I realized, "You know, I'm retired. You can't get me. You can't picket where I work or play. You can't fire me. I don't have to be politically correct anymore." I realized I didn't have to worry about whether or not the minorities were mad at me.§ If I wanna say it, it's gonna get said. If you wanna not like me because of it, then oh well.

Alicia, I have to ask: Do you agree with all his political views?

Alicia: Well, there are many things we disagree on, yes, but at least I see where he's coming from. I feel like part of my job

---

* I think this is called an "orgy," and I can confirm that all liberals are stridently pro-orgy unless, of course, they've actually had one.
† I've had a hard time deciphering the point of Rocker's "Speak English" campaign. First off, its physical manifestation, as far as I can tell from Rocker's Web site, is simply a couple of T-shirts. Also, if Rocker really does want to help solve our nation's immigration problem—if you are willing to grant that it is a problem— shouldn't the shirts say "Hables ingles"? This is not to say that I don't believe anyone new to our shores should *not* make Rocker's Web site their first stop toward cultural education.
‡ This tells you all you need to know about *Hannity & Colmes.*
§ Unless, of course, he's having sex with them.

with him is to help people get past this whole "He's John Rocker" thing, because anything that comes out of his mouth is going to be misconstrued, no matter what he says. I want to help facilitate that.

Rocker: Well, it's not like it's her job or anything. It's not like I said, "Well, I need to hire a black girlfriend to make me look better."

People have said that.

Yeah, she's gotten lots of e-mails. I wish she weren't so accessible on the Web, actually. Honestly, I don't understand why people are so interested in me, and what I'm doing, and who I'm dating.* But people mostly misinterpret the fact that I just don't care. If I were still playing and needed to worry about my image, I might pull some shit like this, dating a black girl, just to throw the old Jedi mind trick on people.† I'm out of the public eye now. People's opinions aren't that important to me, I'm not gonna do something like this just to change the opinion of people I don't care about.

When you guys walk down the street, and people see that you're John Rocker, do they say anything?

I don't ever make eye contact with people on the street. I've become like a New Yorker in that way. People want to say, "Hey, has John Rocker changed, has he turned over a new leaf?" I haven't changed at all. I don't understand why it's so hard for journalists to admit that I haven't changed; they were just wrong. Maybe they made me change by writing an article or something. That song by Joe Walsh, "Life's Been Good to Me So Far," that's totally how it is.‡ I haven't changed.

Just to ask for the millionth time: Do you regret the interview? You didn't really pitch much after that.

---

* I think I'm probably the only person who cares . . . and I really don't care that much. (Really.)

† A universe in which John Rocker was capable of pulling the Jedi mind trick on people would be an exciting universe indeed.

‡ Totally.

If it would have been portrayed in the correct version, no. The way the sucker punch was done, yeah, it was horseshit. Every dark cloud has a sun behind it, though; there's a lot of things I can do now that I wouldn't have been able to do had it not been for that article. It's opened a lot of doors. I know a lot of players who had a lot better careers than me, but when they retire d, you never see or hear from them again. For some reason, people still have interest in me. Without that article, I wouldn't be writing a book.* When you go into a restaurant and the maître d' says, "Come on in, sit down," that's when you don't mind it. When you're at Bungalow 8, and the bouncer won't let you in because he's Dominican, well, that's when it's not so good.

That really happened?

Yeah, even though two or three of my best friends are Dominican or Puerto Rican. And her, of course [points to Alicia].†

Did any players ever give you any crap about the interview?

Not really. Most players have been misquoted before, so they know how it goes. It happens on some scale to pretty much everybody.

So when I told most of my friends who don't know anything about sports that I was interviewing you, they all knew who you were and wanted me to ask you about Michael Richards.‡

Well, it was bad, but I bet he ends up getting work in a few years. That's not what happened to me. People still bring it up today all the time. People act like they're gonna "get me" or something. Journalists act like they're the first person to ask me about racism. I apologized and everything, but it didn't stick.

---

* Another moment of clarity from Rocker. I appreciate that he understood, after all this time, that no one would have ever cared about him otherwise. If Rocker never does that interview, he's Steve Karsay. Whether the fact that it's ultimately leading to a book *written by John Rocker* is a good thing or not, well, we'll leave that to the historians.
† Honestly, he's the best.
‡ The majority of my friends know nothing about sports, and every single one of them knows who John Rocker is. Rocker is better known by non–sports fans than Peyton Manning. This is how the planet works.

I think it's because I was a white man from the South. My favorite show is *South Park,* and those guys are probably liberals, they're from Canada, but their perception is that the South is dumb, ignorant hicks.* They don't see it as the cultural center that it really is. The liberal side of things, they try to pin the South as the racist place in the world. We can connect John Rocker to the South, which equals racist, which equals John Rocker is a racist.† The South is just a bunch of fucking racists, that's what they want to see it as, and I just got caught up in that. Michael Richards is lucky he's not from the South. If I'd been Ozzie Guillen, no one would have cared. But I'm not. I'm from the South. It's just a gross double standard. I have a chapter in my book about double standards.

That's the thing, though: When people have an agenda, that's all that matters. Jeff Pearlman is who he is: a liberal Jew from New York.‡ He's one of their own, who spent a couple of hours with me, pulled things out of context, and you're trying to create a persona of an individual when you don't know them. You look at Michael Irvin, and Michael's a friend of mine—

You're friends with Michael Irvin? Really?§

Yeah.

I would like to watch you two talk to one another.

He's a very nice guy. I see him at a lot of parties.¶ Anyway, it's not like when he goes on to do his morning show, people don't call him the crackhead womanizer, though he's been caught twice with cocaine and prostitutes. I've heard from

---

* Trey Parker and Matt Stone are not from Canada.
† It's math!
‡ I interviewed Pearlman once for Deadspin—his book on Barry Bonds is excellent, and I'm not just saying that because it was published by the same people who are publishing this—and I found him friendly but a bit skittish and overemotional. After reading this Rocker interview on Deadspin, Pearlman wrote a piece for ESPN's *Page 2* in response, saying, "As I write this, my hands are shaking. My heart is beating unusually fast. I am pissed off like few times before." This seemed like a bit much.
§ This is one of the most insane things I've ever heard. Just the mental image of this makes me think someone slipped me psilocybin.
¶ I need to go to more parties. Actually, no, I don't.

people who have worked with him on movie sets that it's not a once-in-a-while type of thing, that it's more of a lifestyle thing. So I sit back amazed that people still don't give me any slack on it.

I'm not sure how long your friendship with Michael Irvin is going to last.

No, we're friends, we're friends. Honestly, people in this world just need to stop being so sensitive. Sure, if you go take a lead pipe to someone because they're a different ethnicity than you, then yes, you've got problems.* But someone's gonna call me a cracker or a honky? Come on. I think the Islamic religion is the most sensitive group of people ever. These people lose their minds over anything. I'd like to see someone make a comment about Muslims, Muslims get mad, and have the person say, "Take it, and ram it right up your ass. Get pissed all you want, I'm not taking it back."† You see people ripping on Jesus or the Virgin Mary or Jewish religious stuff, and people can take it. Get on Muslims, though, they get on you quick. At some point, someone needs to just be irreverent. I like Carlos Mencia, I like Dave Chappelle, they can dish it out and have fun with it. The crying and bitching and whining for people to not express their dislike of you, it's no way to bring people around to you.

Do you think if the story hadn't come out, you'd still be playing?

I don't think so. When I played in Long Island last year, I stunk, man. It had been two years since my shoulder surgery, and I was throwing 88 mph on a good day. It would take me 40 minutes to get loosened up for one inning. The shoulder would have blown out regardless. In 2000, I had an ERA under 3.00. The next year I led the league in saves. But then I got traded to Cleveland, and I was pissed to leave Atlanta. I pitched well for

---

* This is true.
† There's supposed to be a cartoon of Muhammad right here, but the pussies at HarperCollins said no. You guys have no balls.

the first month I was there, then I stunk, and then I went to
Texas, and I was kind of pouting.

*If it hadn't been for the story, you might have stayed in At-
lanta.*

Yeah. [Braves general manager] John Schuerholz traded me.
He's a real asshole. I'm gonna absolutely crucify him in my
book.* The credibility that guy receives for the Atlanta Braves
dynasty . . . he is an imbecile. Every player who took that team
to the playoffs were people who were already there. All his
good acquisitions were no-brainers. Schuerholz tries to take all
the credit, but he's a complete moron. It's amazing he gets so
much credit for it. We had a bad arbitration case, he and I. He
just sat there and motherfucked me to death, you suck, you're
horrible, and I lost the case. I never spoke to him again. He'd
walk right by me and say, "Hi, John," and I'd just ignore him.
He has the worst case of Little Man Syndrome I've ever met.
He's about 5-foot-5. He's a piece of shit.

*I don't know why I'm asking this, but what do you think of
the war?*[†]

I'd like to go into politics someday. I'm a little young now,
but I think I'd be good for it and people would get behind me.
I'm not a George Bush fan, but I'd like to see him work with the
Left a little more. But we need to help those people. They were
living under the iron fist of a dictator, and we have to help them.
But I don't know. It's a damned if you do, damned if you don't
type thing. But it's Islam and the Middle East. It's not gonna get
better.[‡]

Thank you for your time, sir.

Thank you. Congratulations on your Cardinals, by the way.

Thank you.

---

* By now, Rocker was pretty blitzed.
† I have no idea why I asked this.
‡ My God, he's right!

GLOSSARY

Anthony, Carmelo. All-Star guard for the Denver Nuggets whose reputation constantly wavers between up-and-coming superstar and out-of-control thug. Caused "controversy" in 2004 when he appeared in an underground *Stop Fucking Snitching* video, made by Baltimore gangs to discourage members from talking to police. Lost respect from fans for resisting the temptation to punch Isiah Thomas in the face during a 2006 brawl at Madison Square Garden.

Arenas, Gilbert. Charmingly insane guard for Washington Wizards whose nickname, "Agent Zero," was coined by bloggers (and he is now a proud blogger himself). Once bragged that his favorite activity is ordering merchandise from infomercials, including a colon cleanser.

Armstrong, Lance. Genetic freak Texan who defied the laws of reason by sparking a brief interest in the deathly boring sport of cycling. Despised by the French for constantly winning their only contribution to the sporting landscape while never testing positive for blood doping, which, along with his contributions to cancer research (and ugly wrist jewelry), is the only reason he remains popular with the public. Friends with both Matthew McConaughey and George W. Bush.

Artest, Ron. Sort of a modern-day Dennis Rodman, without the cross-dressing. In constant danger of taking out half his team and himself with a machete. Once, as a Chicago Bull, applied for a job at a Circuit City just to earn the employee discount. Famous Palace Brawl between Artest's Pacers and the Detroit Pistons was allegedly started by Artest telling Ben Wallace "you can suck my balls." Was punished for his role in the brawl with suspension for the rest of the season, then banishment forced to play for Sacramento.

Beckham, David. Over-the-hill pretty boy shouldered as the 45,212th person to Make Soccer Popular in America, a Sisyphean task that has been failed by people who *aren't* married to a Spice Girl and prone to wearing sarongs. Has a tattoo on his arm of his wife's name in Hindi, but it is misspelled.

Benson, Kris. Oft-injured pitcher more famous for his crazed ex-stripper wife, Anna, who continuously steals the spotlight from her husband even though she's not that hot. Anna's personal Web site is renowned for her unhinged rants, including an anti-PETA screed that claimed "[Animals] have, like, two cells in their little animal heads, but I think natural instinct helps them understand that they are here to eat and be eaten."

Bonds, Barry. One of the greatest baseball players of all time who, unfortunately, overdid it in his late-career experimentation with steroids to the point that he made his body resemble a space alien. Hated by almost everyone, and wouldn't have it any other way.

Brady, Tom. Golden Boy Patriots quarterback known for impregnating models and maintaining a clean public image. His unexpected rise to the top of the NFL now seems inevitable; it's impossible to imagine him backing somebody up and holding a clipboard.

Bryant, Kobe. Notoriously insecure and socially awkward scoring machine whose arrest for rape in 2003, in the twisted logic of NBA fandom, made him more popular. Court reports from his arrest feature the bizarre tidbit that, while being questioned by police, he threw a T-shirt he claimed to have ejaculated in toward a police officer, who caught it around the neck; Bryant said "he hadn't shot it up that far." Considered the least menacing person to ever be arrested for rape, even while many consider him guilty of the crime.

Canseco, Jose. Patient Zero in baseball's steroid scandal of the 1990s, an incredibly unlikely but undeniably vital point man in the maelstrom that was the mainstream reaction to grown men sticking needles in the fatty tissue of their ass. Predictably, has decided he wants to become an action movie star, even putting together an "audition tape" that featured him doing judo air kicks and besting imaginary ninjas.

Clemens, Roger. Reportedly fingered by Jason Grimsley as a steroid cheat, which Clemens denies, whose yearly dance with whether or not he will retire would be exhausting even if it weren't so predictable. Self-regard evidenced by his habit of naming all his children with monikers that start with the letter K. Big fan of Asians: When asked about the popularity of the World Baseball Classic, he said he knew it was popular in Japan because while it aired he "couldn't get [his] dry cleaning done."

Daly, John. Robust, flatulent, lovable golfer renowned for smoking cigarettes and drinking beer on the course. Surprisingly, still breathing. The world's only interesting golfer.

Davenport, Najeh. Journeyman running back most famous for a college exploit, in which he sneaked into an ex-girlfriend's dormitory and vengefully defecated in her closet. Was arrested for the incident and subsequently dubbed "The Hamper Shitter."

Eckstein, David. "Scrappy" Cardinals shortstop whose heroic traits of "grittiness" and "guttiness" are common media buzzwords for "short white guy." Not Jewish.

Favre, Brett. "Gunslinging" quarterback and recipient of every white sportswriter's adulation for ten years past the sell date. Somehow has everyone hanging on his every word about whether or not he will retire every year, even though he's never retired (despite his team's practically begging him to do so).

Loves trotting out the myth that he'd just as soon be home working on his Mississippi farm.

Federer, Roger. Dominant tennis player, helplessly boring, likely a cyborg.

Freel, Ryan. Cincinnati Reds outfielder who boasts of his imaginary friend "Farney." Once told the *Dayton Daily News:* "[Farney is] a little guy who lives in my head who talks to me and I talk to him. That little midget in my head said, 'That was a great catch, Ryan,' I said, 'Hey, Farney, I don't know if that was you who really caught that ball, but that was pretty good if it was.' Everybody thinks I talk to myself, so I tell 'em I'm talking to Farney."

Giambi, Jason. Proof that steroids are good for you and will make you money. Signed nine-digit contract with the Yankees after years of steroid abuse, a contract that cannot be voided.

Griffin, Eddie. Journeyman NBA player once arrested for a car accident outside a grocery store that took place while he was masturbating to the adult film *Privates,* which has to be the worst name for a porn film of all time. Was killed two years later, when he crashed his car into a train.

Grossman, Rex. Chicago Bears quarterback responsible for all-time worst Super Bowl performance, thanks largely to his "Fuck It, I'm Throwin' Deep" attitude toward game management. Nicknamed "The Sex Cannon" by popular NFL blog Kissing Suzy Kolber, plays football like a Madden-addicted teenager who goes for it on fourth and 35 from his own 10-yard line.

Hardaway, Tim. Retired NBA guard known during his playing days for his crossover dribble, and during his post-NBA career for gleefully proclaiming that he "hates gay people" on national radio. Indicative of a larger antigay bias in the NBA than most players will admit. Probably made the comments to cancel out a moment in his past in which a group of gay men invaded his home and took turns anally raping him until he became One of Them. Heroically, resisted.

Henry, Chris. Oft-arrested Cincinnati Bengals receiver. Hit the Grand Slam with six arrests in four months, once while

wearing his own jersey, on an undercover operation that perhaps should have been rethought.

Holyfield, Evander. Elderly punch-drunk boxer who insists
he will someday retake the world championship even though
he's been fighting—and has had serious brain damage—since
before boxers used gloves. Might benefit from a profession that
does not require taking repeated blows to the face.

Jackson, Stephen. NBA crazy man whose violent instincts
remain underrated. Started swinging at anyone in sight during
the Pacers-Pistons brawl, and has had several incidents, many
involving guns, at various Indianapolis-area strip clubs. Has
since been traded to Golden State, in Oakland where, hey, what
could possibly go wrong?

Jeter, Derek. Beloved Yankees shortstop best described as
"looking like The Rock's retarded little brother." Somehow has
navigated the New York media rigmarole so that he is beloved
regardless of what his actions and however many vapid quotes
he gives. Has his own cologne.

Johnson, Chad. One of the few Cincinnati Bengals not to
have been arrested, his end-zone touchdown dances manage to
be self-aggrandizing in an appealing way. Once mocked Bears
linebacker Brian Urlacher—who had been involved in a paternity suit with, of all people, *Riverdance* creator Michael Flatley—
by dancing Irish-style after scoring. Once threatened to drape a
dead deer over his shoulders upon reaching the end zone; sadly,
did not.

Jones, Pacman. The man credited with introducing the
phrase "Making It Rain" to a grateful nation of white people.
The Titans' cornerback was suspended by the NFL for an entire season, even though he had yet to be convicted of anything, and now he's farting around low-level professional
wrestling, cutting his dreadlocks and waiting to be let out of
Goodell Jail.

Jordan, Michael. Absolutely, in no way, suspended by commissioner David Stern for gambling in the mid-'90s. Nope.

Kidd, Jason. New Jersey Nets point guard and walking advertisement for the sanctity of marriage. Dueling lawsuits with wife, Joumana, have featured accusations of spousal abuse and repeated infidelities, all played out in the New York City tabloids. Children likely to be less stable than Frances Bean Cobain.

Leinart, Matt. Superstar college quarterback known for bedding coeds and hanging out with Nick Lachey. Lived the American Dream in college, but obviously used up his karma, being drafted by the Arizona Cardinals and accidentally impregnating an ex-girlfriend within a three-month span.

Manning, Eli. "Slow" younger brother of Colts Super Bowl hero; the Billy Carter of sports, if Billy Carter were the president of a large third-world nation that lacked running water, electricity, and any sort of legislative organization.

Manning, Peyton. Socially stunted, playbook-memorizing, frantic Colts quarterback whose skills and Super Bowl ring are unlikely to ever release him from that gawky yokel appearance. Has no commercial sponsors.

Manning Jr., Ricky. Backup Bears cornerback who once beat up a man at an International House of Pancakes because he was using a laptop computer. Constantly on the lookout for nerds to pummel.

Myers, Brett. Philadelphia Phillies pitcher who punched his wife in the face in front of sizable number of Boston witnesses before a Red Sox game; he convinced her later not to press charges. A tae kwon do specialist and all-around class act.

Nash, Steve. Canadian, socialist point guard who somehow seems a freewheeling, liberal man of the people despite having sex with Elizabeth Hurley.

O'Neal, Shaquille. Jovial and monstrous NBA legend whose obsession with pretending to be a police officer would be cute were it not for one incident—accompanied a SWAT team invading a house where officials believed the owner had been downloading child pornography. When the house was entered, police quickly realized that they'd come to the wrong house and that their guns were pointed at the wrong people; this would have been bad enough had the poor family *not* looked up and found Shaquille O'Neal staring down at them from the barrel of a shotgun. Starred in a movie in which he played a big purple genie.

Orton, Kyle. Bears backup quarterback renowned for his off-field drinking exploits; various online photographs of Orton downing bottles of Jack Daniel's while shirtless and sporting a neck beard have entertained countless Web denizens.

Owens, Terrell. Slightly more successful during the last few years at football than he has been at suicide . . . but there is always room for improvement. Has potential and many fans rooting for him to succeed.

Perez, Odalis. Lousy pitcher, but expert in public relations. Spoke for athletes everywhere when, after he was demoted from the Los Angeles Dodgers' starting rotation and was asked if he would continue his "O's 45" program (which allowed poor inner-city children to attend his starts), he said no way. He added, "When you spend your own money you want to be recognized for that. I don't want to be a hero, but just pay more attention to what I'm doing. People don't want to give me the recognition for it." Never restarted the plan, even when he rejoined the rotation.

Piazza, Mike. Not gay, and stop asking. Oh, and pass the highlighter.

Plummer, Jake. Failed Broncos quarterback best known for his antiwar speechifying, inspired by the death of his college friend and pro teammate Pat Tillman. Proof that all political discourse is more convincing when the speaker is having sex with a Denver Broncos cheerleader.

Porter, Joey. Batshit linebacker constantly battling the enemies in his own brain, inventing people who "disrespect" him so he will be more inspired to smash his helmet into their solar plexus. Rhodes scholar.

Portis, Clinton. Wildly eccentric Redskins running back known for his multiple personalities and various costumes and wigs, most famously "Sheriff Gonna Getcha" and "Coach Janky Spanky" (in which he impersonated anyone who ever ran a gym class).

Pujols, Albert. Future Hall of Famer who has never done anything wrong in his life, ever, and might have been sent here by God to demonstrate what our species might be capable of. Rumored to have wings and the ability to heal cancer with his mind.

Ramirez, Manny. Dingbat Red Sox slugger. Key story: While playing for the Cleveland Indians in 1994, he was told that police were "chasing O.J." His response: "What did Chad do?" in reference to teammate Chad Ogea.

Randolph, Zack. Troubled NBA forward once accused of the most depressing pseudo-rape on record. Quoth a police report: "The woman who filed the complaint said Randolph was disappointed that the [paid] sex show had only simulated sex and refused to pay her. After the show, she said, she had consensual sex with Randolph's friend and then fell asleep or 'passed out.' She claimed she awoke and found Randolph trying to have anal sex with her. She told investigators she awoke and 'slapped' Randolph away twice, and he went back to sleep." Proof that the NBA is the most glamorous league on earth.

Roethlisberger, Ben. Super Bowl winner who followed up on his greatest professional triumph by being photographed drunk in every Pittsburgh bar, crashing his motorcycle while helmetless, and having an emergency appendectomy. Has nasty beard.

Schilling, Curt. World Series hero/blowhard who has been known to e-mail everyone from random Red Sox fans to obscure sports bloggers whom he's unlikely to meet. Will not be satisfied until he is deemed king. Not to be underestimated, even for a Bush supporter.

Smoot, Fred. The ringleader of the famous Minnesota Vikings sex boat, he certainly seemed to have the most fun in the whole ordeal, notoriously "pleasing" two hookers at once with what the kids call a "double dildo." Has helpfully contributed the verb "to smoot" to the lexicon.

Stewart, Kordell. Retired quarterback rumored to be gay throughout his career, rumors which he helpfully put to rest by explaining to his teammates, with pictures, what his favorite sexual positions were. With women. Ladies. Chicks. Girls. Whatever.

Thomas, Isiah. The NBA's reverse-Midas touch; has destroyed every franchise/league/player he's ever placed his hands on. That's not to mention the Madison Square Garden employee who sued him for sexual harassment and won. Also sells popcorn on the Internet.

Tyson, Mike. Former heavyweight champion and video game star of *Mike Tyson's Punch-Out!;* at the age of thirty-two, I still find him nearly impossible to beat as Little Mac.

Urlacher, Brian. Stud Bears linebacker with an off-field life that seemingly belies his intense on-field persona. One of the few people romantically linked not only with Paris Hilton, but also a woman who has slept with Michael Flatley. Okay, not one of the few.

Vick, Michael. Mexico, Ron. Do not ask him to pet-sit.

Weir, Johnny. "Flamboyant" figure skater whose "flamboyant" (and amusing) nature constantly offends the non-"flamboyant" rulers of the figure skating world, who seem surprised that a male figure skater might be "flamboyant." Also, does it with guys.

Woods, Tiger. Hits golf balls a long way and is friends with Hootie from Hootie and the Blowfish. Rumor has it he's black: incorrect.

PART II: OWNERS

In which your already exhausted typist:

- opines on matters economic despite a rather gruesome credit rating (page 87);

- tackles the highly controversial topic of beer advertisements (page 93);

- kids himself that people care enough about the Olympics to read an essay about why you shouldn't care about the Olympics (page 97);

- pens a love letter to NFL commissioner Roger Goodell (page 105);

- takes down the otherwise beloved Peter Angelos (page 109);

- casts himself as a blue-collar working man in a trip to Yankee Stadium (page 113);

- lists five terrible sports owners, because five is a big round number and ten would have been too many (page 119);

- retells an old story that has nothing to do with sports but does involve public masturbation (page 123);

- fills some pages with quick, easily digestible glossary entries (page 127).

AN ASSHOLE IN A SUIT IS WORTH TWO WEARING PADS

It is perfectly legitimate for fans to look at the continued labor woes of pretty much every major professional sports league and not be able to resist the urge to tell them all to fuck off and die.

It's a natural reaction. Anytime there a strike or lockout in pro sports, analysts always describe the conflict as two sides "fighting for pieces of the big pie." This ignores the real power brokers in the dispute, which of course are the fans. And that's not just populist claptrap either. The "pie" that owners and players are fighting over is the vast amount of cash that comes directly from the fans. There are platitudes about not alienating the fans, but, ultimately, owners and players assume we'll come back, once they get all this settled.

This is a largely correct assumption. Every major professional sports league has had a labor disaster that was expected to derail the funnel of cash—but the cash flow never stops. The NFL gave us Keanu Reeves and a ragtag bunch of lovable miscreants as replacement players; the NBA took half a season off and returned with seemingly every player thirty-five pounds and two illegitimate children heavier; baseball actually *canceled the freaking World Series.* These are death penalty–deserving offenses. But, what can we say? We like sports. If there were no sports, we would be forced to speak to our families, become responsible citizens, maybe even vote occasionally. And we can't have that.

That is to say: The claims of thinking about the real victims, *the fans,* are just crowd-pleasing bromides. Players and owners will always act as if we will keep handing them cash ad infinitum, and they will always be correct. No sense pretending otherwise.

So, then I ask, with honest curiosity . . . why do we always assume that when players are asking for more money, they're whiners who don't appreciate what they've been given, but that owners are just "reacting to marketplace realities"? Why do we assume the owners have more right to our money than the players? Why does it bother us so much when a player cries for a raise, but not so much when the owner refuses to give it to him?

A case study: Javon Walker, formerly a wide receiver for the Green Bay Packers. In 2004, Walker, still working off his locked-in, barely negotiable rookie contract from the 2002 draft, had his best season as a professional, catching 89 passes for 1,382 yards and 12 touchdowns. He was the No. 1 receiver that Packers fans—and drama queen quarterback Brett Favre— had been waiting for. All was well.

But in the summer of 2005, right after his breakthrough season, Walker held out of training camp, claiming he wanted to renegotiate his contract. The Packers, mindful of the stridently pro-ownership labor rules of the time, pointed out that his contract had two years remaining and refused to talk further about it. They even enlisted Favre, who really must have his public relations person following along behind his storied Kiln, Mississippi, tractor at all times, to call Walker out in the press for lack of team-oriented ethic, whatever that means. Walker pointed out that even though, yes, he was under contract, if he were somehow injured and unable to play for the team, the supposedly sacred contract would be nothing to the team; they would just cut him and not have to pay him. Which is true. Which is insane.

Not that it mattered; Packers fans, and football fans in general, excoriated Walker for his selfishness, and eventually he caved and showed up to camp, his bluff officially called and exposed for the world to see. In the first game of the 2005 season, Walker caught a 55-yard pass from Favre and promptly tore his ACL (anterior cruciate ligament) and was out for the season. Only Favre's sheepish backtrack of begging Packers management not to release him allowed Walker to receive a paycheck at all; the Packers, had they wanted, could have just cut him right then and there. He'd have been injured, his entire career in question, and they could wipe their hands of the whole mess. In other words, they could have torn up his contract . . . the very same whose sanctity Walker had supposedly defiled in the off-season. Eventually Walker requested and received a trade to the Broncos, saying, "They want players to come up there and play hard and work hard, but when it comes time to be compensated, it's like, 'We forgot what you've done.'" He signed a new contract with the Broncos, one that could just as easily be ripped to pieces if he were injured again.

But still, Walker was perceived as a selfish player. A player wanting to garner more money from his team is a cocky bastion of greed. An owner who doesn't want to give him the money, though, is just trying to do his best to put a good team on the field. This makes absolutely no sense.

For reasons that escape my intellectual capabilities, the average fan seems to think that players are just lucky to be blessed with athletic ability, whereas franchise owners have *earned* their money. They made it in the real world; players just make it in this dream world they're fortunate to inhabit.

So let's compare the life of an athlete to, say, my life.

My life is simple. I get up in the morning, I write a bunch of jokes about sports all day, I answer a lot of e-mail. It's more work than people realize, but not *really;* I have a fifteen-second commute, and this commute does not require that I wear pants. I'm in no position to complain, and I won't. Most important, I am allowed bad days. If one day the jokes aren't clicking, or

I had too much to drink the night before and am unable to speak in any language other than Esperanto, the odds are good that no one will really notice. I work hard, but, like the rest of America, I can fake it every once in a while. If I had to work at my peak capacity every second of every day, with the entire world watching my every move, well, let's just say a lot of people would be dropping me from their fantasy team. I always think of an old job I had working on a magazine paper-assembly line. If I messed up and left my station for longer than sixty seconds, the machine would run out of feeding paper, jam up, and stop, setting off a loud alarm and flashing red light. Everyone in the plant would look at me and know that I screwed up. If this happened in your office, with a flashing red light above whatever cubicle that ceased being productive for a sixty-second stretch, corporate America would look like a rave party. (Wait: Do they still have raves? There still have to be people raving, yes? I don't get out much.) This is not to say that we are lazy. It is just that we don't have to prove ourselves every minute of the workday. This is hardly a bad thing.

You can argue that I am a bad example in this postulate, that my job is not as difficult as yours, offers little to society, and is more likely to cause carpal tunnel and bed sores than a rotator cuff injury. I am sure your job is more difficult. That is fair, but still beside the point.

Because you *really* have to earn your way onto the roster of a professional sports team. (Rare exceptions include Drew Henson, Jeff George, and the 2002 Pittsburgh Pirates.) Unlike your job, there are hundreds of thousands of people who would love to have the job of professional athlete, and hundreds with the physical prowess to attempt it. You don't get ahead as an athlete by making friends with the right people, or having the right number of alumni in the right managerial positions in your field, or scoring the right amount on a mathematics test. You get ahead as an athlete solely by being better than those who are trained to do the exact same job as you. And this is not a grandfathered situation either. It doesn't particularly matter what you did last year, or last week, or yesterday; if you are unable to perform at the level your employer expects you to, every single day, they will find someone who will. The past is immaterial; you are forced to go out and prove yourself, all the time.

This is not to say that players are not generously compensated for their efforts, or that they are somehow anonymous drones enslaved by a corrupt system. This is also not meant to be a spirited defense of athletes; remember one of the fundamental rules of sports fandom: *If you knew any of these people in real life, you would hate them and they would hate you.* But to somehow believe that these men are successful and able to play athletics at the highest level merely because of God-given skill is to bring personal biases and regrets into a situation where they should not apply. Athletes are required to constantly prove why they have their position on the most public of stages; otherwise they will be discarded. That's just how it works.

And you know who is not required to constantly reaffirm why he has his position? The owner.

We think the players earn the money the easy way, while owners somehow worked their way up the corporate food chain, like real Americans, compiling their billions through blood, sweat, and hedge funds. This is hardly the case. In the NFL, an owner couldn't lose money if he tried. In the MLB and the NBA, any team with half a clue is at least able to exist in the black. Never mind that many of these franchises, particularly in the NFL, are family heirlooms that even the biggest dunderhead couldn't screw up, profit-wise; we Arizona Cardinals fans know this all too well. Fans treat the players' complaints as sour grapes; ownership is afforded far more leeway.

The reason for this, I suspect, is that it is nearly impossible for most of us to imagine being a billionaire—but a scrappy second baseman? Man, we could have totally made the bigs if we had just caught a break here or there. Playing sports is something we can relate to. When a player makes a mistake, we, from the couch at home, can envision ourselves executing the play correctly. *How can this guy miss that ball when he's making $1.3 million a year?* But we don't see owners' mistakes, at least not in such plain view.

It's not like fans have sympathy for the owners; it's just that we have none for the players. Rather than perceiving the matter as simply the workers earning their wages from the owners, we think they're taking money from *us*. They are, of course, but we don't hold the owners up to the same standard. We're not supporting the owners; we're supporting the *team*. We put the burden on the players, because, jeez, playing sports is supposed to be fun! We'd do it for free! Why can't they?

Therefore, when ownership raises ticket prices or charges fans admission to visit training camp, they're simply being jerks; when Alex Rodriguez strikes out four times, he's *robbing us.* We insert ourselves into the equation, which is fair, but we do it in a consistently one-sided way, which is not.

The logical way to react to this, of course, would be to boy-cott the games and merchandise until both sides come to their senses. But let's not start talking crazy. We hang out with our families enough as is.

So when the players strike, or the owners lock them out, we save a disproportionate amount of our vitriol for the players, when, at the end of the day, we should probably just tell them both to, you know, fuck off and die.

COORS LIGHT THINKS YOU'RE A MONSTER

If you want to know what advertisers—providers of the real reason you're allowed to watch sports on television, with the actual games simply filler between hucksters pitching unhealthy "sports drinks" and boner pills—really think of you, the sports fan, all you need to do is watch any set of commercials during an NFL game.

One Coors Light commercial is the ultimate example of the fact that advertisers not only think we're morons, but also that we're monsters. The ad is for a new type of Coors Light bottle, in which the label turns blue when the beer is fully chilled. (This is extremely helpful; for years, I have struggled to decipher when, exactly, my beer is cold enough to drink. The years of anguish caused by warm beer are now, thankfully, in my past.) In the commercial, a man and a woman are in a small apartment. The woman is in the bathroom, fidgeting with what appears to be a home pregnancy test. The man is in the kitchen, staring into the refrigerator.

From the bathroom comes a call. "It's blue!" the woman yells, smiling. "It's blue!" Cut to the man, with an even broader grin. "Yes it is!" he yells. "It's blue!" That's the initial punch line; cut to a close-up of the Coors Light bottle and a voice-over about the virtues of the "when it's blue, it's cold" concept. And then they cut back to the couple. The woman stomps into the bathroom and slams the door, while the man, bewildered, says, "But I'm so happy it's blue! What's wrong?" And then he smiles as he opens the bottle of beer.

Mind you, this commercial doesn't have anything to do with sports. But you will only find it playing during a sporting event. (I don't watch much *Oprah*, but I'd say the odds are good that Coors isn't filling ad space there with this one.) Coors (which is the official beer sponsor of the NFL), for its part, claims the ads are uplifting, not exploitive.

"We've been careful not to make this all about babes," Coors then–marketing chief Ron Askew said. "All the women in the spots are leaders, not followers. The women are in control. They're the ones inviting you into the party at 4 A.M." The only person who could say that with a straight face is someone who claims Coors Light is a drinkable beverage.

Listen, I'm no moral policeman, and I have few qualms about looking at an attractive woman. But a stray glance at any sports commercial reveals how cretinous these advertisers— and networks—consider consumers to be. A friend of mine once dated an actress who constantly went on auditions for beer commercials. She said, without fail, the role was for the hot woman that a man inevitably casts aside for a beer. She called them "Me or the Beer" parts. "I always lost, and usually, at the end of the commercial, I'd be bonked on the head with something, or fall down some stairs."

Look at any commercial that attempts to show what average sports fans are like. Inevitably, they're a group of screaming lunatics, usually shirtless, with their faces painted, yelling whooping noises. I do not deny that these sad genetic anomalies do exist, and they usually do end up with cameras in their face. (Extra credit if they have one of the letters "ESPN" written on their bare chest during freezing weather.) But this is not the typical sports fan. Is this what they really think of you? Imagine if a financial services company portrayed all its investors in ads as cocaine-addled, pill-popping Patrick Bateman Masters of the Universe.

This is to say: There's no better way to grasp what the real money men in sports think of the average fan than to look at the way they are stereotyped in advertisements. And don't think that our leagues aren't beholden to the beer companies more than any other major corporations.

Our sports leagues are so indebted to the world of beer that it's impossible to separate the two; when Cardinals pitcher Josh Hancock was killed in a drunk-driving accident in May 2007, the team made a big show of banning alcohol from the clubhouse. This, of course, while they were playing games in *Busch Stadium*. Warriors coach Don Nelson brought a Bud Light to his postgame press conferences during the 2007 NBA Playoffs— until the league, in the post-Hancock fervor, ordered him not to, thus making Nelson's press conferences the *only* aspect of the NBA Playoffs in which beer was not prominently displayed. Sports and beer are inextricably linked; jeez, in Milwaukee, even the child-friendly mascot slides into a mug of beer when the Brewers hit a home run.

I certainly down my fair share of beer. But consider who the real power brokers are in sports—it's not the players, or the coaches, or even, often, the owners. It's the advertisers—and they're often advertising the major beer breweries. And if their commercials are to be believed . . . we're all morons.

IT'S AMERICAN TO ROOT
AGAINST THE U.S.A.

A confession: I hate the Olympics. I'm not sure any real sports fans like the Olympics anymore. We feel like we're supposed to watch; we have these nostalgic images in our minds of Mary Decker and Carl Lewis and Mary Lou Retton on all these Wheaties boxes, L.A. Coliseum's Olympic torch burning in the background. We feel obliged to fire ourselves up to root for the U.S. of A.

But then you sit down to actually watch these events, and you realize that they appear to have been beamed in from another decade, century, millennium. First off, it's almost literally so: With time delays, by the time the events are shown in the Eastern Time Zone prime time, thirteen hours have passed and anyone who has figured out how to use their mouse has long since uncovered everything that has already happened. It turns the telecasts into something like an Oscar telecast, minus the actual suspense, musical numbers, and the sublime pleasure of imagining what Melissa Rivers would look like being ripped apart by wolves. The joy evaporates before we even have the opportunity to find out if it's there. Also, most of the pomp and circumstance surrounding the Olympics feels dated. It's like watching old newsreel footage of a squirrel water-skiing. The time when these athletes were lone wolves coming together to honor their country has long since passed; most of them were separated from their families to train at such an early age that they have no idea how to interact with other human beings. The planet is a background player in their odd quest to master the art of skiing while holding a weapon.

And the events themselves . . . well, I'm more addicted to sports than anyone I know, and there's still not a damned way I'm ever going to understand what's going on in luge. The Olympics are hardly the most telegenic event; inevitably you just watch people in tight spandex and thick goggles zipping by faster than you can soak in. You can't tell what they're doing right, what they're doing wrong, what the difference is between them and the poor Ugandan kids freezing in eighteenth place. The Olympics are pure spectacle. All traces of competition are lost in a frenzy of garish graphics and loving portraits of scrappy underdogs. We pay no attention to these people the rest of the year, and I'm pretty sure that the soft-focus features on them are entirely fabricated. (*"Lars Jorghennsenn was born with four calf valves and a blocked aorta, causing him to bleed profusely from the ear, walk around in circles with a pronounced limp, and only able to utter the words 'yak broth.' It was from this hardship that Jorghennsenn learned his love of the curling broom, and his intestinal fortitude made him a champion . . . and allowed him to buy his peasant parents their first home, a small cottage on the outskirts of Gudmunsdottir."*) This is what networks pay billions of dollars for? And *Arrested Development* can't stay on the air?

Why is it that we have to pretend to care about the discus throw every four years? Never mind the fact that no team sport has anything resembling the motivation Olympians bring to injecting his/her body with every undetectable performance enhancer. Olympic sports appeal only to those single-minded enough to devote their entire lives to them. Have you ever attended a track meet in person? There are thirty events going on at any time.

The only Olympic sport I truly enjoy watching is figure skating, because I can roughly tell what's going on. That is to say: Sometimes they fall down. Call me a sadist, but nothing in the Olympics thrills me more than watching a figure skater fall down. You think about all the dreams they've harbored, all the hard work they've put into their craft, and then the entire planet witnesses them fall directly on their ass. (You can't fall elegantly while wearing skates, no matter how many sequins you're wearing.) And even if they do somehow remain upright through their entire program, their fate is entirely in the hands of faceless, corrupt judges. Judges! *There's no scorecard.* A major Olympic event, the most popular one, crowns its champion using the dog show method. You could say the same thing about gymnastics, but, frankly, the concept of watching prepubescent girls—desperate to stave off the aging process and the horrific notion of growing breasts so that they may remain waifly nimble—get screamed at by balding mustached men while wearing grotesque leotards is too gruesome to even contemplate. If you meet someone who is feverishly into gymnastics, make sure that they register with the local sheriff.

But I'm hardly alone; Olympic ratings fall every year and the exhibition is slipping further and further into irrelevance. The only reason any fans pay attention to the Olympics anymore is because they're conveniently scheduled during times of the year where there are no other sports on. Try programming the Olympics against the Super Bowl or the NCAA Tournament, and let me know if anybody cares who the hell Bode Miller is.

So if no one is actually enjoying the Olympics—except for women who don't really care much for sports and mostly enjoy, well, watching other women fall down—then why are we supposed to be so invested in them? The reason, I'm afraid, lies in a field that's far from sports and light-years away from why we enjoy them. The reason is nationalism. The reason we're supposed to care about the Olympics is because these athletes are not trying to win gold medals for themselves or their sponsors; they're trying to win *to honor America.*

This might have once been possible, back when all the Olympians were true amateur athletes, unable to get paid and cash in on their success. Those days have obviously passed, and that's for the better; Bode Miller excepted, you usually end up with people thriving more at their chosen pastimes when they know there might be a check at the end of the day. But it eliminates this idea of the selfless athlete striving to bring glory to his nation. We hold a romantic image of Jesse Owens sprinting past Adolf Hitler's notions of genetic superiority, taking a stand for America, letting the planet know that the United States is the strongest nation on earth, that its sense of freedom and fair play can thrive in the face of fascism, that America is the place where hard work allows you to thrive. (Well, except for all the black people *other* than Jesse Owens . . . but that's probably a larger issue.) But this hasn't been the case for decades. Half of these fiscally motivated athletes probably couldn't tell you who the vice president is. When Shaun White, the gawky redheaded ginger kid with the overbite, won the gold medal in the halfpipe in 2006, he stood on the podium with the medal hanging from his neck, befuddled by everything, from the national anthem on down to the lady in the ski suit who kept patting him on the back. What do you think Shaun White—by all accounts, a great kid, but a kid nevertheless— was thinking about when he was on that podium? Do you think he was contemplating how he stood up for his country in a time of great peril, a time in which the United States finds itself at a major crossroads—with one foot in the police-the-world super-power past and the other in the globalized, decentralized future? Do you think he was thinking about 9/11? Osama bin Laden? President Bush? Or do you think he was worrying about whether or not anyone would notice his erection when he saw Pam Anderson at the postparty? Or if he'd be able to drink at the party, even though he was underage? The kid was nineteen years old; what do *you* think he was thinking about?

We attach patriotic feelings to him, though, because we have to. Otherwise, the Olympics are just a bunch of people we've never heard of playing sports we could care less about. Root for the Americans! They're short-track speed skating for *liberty*!

Here's the thing, though: *We're the bad guys.* Every instinct we have in our sports decision-making process—whom we root for, whom we consider the evil Cobra Kai villain—would, under ordinary circumstances, cause us to root against the United States. After all, the United States dominates everything on the planet—*for now*—and we're rather insistent on keeping it that way. There was once a time when we battled it out with the USSR for Summer Olympic preeminence and came in fifth or sixth in the Winter Olympics. But that won't do: We're America! So we started adding our own events—the ISOC isn't loath to strong-arm—like the halfpipe and snowboarding, young sports that we invented and already control, and whammo, look! We're second in the medal count. Not enough! Next Olympics: the grilling of meats and the waste of natural resources. We'll rule those. Take that, Sweden!

Note: I love America. What a country, right? ("In Russia, the Olympics watch *you!*") My father is a military man, we have a flag proudly waving in front of our home, I had a crew cut until the age of fifteen—at which time I expressed my independence by growing a particularly mean mullet—and I even own a pair of American flag boxer shorts. (Like Kid Rock!) I have nothing against freedom, and I have nothing but respect for the men and women who fight for my right to scream obscenities at Rachael Ray while eating Cheez Doodles and playing with myself. The Olympics has nothing to do with our country; it has to do with sports, and accepting that we are the bad guys. And embracing it.

Much Sturm und Drang developed in 2006 when the United States basketball team, made up of a bunch of NBA superstars preoccupied with avoiding the accidental impregnation of groupies, lost in the semifinals of the World Basketball Championships to Greece, a team that had previously been best known for its body hair. The body language of the two teams after the loss was telling. The Greeks? They were losing their minds, jumping all over each other, shaving each other's backs . . . it was Crazytown. The Americans? Well, they looked disappointed, but not necessarily because they had lost. They looked like they were going to get yelled at by their agents when they got home. And why wouldn't they feel that way? They traveled halfway around the world to participate in an event for which they're barely paid. Why should LeBron James put aside everything he has in his life to play for America? Will America suffer if he loses? Will we really even notice? All LeBron James had to worry about was not getting arrested for anything and trying to figure out how to get Eric Snow to bury a jump shot every once in a freaking while. That game was *everything* to the Greeks, but to us—not just the players, but all of us—it had the intensity of a preseason exhibition in Sioux Falls. Isn't it worth it to lose that game? Why can't we let the Greeks have their fun? The joy they experienced in winning far outweighed any relief we would have drawn from surviving against highly motivated opponents. Why bother?

We'd all be a lot better off accepting that the god of our sports is not America; it is money, which, for once, isn't the exact same thing. The less importance we attach to these international competitions, the less we'll gnash our teeth when we lose them and, consequently, the less other countries will glory in our defeat. If the Greeks had really known how little we truly cared about that game, would they have celebrated that much? Anybody feel the need to tell them?

The only people who care about how the United States does in international competitions are the sponsors shelling out big cash to have their logos splashed across such "pure" events and those who only pay attention to sports casually and therefore can act all ashamed and shocked when we don't win everything all the time.

So let's just all agree, okay? We don't have to pretend we care about the Olympics anymore, and if we do, it's just to root for the upstart underdog nations to knock us on our cans. It will make them happy, it will help them to look past the fact that we pretty much control every other aspect of their lives. Sure, every restaurant you see is a Kentucky Fried Chicken, but you kicked our ass in ski jumping. Congratulations. Now if you'll excuse us, we've got some McGriddles to inhale and heathens to convert to Christianity. Carry on.

WHY THE NFL GETS AWAY WITH EVERYTHING

In August 2006, Bryant Gumbel—who considers himself quite the social critic for a guy who used to make omelets on morning television—decided he would make a little political statement on his *Real Sports with Bryant Gumbel.* (This show is alternately known as "The Only Show That Takes Bernard Goldberg Seriously" and "What in the HELL Happened to Frank Deford?") While discussing labor issues in the world of sports via the ascension of Roger Goodell to the office of NFL commissioner, Gumbel said this:

> *Before he cleans out his office, have Paul Tagliabue show you where he keeps Gene Upshaw's leash. By making the docile head of the players' union his personal pet, your predecessor has kept the peace without giving players the kind of guarantees other pros take for granted. Try to make sure no one competent ever replaces Upshaw on your watch.*

Gene Upshaw, of course, is the head of the players union in the NFL, which is not only the weakest in all of professional sports, it's probably weaker than any teachers' union, and teachers make less money than bloggers. (Mostly.) Gumbel, who was blasted by Tagliabue for the comments, was trying to say that despite having the most violent jobs of any major professional athlete, NFL players have the shortest career, make the least money, and have no guaranteed contracts. (And their pension plan sucks, too.) Gumbel was blaming Upshaw for this, which makes sense; when your union has no real power, it's reasonable to assume that the union head is a lackey to management.

But that's not fair to Upshaw. He is not the lackey to NFL management: It's us. Every single one of us, from the players to the media to the coaches to, yes, you the fan. The NFL is judge, jury, and executioner, a dictatorship in the purest sense . . . and none of us would have it any other way.

SHORTLY after taking over from Tagliabue as NFL commissioner, Goodell had a clear problem to deal with: Athletes, particularly ones who played for the Cincinnati Bengals, kept finding themselves in trouble with the law. (Impressively, wide receiver Chris Henry was arrested four times in one year, which is not easy to do even if you are trying.) More pressing, Tennessee Titans defensive back Pacman Jones—so named because of the way he used to suck on his mother's nipple as an infant—had caused a ruckus at the 2007 NBA All-Star Game, starting a fight with a strip club bouncer that ended with the bouncer shot and partially paralyzed.

Jones was under investigation by authorities, and his family was releasing statements that he was out of control. Goodell's hands were tied, however; Jones hadn't yet been convicted, or even indicted, for any crime. But he wanted to send a message. So he simply untied his hands and suspended Jones for a whole season—Henry also went down for eight games—by invoking a newly invented "Standard of Conduct" clause.

"It is not enough to simply avoid being found guilty of a crime," Goodell said. "Persons who fail to live up to this standard of conduct are guilty of conduct detrimental and subject to discipline, even where the conduct itself does not result in conviction of a crime."

This is rather unprecedented; taking away a man's livelihood simply because *you don't like the way he's running his life.* Pacman Jones's lawyers appealed the sentence . . . to Roger Goodell. When it became clear that he'd turn it down, they withdrew it.

In the MLB, or the NBA, fans would be up in arms. But in the NFL, we look the other way. The NFL gets away with everything because the fans are slaves to the violence; we think of NFL players as gladiators; if they can't hold up their end of the bargain, we find new gladiators who will take their place. It's our national bloodsport. The players are all faceless robots, out there to pump up our fantasy team numbers. We don't hold the NFL up to the standards we apply to any other professional sports league . . . or any other business. We've already discussed the "If you do steroids in baseball, you're a pariah, but if you do steroids in the NFL, you're an MVP candidate" dichotomy, but it's instructive: Deep down, we don't want the NFL to have any rules. We just want to see people hurting other people, interspersed with some funny touchdown dances. Athlete malfeasance bothers us less in football than in other sports because it's really tough to imagine playing in the NFL. We can imagine laying down a bunt to win a World Series; we can't imagine pushing a 350-pound man to the ground. Only a very certain type of physical specimen can become a football player; *anybody* can play baseball. You might play pickup basketball with your friends, but you *watch* the NFL with your friends. Every Sunday.

Frankly, the players don't really matter that much in the NFL. Look at the difference between labor disputes in the NFL and in Major League Baseball. When baseball went on strike in 1994, and ultimately canceled the World Series, fans felt a real sense of betrayal. Many vowed they'd never return to the game they grew up loving; they felt it had lost its innocence, become too beholden to money and big business interests. The only thing that brought them back, of course, was steroids . . . but that's another essay.

But the NFL? No one believes the NFL is innocent. When NFL players went on strike in 1987, replacement players swooped in. The reaction was, in part, excitement: Cool! New players! These are anonymous men, twenty-two of them in one jumble in the middle of the field. As long as we have a reason to start drinking at noon on a Sunday, put whoever the hell you want out there. Just don't cancel any games, and we'll be fine. What's the difference between this guy getting JACKED UP and the other guy getting JACKED UP?

I love the NFL, and it would take an investigation that uncovered every NFL owner secretly being a member of Al Qaeda to make me turn away from it. (And even then, it would take a year or two.) But the NFL brings out the worst in us as sports fans. And the NFL knows this. It's why they do whatever they want. Just keep 'em comin'.

PETER ANGELOS KILLS KITTENS AND IS TRYING TO SLEEP WITH YOUR MOTHER

Before 1993, Peter Angelos was known as one of the most dogged trial lawyers in the country. He amassed his fortune through a series of publicity-friendly lawsuits; he went after the pharmaceutical industry, asbestos harborers, and, most lucratively, the tobacco industry. (His 25 percent fee netted him $1 billion.) Then, in 1993, he set his sights on the Baltimore Orioles.

At the time, the Orioles, one of the oldest and proudest franchises in baseball, were on the cusp of a renaissance. Behind manager Davey Johnson, icon Cal Ripken, suspiciously bulked-up Brady Anderson, and stoic right-hander Mike Mussina, they rode a wave of warmth that surrounded the opening of retro-before-it-was-cool-to-be-retro Camden Yards. The Orioles were the envy of the sport. The notion of placing a team in nearby Washington, D.C., seemed insane; the Orioles were primed to dominate the market, and the American League East, for decades to come. Angelos, along with some smaller investors, bought the team for $173 million.

After one final flash of light from Ripken's determined chasing-down of Lou Gehrig's consecutive game record, the Orioles went to hell . . . and fast. The sole source of the destruction was Angelos. To look over his reign of terror feels like watching a really cute puppy get tortured. Here are some key moments in the downward spiral:

- One of Angelos's first moves was to release beloved broadcaster Jon Miller from his contract, reportedly because he was displeased with Miller's candor in describing the team's faults. Angelos attempted to spin this, saying that Miller had wanted to head to San Francisco all along, but Miller spoke with his feet: He still lives in Maryland and is rumored to (quietly, because he's Jon Miller) despise Angelos. Up to this point, Orioles fans were cautiously optimistic that Angelos would pour his millions into the team and cultivate the rabid fan base. This was the first sign that matters could go disastrously wrong.

- The same day he was declared American League Manager of the Year, Johnson resigned as Orioles manager because Angelos refused to give him the notorious "vote of confidence" going into the season. He was replaced by overmatched pitching coach Ray Miller, and the Orioles finished fourth in the AL East eight of the next nine years. (The other year, they finished third. Yahoo.) Angelos would proceed to bully a rotation of general managers and field generals, leading to the spectacle of eight pitching coaches in eight years. And after allowing local hero Mike Mussina to sign with the hated Yankees, he blasted Mussina for not understanding baseball finances.

- Angelos's protests about the MLB's desire to put a team in Washington, D.C., led to an extremely friendly cable package for the Orioles. As a way to show his love for the city of Baltimore, rather than the Beltway area in general, he had the word "Baltimore" removed from the team's jerseys.

- Hall of Famer Brooks Robinson, probably the club's second-most-popular player after Ripken, announced that he would no longer have any association with the club (because he's Brooks Robinson, he said it in a nice way). When the Orioles celebrated the fiftieth anniversary of Robinson's major league debut in 2005, Robinson was not in attendance.

- In 2004, Angelos sent out a memo to Orioles personnel, saying, "Pursuant to meetings last week with Mr. Angelos regarding current forecasts of the club's financial statements, Mr. Angelos would like each of you to immediately review all of your respective cost center budgets." That same year, he raised ticket prices 22 percent.

- An annual tradition pops up at Camden Yards in August. With the Orioles perpetually out of the playoff chase, a collection of fans have filled up the upper deck and, at a predetermined time, stood up and left the stadium to protest Angelos's ownership. In 2006, there were one thousand fans. Angelos responded: "Whoever joins that protest has no comprehension of what it costs to run a baseball team."

Last year, rumors arose that salvation could potentially be found in the person of—who else?—Ripken, who was considering a purchase of the team. Financial analysts dug deep into the Orioles' numbers and came up with a value of the franchise.

The price tag was $800 million, a 425 percent profit margin for Angelos on a franchise he had eviscerated and a fan base he had demoralized. Oh, and then he announced he wouldn't be selling the team after all.

Why do owners and management—Angelos being only the most extreme example—treat the fans with such contempt? Because they can. They not only have nothing to lose, they have a 425 percent profit to gain.

TAKE OUT THE SECOND MORTGAGE: WE'RE OFF TO YANKEE STADIUM!

My parents, still living in the humble rural burg of Mattoon, Illinois, have never quite adjusted to the fact that their son lives in New York City. They've dealt with everything else wrong with their son—the fear of family suburban life, the decision to type for a living rather than getting a real job, the refusal to submit to the musical stylings of Billy Joel—but they just can't warm themselves up to my love of New York. It's all just too much for them; my block in Brooklyn has about as many people as their sleepy town, and that's difficult to wrap one's mind around. I have no qualms with this; I'm not sure why I still live here, either.

One part of New York they love, however, without reservation is Yankee Stadium. Anytime they visit—usually when the Cardinals are in town to play the Mets—they try to sneak a visit to the Bronx. They still have the pre-Giuliani mind-set that they're going to be murdered if they so much as make eye contact with anyone on the subway (according to my parents, New York is pretty much still the way it was in *The Warriors*), but to them, Yankee Stadium is sacred, the home of Babe Ruth, Billy Martin, Mickey Mantle, Lou Gehrig. They see the history, and are blind to all else.

I find this amazing, because, as far as I'm concerned, there's not a stadium in all of sports that's a less enjoyable place to watch a sporting event than Yankee Stadium. It's not just that the park, because of an ill-fated mid-'70s remodeling, has the nostalgic architecture of an International House of Pancakes. (Though that doesn't help.) It's that the mythos of Yankee Stadium, hand in hand with that unique blend of entitlement and narcissism that makes New York what it is, have combined to make attending a game there feel like you've been invited to your extravagantly wealthy uncle's house, the one who never talks to you, works for some evil law firm somewhere, and makes you take your shoes off the minute you get out of the car. Oh, and he charges you forty bucks once you make it through the front door. It's the biggest rip-off in all of sports.

It's not the fans' fault, either. I actually quite enjoy (most) of the fans at a Yankees game. I'm mostly impressed by the cheers. The cheers at Yankee Stadium are communal comedic concertos. Everyone seems to have studied from some sort of crude handbook. When the game starts, they shout out the names of each Yankee on the field until the player waves. Anytime there's a bad call, everyone, in unison, immediately breaks into "ASS-HOLLLLE. ASS-HOLLLLE!" When the grounds crew comes out to drag the field in the sixth inning, to the tune of the Village People's "YMCA," the bleachers make it their own song, finding someone wearing the opponent's cap and screaming, together, to the chorus: "WHY ... ARE ... YOU ... GAY? HOW ... DID ... YOU ... GET ... THAT ... WAY?" It's politically incorrect, awful, wrong, and, frankly, hilarious.

But, God, the Yankees. Let's track a typical evening trip to Yankee Stadium.

5:30 P.M.

You beg out early from work—and only in New York is 5:30 considered "leaving early"—and hop on the subway. (If you are driving to Yankee Stadium, you, frankly, deserve what's coming to you.) At this hour, you're running into rush-hour trains, so they're packed, hot, sweaty and full of handsy people. Guard your wallet, guard your ass, guard your soul, really. Also: If you're foolish enough to wear a hat of the opposing team—particularly if that opposing team plays in Boston or Flushing—it's probably wise to keep some headphones on. Until they knock them off, anyway. Fortunately, your StubHub tickets only cost you $115 for a seat in the upper tier.

6:15 P.M.

Oh, so you know how you brought that bag of work papers with you? (Because you didn't have time to stop at home with a 7 P.M. first pitch.) You can't bring those in the park, because the Yankees are a terrorist target; therefore, your briefcase could have a sniper rifle aimed directly at the temple of Doug Mientkiewicz. So you're gonna have to check that at one of the stores across the street; if the Yanks are playing the Red Sox or Mets, it's gonna cost you seven bucks (it's five for everybody else, unless it's the playoffs, in which case you're running at least ten). A teenager will check your bag in an overcrowded, mold- and rat-infested bin and he will hand you a ticket. If you lose this ticket, you can say good-bye to your bag, and if you hang on to it, you're still pressing your luck. By this point, you have been harassed by a gaggle of drunken teenagers, berated by cops to "keep moving" (even though you're packed shoulder-to-shoulder with the rest of the lost souls), propositioned by scalpers, and wound up inadvertently purchasing a Derek Jeter towel. If you can make it through the unwashed masses to the gate, be prepared to wait at your gate for half an hour as ushers search every woman's purse while simultaneously looking down their shirts.

7:25 P.M.

Congratulations! You're only fifteen minutes late, though you're now looking at another ten minutes until you fight your way to your seat. (Oh, if you smoke, I hope you had one before you came in, because there's no smoking area in Yankee Stadium—unlike every other ballpark in the country.) You should stop and grab a beer first: That will be nine dollars, also the highest rate in the country. The plastic cups are smaller than most ballparks', too. The good news? They fill them to the brim, so you can spill them all over everyone in your (cramped) row as you shuffle to your seat.

8:18 P.M.

Because this is American League baseball, an hour-plus in, you should be in about the top of the second inning by now.

8:43 P.M.

After another half-hour trip to grab a couple more beers and a hot dog (twenty-five dollars, plus tip, and I wouldn't recommend not tipping your server), a man behind you starts his drunken screaming at Alex Rodriguez, for alternately being gay/cheating on his wife/striking out/wearing lipstick/aiding Sirhan Sirhan in the assassination of Robert F. Kennedy. Expect spittle to land on the back of your neck.

9:25 P.M.

Around now, the Yankee Stadium JumboTron, after countless between-inning platitudes of Supporting the Troops and Which Hat Is the Ball Under?, shifts into Paul O'Neill Is an American Hero video montage, scored, bizarrely, to Pat Benatar's "The Warrior." I've never understood why, of all the Yankees stars of the last two decades, Yankee fans lionize Paul O'Neill so much. The guy was a slightly above-average hitter, seemed to genuinely hate himself—to the point that he would punch himself in the face—when he struck out, and wore a mullet perm. *This* is the guy who gets a video montage? Really?

10:05 P.M.

At last! The seventh-inning stretch! The perfect time to leave for the restroom. You better do it fast, too, like midway through the top of the seventh. If you wait, the ushers will actually *chain your section closed so you cannot leave.* Why? Because the Yankees Are More Patriotic Than You Are. Even though every other stadium in baseball (including Shea) realizes it's not September 12 anymore, the Yankees insist on playing "God Bless America" at every seventh-inning stretch. I'm all about America—I love America—but I, and most normal-thinking people, cannot stand "God Bless America." Putting aside the whole church-vs.-state discussion, it's a poorly written and constructed song, sugary, stupidly sentimental, not Irving Berlin's happiest moment as a songwriter. (He even admitted this late in his life.) I'll take "America the Beautiful" any day. But George Steinbrenner—when they poke him with a stick to wake him every couple of weeks—doggedly insists they play the funereal dirge every damn game. And you better stand at attention, or one of the snipers on the roof will take you out. Oh, and once you've appropriately paid tribute, just to keep up the mood, the Stadium plays "Cotton-Eyed Joe," which might be the worst song ever recorded. Honestly, I left Illinois to get *away* from that crap.

10:45 P.M.

Because beer sales ended an hour and a half ago, you're now in that fun purgatory of no-longer-drunk and desperately-needing-to-pee. The bathroom lines are all jammed, though, so, you know, that's why the plastic cups have the wide rims.

11:15 P.M.

At last, the game is over. If the Yankees won, you're listening to Frank Sinatra sing "New York, New York." If they lost, you're listening to Liza Minnelli's version, which has to be somewhat demoralizing to her. It's gonna take another half an hour to make it out of the stadium, which is really no big deal, considering you now have another half-hour line to reclaim your bag . . . if it's still there.

12:15 A.M.

You've made it back on the subway. Don't worry about guarding your wallet anymore: You're completely out of money.

Many have complained that something historic will be lost when they tear down Yankee Stadium next year to build another stadium next door. Not me. Burn it to the ground, I say.

APPENDIX: THE FIVE WORST OWNERS IN SPORTS

Peter Angelos is my personal choice for the worst owner in sports, but here are five others—in descending order of disgracefulness—who are ruining their fan bases' hopes and dreams in order to earn just a little more cash.

5. Bill Wirtz. The Chicago Blackhawks owner, while listening to a pitch from a potential general manager, once responded with: "Don't go thinking about a Stanley Cup title. They're too expensive." Now that's inspiring! (The Blackhawks have gone longer than any team in the NHL without a title.) Despite ticket prices that are among the highest in the NHL, the team blacks out nonsellout home games on local television. Wirtz is also responsible, through Judge & Dolph, Ltd., for a third of all alcohol sales in the state of Illinois, which is a good or bad thing, depending on your perspective. Apathy toward the Blackhawks has grown to the point that the AHL Chicago Wolves rival the Blackhawks in attendance ever year. Would be higher on this list, but this is hockey, and nobody really cares. (He receives no extra credit for having died in September 2007, by the way. In fact, it's why he's fifth, rather than first.)

4. William Clay Ford. Has been running the Detroit Lions, one of the NFL's most storied franchises, into the ground for forty years, but has earned extra credit points for his dogged refusal to fire team president Matt Millen, who handles a sports team the way, say, Kurt Cobain handled a shotgun. Since he took over the team in 1964, the Lions have won exactly one playoff game, despite having Barry Sanders for his entire career. Ford is the grandson of Henry Ford, though he doesn't appear to be a Nazi sympathizer, which is nice.

3. James Dolan. It would seem difficult to destroy the New York Knicks, the beloved jewel of the NBA, with league commissioner David Stern doing everything in his power to prop them up. But Dolan has made destruction into an art form. Hiring Isiah Thomas was actually one of the smarter moves he's made . . . and that's a terrifying concept. Famous for his controlling nature and his tendency to act like an expert in matters that he does not understand, he also famously headlines the "blues rock" band JT and the Straight Shot. The band often plays at various House of Blues venues across the country, and he has been known to order his employees to attend his concerts at BB King's club and restaurant in Times Square. Frankly, if I were a billionaire sports owner, I would make these kinds of demands, too. Oh, and, uh, that whole sexual harassment business could have been handled a bit more delicately.

2. Bill Bidwill. For years, the NFL had considered Phoenix as the next great expansion area, the place where the league could extend its grasp and lure thousands of retirees to adopt a new favorite team. Unfortunately, they allowed Bidwill and his Cardinals to move there, essentially ruining the space before anyone even had the opportunity to tap it. The Cardinals have won one playoff game in the last fifty years, and Bidwill has devastated fans of two NFL cities in the process. (Don't believe St. Louis fans when they say they truly love the Rams. They don't. They're just biding time until the baseball Cardinals start playing again.) Also, Bidwill is ruining the fashion statement that is the bow tie. He's saved from being No. 1 on this list merely because I am a fan of the Buzzsaw That Is the Arizona Cardinals and hope to curry favor. Because I am a whore.

1. Jeffrey Loria. You probably didn't know any of them, but there were, in fact, Montreal Expos fans out there, back in the day. (I once attended a game at Olympic Stadium, where I bought a front-row bleacher seat for two bucks five minutes before the game started. Vladimir Guerrero hit the ball off the roof of the dome, and the hot dogs were microwaved, served in Styrofoam containers, and had hair on them.) What happened to the Expos as a franchise is one of the biggest corporate tragedies in the history of sports, and Jeffrey Loria somehow receives less blame for this than Bud Selig, though he played the central role. Loria essentially stripped down the Expos to nothing. After blasting the Montreal government for not building him a new stadium, he made sure the games never showed on television, effectively spoiling the well such that the Expos couldn't possibly stay in Montreal. He sold them back to baseball with a profit, and showed up with a new team in the Florida Marlins. (He's destroying them now as well.) Not that one could imagine an Expos or a Marlins fan anymore . . . and Loria's the reason why.

BONUS DISGRACE: From the great blog The Feed, here's a quote from former Cleveland Cavaliers owner Ted Stepien, on how to build a popular sports franchise:

> This is not to sound prejudiced, but half the squad would be white. I think people are afraid to speak out on the subject. White people have to have white heroes. I myself can't equate to black heroes. I'll be truthful. I respect them, but I need white people. It's in me—and I think the Cavaliers have too many blacks, 10 of 11. You need a blend of white and blacks. That draws, and I think that's a better team.

I cannot possibly imagine how this guy was not successful.

CARL MONDAY IS WATCHING YOU MASTURBATE

In May 2006, WKYC, a Cleveland television station, featured an investigative report by a man named Carl Monday. The report focused on a nationwide epidemic that most citizens were unaware of: predators waltzing into public libraries, downloading porn, and masturbating. I have no doubt this has happened; after all, the Internet exists for porn. But the report, as is the wont of local television newscasts, acted as if this was a plague that had landed on America's youth. (The report breathlessly pointed out that the computer room was just down the hall from the children's section of the library.) It was not a rip-the-lid-off exposé of an issue threatening national security; it was just an unintentional satire of the excesses of local news. ARE YOUR KIDS IN DANGER OF BEING EXPOSED TO LONELY MASTURBATING MEN WITH MUSTACHES? . . . STAY TUNED!

Mostly, though, the story introduced the phenomenon that is Carl Monday to a national audience. When I first came across the clip on an outstanding college football site called Every Day Should Be Saturday, Monday was the obvious star. Wearing a tan trench coat, silver wisp hair, and a VFW mustache, Monday was a TV Reporter straight out of central casting. And he was out for truth and justice. He introduced the segment by interviewing various employees of the Berea Public Library, all of whom responded in appropriately alarmist tones. And then he met Mike Cooper.

Mike Cooper was a twenty-three-year-old kid who had been hanging out in the library that day. That is to say: He was exactly the type of guy—single, living with his parents, unemployed, mustached—Monday had been waiting for. Alone in a computer lab, in the middle of the afternoon, Cooper began, as Monday would later put it, "having sex with himself." But he picked the wrong day and the wrong library.

Outside the library, on a rainy Wednesday afternoon, Carl confronted Cooper. Here's how the exchange went:

Monday: What do you look up on the Internet?
Cooper: (hesitant) Nothing, really . . . sports scores, stuff like that . . .
Monday: Sports . . . pornography . . . stuff like that?
Cooper: Uh . . . no . . . *why*?
Monday: I don't know why. You tell me why.
Cooper: I don't look up pornography, so, no.

You can probably guess what happened next: Monday showed (mercifully) blurry footage of Cooper in the library, and confronted him with it.

Monday: You ever perform a sexual act at the library?
Cooper: No, I have not.
Monday: What if I told you that we've got video of you performing a sexual act?
Cooper: (hanging head) Well . . . it wasn't me.

Cooper didn't hold out for long.

Monday: You just reached out and grabbed yourself and started having sex?

Cooper: (pale) I did . . . I, uh, wasn't thinking. I made a mistake.

Monday: Based on the fact that there are people out there doing this type of thing, don't you think parents ought to be a little more careful about letting their kids at the library alone?

Cooper: (holding knife to own throat) Yes.

Monday: If you were a parent, wouldn't you be afraid of a guy like you?

Cooper: (plunging scepter into his stomach) I'm not a sexual predator or anything . . . sure, yeah, I'd be afraid. I didn't think I was doing anything wrong at the time, but now I understand.

And then, just to be safe, Monday twisted the knife one last time.

Monday: You live with your parents?

Cooper: Yes.

Monday: What do you think they're gonna say about this?

Cooper: They're gonna kill me.

Monday then *follows Cooper to his house,* where his father throws him out of the driveway yelling, "I'm a combat vet!" and the process of humiliation is complete. The report aired on Cleveland television, and that would have been the end of it, except . . . Cooper happened to be wearing an Ohio State sweat-shirt. That gave me an excuse to run the video on Deadspin . . . and to sit back and watch what happened.

The response was immediate and immense. The video is like a gothic novel, full of rich characters you can't resist returning to and experiencing all over again. The target of the mockery was not Cooper, but Monday, who was seen as all that's wrong with puritanism, local news, and men in trench coats. One reader started printing T-shirts that read "Carl Monday Is Watching You Masturbate," and someone even put together a Dilbert cartoon.

© Scott Adams, Inc./Dist. by UFS, Inc.

It didn't take long for mainstream types to catch on to the story, with the Cleveland *Plain Dealer* doing a cover story on the issue (I was quoted, as was Monday, who, God bless him, stuck to his guns: "I still think it's a serious subject," he said. "People keep forgetting, this was in a public place, in a library, and it was near a children's section. We weren't trying to single out Cooper necessarily, but it certainly was part of the story, and that's the part of the story people seem to remember. Once that got on the Internet and on the blogs, all hell broke loose.")

"All hell broke loose" is an understatement. Eventually, *The Daily Show with Jon Stewart* sent "reporter" Jason Jones to confront Monday with the repeated refrain, "You Jackin' It?" Monday would have been a quiet, weird local television reporter; by accident, Deadspin made him a star. Not quite perhaps the type of star he'd like to have become, but hey: When you're doing the Lord's work, sometimes there are unforeseen consequences.

Despite repeated e-mails, I've never spoken to Carl. I'll always feel I owe him something.

GLOSSARY

Belichick, Bill. Napoleonic Patriots coach whose on-field success is only exceeded by increasing antipathy from anyone who happens not to work for him. Allegedly he's been carrying on an affair with a married New Jersey woman for decades, supplying her with a house and countless material goods. He must be the least likely home-wrecker in recent sports history. Inexplicably, is friends with Jon Bon Jovi. Also: cheating.

Benson, Tom. Owner of the New Orleans Saints known for carrying a ridiculous French Quarter umbrella after the team's rare victories, now holds the dubious distinction of being the only owner in sports history to refuse to commit to keeping a team in a city that has been devastated by a national disaster. Complains constantly about the Superdome, but, strangely, not about the fact that it once held floating dead bodies. If the Saints end up in San Antonio, expect him to be assassinated by Anderson Cooper.

Bidwill, Bill. Owner of the Buzzsaw That Is the Arizona Cardinals, the most poorly run franchise in American sports. Sadly, resisted an advertiser's suggestion to name his new state-of-the-art home field "Pink Taco Stadium." Even Pat Tillman disliked him.

Bozeman, Todd. Former California Bears coach who paid a

recruit nearly $10,000 and was subsequently banned by the NCAA for eight years. After his suspension ended, was hired as coach of Morgan State University and was cited for attacking a restaurant owner because he provided his team with ham sandwiches rather than chicken.

Cox, Bobby. Longtime Braves manager whose slouching, portly, affable nature is belied by a former spousal abuse charge.

Cuban, Mark. Obnoxious Mavericks owner/blogger whose Everyman persona (and tendency to head out and get drunk with college students) keeps him popular with fans even while his players and coaches wonder how this crazy man could possibly have ended up with his name on their checks.

Davis, Al. Skeletor-esque Raiders owner who eats children to sustain life.

DeWitt Jr., William O. Principal owner of the St. Louis Cardinals and major booster of President Bush and the Republican Party, driving about 15 percent of Cardinals fans crazy—at least the ones who live in New York City, vote for Obama, and write books—by opening the final season of Busch Stadium with Bush throwing out the first pitch while wearing a Cardinals jacket.

Dungy, Tony. Beloved Colts coach who overcame the suicide of his son to become the first black coach to win the Super Bowl despite not really being black, not really.

Glass, David. Bumbling Royals owner who led a once-proud franchise into the gutter of Major League Baseball. He never spends any cash and is happy to pocket the millions in revenue sharing, with the exception of every four years, when he signs an insane contract just to try to make his fans think he's trying. He isn't. Brilliantly satirized by baseball Web site The Dugout.

Guillen, Ozzie. Politically incorrect/borderline psychotic White Sox manager who would take a lot more heat from the media if he didn't occasionally attack *Chicago Sun-Times* columnist Jay Mariotti—whom he called a "fag"—and therefore engender goodwill through Mariotti's rampant unpopularity among his colleagues. Dislike of Mariotti doesn't necessarily make him less crazy, just more likable.

Jackson, Phil. NBA coach who, quaintly, tries to get his players to read. Somehow not the least bit lambasted for sleeping with his boss.

Jones, Jerry. Face-lifted Cowboys owner whose rampant egoism has now finally physically manifested itself on his grotesque skull.

Jordan, Michael. Charlotte Bobcats "president." Ha. Sorry. No, really, he is. Absolutely. Scouting golf courses and casinos everywhere for top basketball talent.

Knight, Bobby. Legendary coach—the all-time college basketball wins leader, if you can believe that—who's in a desperate race to retire with his dignity intact before ripping out the trachea of a player at center court in front of twenty thousand screaming fans. It's going to be close.

Krzyzewski, Mike. Elfish, evil Duke basketball coach whose "fuck"s on the sideline are legendary. Single-handedly making the white basketball player matter again. Not a basketball coach; just a leader who happens to coach basketball.

LaRussa, Tony. A vegetarian, animal-loving lawyer baseball manager who, as a field general, acts like the exact opposite of a vegetarian, animal-loving lawyer. Won a World Series in St. Louis, finally, so reputation as a postseason choker is probably excised. Not that it's stopping the whole sunglasses-at-night thing. Careful drinking wine with him.

Lewis, Marvin. Long-overlooked assistant NFL coach who, upon finally getting his chance as a head coach with the Cincinnati Bengals, inherited a team that notched a record eight arrests in one season. Inevitably took heat for having an out-of-control team. One suspects, though, that if he could figure out a way to make marijuana evaporate when lit, he would.

Leyland, Jim. Weathered baseball manager perpetually referred to as "crusty." A devoted smoker, once appeared on an

ESPN program and was asked whether he felt he needed to apologize to children for his habit. Leyland paused for a moment, put his head down, and delivered the obligatory platitudes about how bad smoking is for you, how children should avoid smoking. Then he looked directly into the camera, his eyes very wide, and said, "Still. Smokers out there, you know what I'm talking about. That moment, after you've had a huge meal, say at Thanksgiving, when you step outside in the cold, light up a cigarette, and take a deep inhale . . . that's about the best moment in the world, you know? All the smokers out there, you know that feeling. Sometimes, smoking is fantastic." Chris Myers quickly cut to commercial, and Leyland has never been on the show since. It's pretty difficult not to love Jim Leyland.

Maloof, Brothers. Crazed gambling-obsessed Sacramento Kings owners who prove that in today's sports environment, you can do little more than play blackjack, have sex with Playboy models, and drink vodka . . . and still make millions if you own a franchise.

Parcells, Bill. Coaching figurehead boosted mostly by his manipulation of the New York media—no small feat. Made an ill-advised decision to return to coaching with the Dallas Cowboys, where his owner saddled him with Terrell Owens. This forced him to retire and, hopefully, do something about that terrifying middle section he has.

Paterno, Joe. Beloved Penn State coaching hero who, slowing down late in his career, sprinted off the field in order to avoid soiling himself, which is not something that has happened to, say, Rick Pitino.

Pitino, Rick. Has never soiled himself before a game.

Pollin, Abe. Elderly Washington Wizards owner once immortalized in a poem written by his team's center, Etan Thomas, that was devoted entirely to the owner's prostate. Really.

Reid, Andy. Rotund Eagles coach whose children were arrested on the same day in two separate driving incidents, one of which involved heroin.

Riley, Pat. Aging relic from the 1980s, back when Gordon Gekko was an inspirational figure. Now spends most of his time skipping out on his coaches-itself team, and soaking in the glory of success. It is possible that Pat Riley is a terrible coach and everyone's afraid to say it.

Snyder, Daniel. Tiny little man who tends to surround himself with other tiny little men, like Steve Spurrier and Tom Cruise.

Steinbrenner, George. Yankees "owner." Died in 1994 and is now played by Larry David in a fat suit.

Thomas, Isiah. As a sort of reverse Midas, he has destroyed everything he's ever been a part of, except for former employee Anucha Browne Sanders, a successful woman who sued him for sexual harassment. (And won!) Gives hope to all fans who, deep down, think they really could be a general manager of a sports franchise.

Torre, Joe. Stoic New York man who is incredibly effective at convincing fans that the reason teams win baseball games is not because of $190-million-a-year players but, in fact, some old man sitting on his ass for three hours, chewing gum.

Weis, Charlie. Corpulent Notre Dame coach who once sued a doctor who messed up his gastric bypass surgery. Trial was suspended when juror had a heart attack, disappointing those who had Weis, at 1:1 odds, as the most likely participant to have a heart attack during the course of the trial. Amazingly, still alive. Not even that great of a coach, actually.

PART III: MEDIA

In which the sad little midwestern boy:

JUST BECAUSE SOMEONE ALWAYS HAS PENISES IN HIS FACE DOESN'T MEAN YOU SHOULD WANT HIS JOB

So here's the story of how Robert Traylor's penis ended up in my face.

In 1997, I was twenty-one years old, a senior at the University of Illinois, and a reporter for the *Daily Illini*, an excellent student newspaper. One day an editor at the *St. Louis Post-Dispatch* called, asking if we had anyone who would be willing to write shorter versions of game stories about the Illinois basketball team for their paper. This looked, of course, to a college journalist, like Moses on a stick. I was already following the Illini around the Midwest for the *DI* anyway; spending an extra forty-five minutes to write up a game story that would be in a *major newspaper*, in *St. Louis*, with *my name on it* was the ark of the covenant.

Writing for the *Post-Dispatch* gave me instant credibility, which didn't mean much more to me at the time than the possibility that it would lead me to an instant postcollege job. I had already decided that graduate school wasn't for me—I am not meant to be a student; I honestly cannot sit still that long—so once May came, I either had to find a job in this journalism field I had chosen or see if the Wal-Mart in my hometown was hiring. (I'm not kidding about this; the Mattoon *Journal Gazette* and the city of Mattoon have lost so many jobs in the last decade, at least three of their former reporters wear Wal-Mart vests now.) So every little bit helped.

Besides, it was *Illini basketball.* I had grown up just forty-five minutes south of the university and had watched their games on WCIA Channel 3, with Jerry Slabe and Judy Fraser and Mr. Roberts, as long as I could remember. The connection of Illinois basketball to the large wheat and soybean swaths of the state of Illinois that *aren't* Chicago is not to be underestimated. An old WCIA commercial perhaps best illustrates this fact. In it, a father—stoic, determined, rock-jawed—is working out in the field, at his farm, hauling a bale of hay maybe, or, uh, lifting a cow or something, while his son, probably thirteen, dutifully assists him, eager to learn and to please. Deep into the task at hand, they barely notice when Mom opens the back door, wearing an apron, hair balled up tight, holding a rolling pin—I remember a rolling pin—in one hand and waving to them with the other. "Boys!" she yells, full of good cheer and pride. "You boys wrap it up out there." Pause. Broad smile. "The Illini are on!" The son casts a hopeful glance at his father, who nods, *We've done good work out here today, son.* They load the next bale of hay on the truck and saunter into the house, father's arm draped over son's shoulder. "ILLINOIS BASKETBALL ON WCIA. GOOD FOR YOU. GOOD FOR YOUR FAMILY." (The slogan was as simple as it was bizarre: Did Illinois basketball lower the divorce rate? Did it provide adequate health insurance? Did it contain calcium for strong bones, healthy teeth, and a winning smile? Did it guard against gum disease?) Every time this commercial came on, my mother would look at my father and me and give us a bemused grin, before yelling at me to stop chewing on the couch.

There are times I believe my father based his entire parenting strategy on this commercial. It seems as sound as any.

A lifelong obsession culminated with covering the Illlini. And doing it for a major newspaper! While still in college! Surely, there would be no stopping my meteoric rise through the ranks of sports journalism.

The schedule was simple. Go to class during the day (right), stop by the newspaper offices to pick up the *Daily Illini* car—a white Ford Escort that started vibrating anytime you approached 55 miles an hour—and drive to wherever the Illini happened to be playing. Iowa City, West Lafayette, Evanston, East Lansing . . . the Big Ten is full of exotic locales. I'd arrive at the arena, grab the free buffet, plug in my laptop—in 1997, the *Daily Illini* laptop actually ran BASIC; it was a grand joke to type "10 PRINT "WILL LEITCH IS HUNG LIKE A HORSE 20 GOTO 10 RUN" and watch the words scroll infinitely across my screen—and just go to town. The game stories were, by definition, quite dull. "Clever" opening paragraph, mention of leading scorer and final score, quote from coach about how the game went, description of key moments, quote from key player, look ahead to next game. I could put them together in about twenty minutes, and that was if I was distracted by a blonde who worked in the school's PR department. It was easy, and I couldn't have been happier.

And then we went to Ann Arbor. The 1997 season was not one of Illinois basketball's most historic ones, and the Wolverines were a superior team. They were led by Robert "Tractor" Traylor, an obese center who used his girth to dominate the paint. It took one guy to block him out on rebounds and another to block out his ass. He was nicknamed "Tractor" because he drank diesel fuel.

After the Illini lost, the gaggle of reporters—all of whom had about twenty years on me, though I consistently bested them in the "lack of a toupee" department—were herded into the Michigan locker room. We knew the drill. Ask bland questions, receive bland answers, return to bland press box, write bland game stories, go home to bland lives. I was young enough not to get destroyed by this routine. Most were not as fortunate. The press box banter usually revolved around the dryness of the buffet chicken and the lack of satisfactory Ann Arbor strip clubs. The other reporters, at more established papers like the *Peoria Journal Star* and the *Aurora Beacon News,* looked defeated. Of all the emotions chiseled onto their faces, "enjoyment of an athletic contest" was in dead last, just behind "worry about whether or not the iron was left on." I would like to say that, at the time, I looked at them and had visions of my own sad future. But mainly, I was just jealous they had better computers.

Traylor and his ass had controlled the game, and he was the key factor in the victory. So we had to talk to him. We death marched to his locker, where he was clad in a towel and flipping through a copy of some rap magazine that none of the white reporters had ever heard of. My vague memories tell me it was called *Booty.*

Traylor saw the reporters approaching and put down his magazine. We stood in a haunted semicircle around him, and because I was new at this, I had the worst spot, sort of crouched down, other scribes using my back as leverage for their notebooks. I palmed my own pad and hunched over, waiting to document Traylor's wisdom.

He looked at us and flashed a lopsided, toothy smile. And then he did something strange: He took off his towel. He wasn't getting dressed or anything; he just took off his towel and let his large, uncircumsized penis hang there for all to see. He looked at us, as if to dare us to say anything, and, knowing full well we wouldn't, said, "Okay, whaddya got?"

It was a power move, of course: Traylor, all 320 pounds and twenty years of him, knew that we men would sit and write down whatever he had to say, no matter what. His job was to knock people over with his ass and ours was to ask him his opinions on the matter. *Y'all are so pathetic,* his eyes said, *that I can whip out the old hog here and not only will you not say anything about it, you'll try to pretend it's not there and go about your business.*

He was absolutely right.

"So, er, Tractor, did you, uh, feel like the Illini should have double-teamed you more?"

"Ah, uh, did you, um, feel good coming into the game?"

"Was this, eh, a big game for you guys?"

This went on for about fifteen minutes, eleven lost souls in dead ties and pit stains, scribbling notes in our notebooks now placed strategically lower than eye level. No way to avert my eyes, no escape, I hunched over, hearing Traylor prattle on about the key run the Wolverines made early in the second half, writing it all down as if it mattered, as if I cared, as if anyone cared, while his big damn cock flapped within inches of my nose.

I thought a lot differently about sports journalism after that.

YOU see, as it turns out, Robert Traylor's penis was *important;* Robert Traylor's penis changed my life. And I think it could change yours, too.

Whenever sports reporters try to justify their place in the world, they talk about how they are the middle man between the team and the fan. They are the ones who keep players honest and the consumers informed. Without them, we would be lost in the wilderness of . . . well, something. They're out there on the front lines, documenting what they see and delivering it to the starved, rabid fan. Sure, anyone can watch a game, but they *interpret* it for us.

This, of course, is a crock of dung.

Athletes don't like reporters. Reporters don't like athletes.

Their entire relationship is founded on a base of suspicion. There is no reason for an athlete to ever say anything of interest. Anything that deviates even slightly from Athlete Speak is bound to make headlines, and almost always in a negative way.

Yankees shortstop Derek Jeter is considered a boring person after games, because he always delivers the same banal "analysis" designed to make him look accessible but gently coax the reporter away from his locker and toward someone else's, preferably Alex Rodriguez's, who is likely crying. The thing is, though, there probably isn't an athlete who lives a more interesting life than Derek Jeter. Do you *realize* how much sex this guy has? What is it like to be considered a legend and Everything That Is Right About Sports, yet, at the end of the day, just be another thirty-two-year-old guy who's chasing skirts, paying bills, and wandering around this planet like the rest of us? Derek Jeter is a guy who hits and catches a baseball for a living and has turned this into a life where he is one of the most famous humans on earth. *Without ever saying anything that affects anyone's life in the slightest fashion.* And Jeter, because he seems smart—not like I or anybody else actually knows—is aware that the engines of Derek Jeter, Inc., run because no one really knows anything about him. He lives off the public construction of a persona, and he is canny enough to feed it by remaining, in public, a total blank slate. Derek Jeter could collect stamps, molest kittens, or cover himself in tapioca every night, and we'd never have any idea. And these hobbies wouldn't affect his ballplaying, or our love (or hate) for him. Why are we fetishizing him again? We don't even know him. No one outside a very small circle of people knows him. So why are reporters asking him so many questions? They know what he's going to say.

If you and I were both athletes, we'd like to think that we'd be pals with all the reporters and go out drinking with fans and generally be the same cool person we are now. But of course we wouldn't be. Those weird thoughts you have about communism, or three-way sex, or Celine Dion, those ones that don't necessarily define you as a human being but sound prurient or are easily condensed into a headline, they don't mean anything when you're an accountant. You could tell them to anyone, and no one would care, unless they happened to be Celine Dion. But when you are an athlete, any statement that deviates even slightly from the norm can only hurt you. If I were a professional athlete, I would sound exactly like Derek Jeter. And then I would go home and bathe in my tapioca.

Here's another story from the front lines—this one from the '80s. David Hirshey, now a book editor (in fact, *this* book's editor) and a former sports reporter for the New York *Daily News*, heard that the Yankees' Reggie Jackson was a fan of the O'Jays and decided to write a story about it. As recounted in a *GQ* magazine piece called "The Death of Sportswriting," Hirshey said, "I walked up to him at his locker, and asked, 'Reggie, I know you can carry a team. Can you carry a tune?' He was facing me. He turned around, lifted a leg, farted, and said, 'How's that for a motherfuckin' tune?' It was shortly thereafter that I left sportswriting."

Sports reporters, this is what the athletes think of you. There is no reason for them not to fart at you. Why are you doing this?

Seriously, why? Let us break down what information traveling with a team and documenting their every move actually can provide us.

1. A player has hurt his hamstring/knee/shoulder/groin/
   epidermis. The reporter asks the player if his hamstring/
   knee/shoulder/groin/epidermis hurts, and he says, "Yes. It
   hurts." Occasionally this sentence construction is modified
   with either "a little" or "a lot." Typically, "but I'll be ready
   to play" or "we're just going to keep working on it and see
   what happens" ends the phrasing.

2. The coach of a team, in a rare moment of public openness, yells at a player in the locker room, and the player responds by putting the coach in a headlock, picking him up, turning him upside down, and depositing his head in the toilet. This could be an entertaining story to make a weekend notes column.

3. A player has performed well on his field of frolic, and the reporter asks him if he is happy about the performance. "Yes, I was happy," the player says. "I played well today. But you have to take one game at a time and give 110 percent. That's all you can give." (Actual quote from former Illinois quarterback Johnny Johnson.)

4. A member of the team, mindful of positive publicity, has started a charity to feed the homeless/stop gang violence/ teach children with Down syndrome how to juggle. The reporter can learn about this charity, write a story about how the athlete is "active in the community," and within a matter of days, no homeless person in America is hungry, all gangs have disbanded, and children with Down syndrome are flipping chain saws down the street and giggling all the way.

I don't think I'm missing anything. Only one of the above is useful, and pretty much just for gambling and fantasy sports purposes. There's nothing else the average fan can't get on his own, without the tired dance between annoyed athletes and bored, embittered sports journalists.

I decided I didn't want any part of locker rooms or sports journalism anymore. And not only am I happier, more pleasant to be around, and not only do I see far fewer penises than I used to . . . but I'm also a more well informed fan in just about every possible way.

Because I don't need them, and neither do you. In the latter half of the first decade of the twenty-first century—a pretentious way of saying "now"—we have no reason not to be flooded with information about our favorite teams, sports, players, and anything else that's clad in our preferred colors. We can get everything on our own.

Need proof? If you're a fan of, say, the San Diego Padres, not only do you not need a subscription to the *San Diego Union-Tribune*, you *don't even need to live in San Diego*. All you need is:

1. *Digital cable and the MLB Extra Innings package.* This is $109 or less a year, about 65 cents a game. Admittedly, the draconian partnership between DirecTV and the NFL makes this somewhat more difficult in football.

2. *A Web connection.* Most postgame press conferences— which rarely feature questions much more complicated than those we've illustrated above—are featured on the individual teams' Web sites. If you are looking for what your fellow fans are thinking, you'll always find a much more lucid viewpoint on fan blogs and select message boards. These are not difficult to find; the Padres currently have twelve daily updated blogs discussing the home team, and this is San Diego, a place where half the population spends less than 5 percent of their time indoors.

3. *A mute button.* Vital. This takes care of the hometown announcers.

That is *it*, folks. The charade of teleconferences, press credentials, publicity departments, petulant quote machines ... it is all *entirely unnecessary.* The current paradigm of sportswriting is dead, even if it doesn't know it yet. I'm just fortunate to have gotten out in time, even if I needed to experience some of the most extreme circumstances to realize it.

Though I suppose if you feel Robert Traylor's huge dong is an important part of your sports experience, you might disagree with all this. You could probably just call him, though, and have him come over. Last I heard, he's available. Make sure you have plenty of snacks.

YOU'RE WITH ME, LEATHER

This is one of the more famous stories to emerge from my little Web site. The legend begins with an e-mail we received from a baseball reporter who recalled hanging out in a bar one spring training night in the late '90s. As reporters in bars on the road are wont to do, he had been chatting up a woman. She happened to be wearing a leather jacket. The reporter chatted with the woman for about two hours and thought he was doing well; he was even thinking of asking her to come back to his hotel room.

Then, with a whoosh and a clatter, the door to the bar burst open to reveal ESPN's portly "personality" Chris Berman. As high on life as ever, Berman waddled up to the woman, pointed at her, and bellowed, "You're with Me, Leather." And it worked. She smiled.

I told this story on the site, thinking it would be a fun little one-off and no one would think all that much about it. I was wrong. Within twenty-four hours, the phrase had taken off, with mock T-shirts, Photoshop illustrations, and constant references littering my site and others. A catchphrase was born. Within a week, Tony Kornheiser had mentioned it on his radio show—he claimed he'd use it as a touchdown call on *Monday Night Football*—and he was followed by Keith Olbermann on his cable program, Neil Everett on *SportsCenter* (allegedly earning him a brief suspension), and, most insanely, MTV *Total Request Live* host Damien Fahey, who displayed a "YWML" T-shirt to a confused smattering of fourteen-year-olds. Eventually, the television show *Las Vegas* dramatized the incident, complete with an older gentleman successfully courting a woman at a bar with the line.

Why did YWML take off so fast and go so far? I certainly can't take credit for it; the phrase has become so huge that most people don't even know Deadspin originated it, and it has a Wikipedia page that's twice the size of Deadspin's. I think it's because it *sounds* like an ESPN catchphrase—"You're with Me, Leather" is the perfect way to describe a shortstop snagging a ground ball—and, in a roundabout way, it became a way to satirize the ESPN-ization of sports in general. You want catchphrases? *Here's* a catchphrase. It was a way of mocking ESPN without actually having to say the call letters.

As for Berman himself, he's only acknowledged the story in public once, at a golf outing, when he said it was something that happened "years ago" and that he's only out to make people happy, or some such Disney nonsense. His on-the-road exploits are epic and constantly recounted—I found a photo of him getting a lap dance before the Super Bowl in Jacksonville a few years ago, and it's even scarier to look at than you think it is—but rather than embrace his exploits, Berman continues to run from them. I've always thought it would be smart of Berman to make this all an in-joke, maybe introduce David "You're with Me" Weathers on *Baseball Tonight* or something, but that would require a modicum of self-awareness that I'm not sure exists in Berman's melon. At this point, it's obvious that "You're with Me, Leather" will end up on Berman's headstone, and sometimes I fear it'll be on mine as well.

TEN EXAMPLES OF HOW ESPN IS RUINING SPORTS

When old-school sports fans complain about the corrosive influence ESPN has had on the games they grew up loving, they often grouse about the gimmicky nonstop highlight parade of dunks and touchdown celebrations, and the glorification of the individual over the team unit. I've never much cared for these criticisms; sure, they're true, but that's a cultural trend that would have happened with or without ESPN. (Besides, we're not all high school coaches. Not to sound like a punk kid, but sometimes I find a ferocious dunk more exciting to watch than a well-executed bounce pass. Sorry.)

Mostly, these criticisms help mask the real damage ESPN has caused, and continues to cause, on a daily basis to the world of sports. They're like the Imperial Forces from the *Star Wars* movies; controlling everything with a dark hand, ESPN does not want you to notice that it's warping everything you see. (They currently lack the ability to control your thoughts, but as soon as Disney figures out a way to capitalize on that, you can count on it.) ESPN has its own interests in mind, not the interests of its average sports fan audience. Here's a look at ten recent examples of ESPN's self-promotion abilities, and how it's sucking the soul out of our games.

Around the Horn

In 2002, ESPN introduced a daily program called *Pardon the Interruption,* which featured *Washington Post* columnists Tony Kornheiser and Michael Wilbon carrying their mock dislike of each other into a daily rundown of the day's events in sport. Both Kornhiser and Wilbon are smart, likable fellows, and their show was sharp and revolutionary. It took *Crossfire* and gave it a clock, buzzers, and flashy graphics. Remembering our enjoyment of it now doesn't necessarily excuse the demons it spawned.

So ESPN launched *Around the Horn,* which was like *Pardon the Interruption* injected with steroids and whacked repeatedly across the skull with a polo mallet. On *ATH,* the entry requirements for punditry were set far lower than on *PTI.* Basically, it took middle-aged sports columnists, the very people who had been coasting on free press-box food and churning out pablum for years, and turned them into television monsters. The show primarily involved nontelegenic writers screaming at each other inside some sort of convoluted "point" system. This was not only excruciating to watch, it extended the arm of ESPN into every major newspaper in the country. Not only did it dumb down every not-that-complicated-in-the-first-place "writer" who appeared on the program, its substantial paychecks assured that only the most self-immolating scribes would dare criticize the network in the pages of their papers, lest they be put on the network's infamous "blacklist" and get banned from appearing on the network—and collecting those appearance fees. (Being on this list is one of the highlights of my career.) *Los Angeles Times* writer T. J. Simers appeared on early episodes of *Around the Horn,* and then wrote about the silliness of the show in his paper. The edict was fired off to him immediately: Stop, or you're off the show. He didn't, and he hasn't appeared on ESPN since. Most columnists got the message.

The show not only made the discussion of sports 57 percent

dumber—a scientific fact!—but it also stifled dissent. Dan Sha-noff, a former columnist for ESPN.com, tells the tale of when he made four appearances on the show—making him the lowest-ranking member in the show's high school cliquelike totem pole—and was handed a packet of ready-made "viewpoints." He felt pressured to take a certain side on issues, a side not his own, selected only because it would clash with the other panel-ists and therefore "create debate." (Because he was new, he was stuck with the most unpopular positions.) How anyone who regularly shows up on *Around the Horn* can, with a straight face, call himself a journalist is beyond comprehension. But the show remains the Holy Grail for scribes looking to build their own brand (not, mind you, those looking to build an audience or foster a discussion). And it has assured that fans looking for a place for honest debate will not find it on television, where journalists put on fake faces, lest they be forced to live off a pid-dly newspaperman's salary.

The Steve Phillips Fake Press Conferences

In 2005, looking to jazz up its off-season baseball coverage, *SportsCenter* decided to try something new. Inspired by the famous Red Sox resignation press conference by general man-ager Theo Epstein—who had escaped reporters by wearing a gorilla suit—the network assigned baseball analyst Steve Phil-lips, a former (and failed) general manager with the Mets, to run a week's worth of "mock" press conferences. The conceit was that Phillips would play a different team's general manager, an-swering questions for a clamoring press corps about off-season plans.

This concept was odd enough in theory—let's talk about these imaginary situations while playing dress-up—but in prac-tice, it veered toward the surreal . . . and the degrading. First off, ESPN insisted on considerable theater, with Phillips sitting at a desk lined with microphones and an epileptic fit–inducing smattering of flashbulbs from the audience. The "press corps" was littered with depressed-looking interns, jumping up and down, waving their arms in the air, clamoring to have their "question" "answered." (I cannot begin to imagine what sordid, humiliating tasks an ESPN intern is charged with. "Hey, Ben, come over here and rub Kruk's feet!") But sprinkled among the gaggle of interns were, sadly, legitimate journalists who worked for ESPN, like Buster Olney, Sal Palontonio, and Jeremy Schapp. These are hardworking, respected journalists—not like the Mariotti and Plaschke blowhards of *Around the Horn*—who, at one point, decided that the big bucks and exposure of ESPN were worth the inevitable conflicts of interest that would arise. And the humilation.

Indeed, these "press conferences" had ample opportunities for humiliation. Buster Olney, a former *New York Times* reporter who has written several outstanding baseball books and runs an excellent baseball blog on ESPN.com, was forced to stand up, wave his hand in the air, and ask a question. My favorite part was when Olney (or Schapp, or whoever) would ask a question, and Phillips would respond, "Well, that's a good question." Of course it's a good question, Steve, *you wrote it*! It all added up to this bizarre, demeaning Kabuki theater that revealed the network's secret thoughts about journalism's place in their world of sports: It's all just an act. The scary part was, if you didn't know Steve Phillips wasn't actually a general manager anymore, you might have mistaken this all for reality. After this, *Who's Now* was a logical next step.

John Amaechi

The promised land, the great white whale, for many of today's "socially conscious" sports reporters—read: Those who still worship at the altar of Frank Deford, decades after he dissolved from a legitimate writer into a dirty old man writing three-thousand-word odes to Anna Kournikova's breasts and calves—is to report the story of the first openly gay athlete. Because there's no real benefit for any active gay athlete to come out of the closet, they've had to make do with minor retired athletes, like John Amaechi.

Amaechi was an entirely forgettable basketball player, a plodding space-filling center whose job was mostly to pick up fouls and grab scrap rebounds here or there. (His main point of interest was that he was British.) Four years after he retired, word circulated among publishing circles that he was shopping a memoir about his life as a gay NBA "star." Most publishers and editors—including the one responsible for the swill you're reading right now—rejected it, with the perfectly reasonable rejoinder "Who the heck is John Amaechi?" But it found a home in the relatively new ESPN Books corporate arm.

ESPN Books had released one big hit—Bill Simmons's *Now I Can Die in Peace,* which was like this book, but better written, entirely about the Red Sox, and featuring nothing but previously published material—and a few duds, including the genius that was *ESPN Baseball Sudoku.* (It was like regular sudoku, but featured the baseball positions rather than the digits 1–9. Outstanding! How could it *not* sell?) The initial concept of ESPN Books was to allow the ESPN promotional machine to churn out cross-platform mentions—"news"—to the benefit of no company other than Disney. The Amaechi story provided the perfect opportunity. A gay athlete! Coming out! On newsstands now! That Amaechi was unknown and uninteresting—okay, fine, he's British, that's *something,* I suppose—was beside the point. You were going to hear about John Amaechi whether you liked it or not.

Though Amaechi seems like an affable enough fellow, the boring book is filled with the usual tales-from-the-road, with the occasional doin'-a-dude scene. (Always chaste and palatable, of course.) The book was uncontroversial; hardly worth a mention, really. So the ESPN machine went into motion. Suddenly, every ESPN platform—television, radio, Web, carrier pigeon—was discussing Amaechi's book, what it means to be

gay in sports, how players would react, so on and so forth. The
problem, though, was that most athletes—smart enough these
days to know what they should and should not reveal to
reporters—gave the usual answers like, "as long as he's a good
teammate." The story was in danger of being extinguished before it could be appropriately cross-promoted.

So they kept trying, asking every athlete they could find,
past and present, what they thought of John Amaechi, hoping
someone would slip up. And they finally found someone who
did.

On ESPN Radio (of course), host Dan Le Batard asked former Miami Heat point guard Tim Hardaway what he thought
of Amaechi, and gay athletes in general. His answer was a gold
mine.

"First of all, I wouldn't want him on my team," Hardaway
said. "And second of all, if he was on my team, I would, you
know, really distance myself from him because, uh, I don't
think that's right. And you know I don't think he should be in
the locker room while we're in the locker room. I wouldn't even
be a part of that. . . . You know, I hate gay people, so I let it be
known. I don't like gay people and I don't like to be around gay
people. I am homophobic. I don't like it. It shouldn't be in the
world or in the United States."

We got one! The backlash was immediate, immense, and
exactly what ESPN had been hoping for. The NBA banned
Hardaway from the upcoming All-Star weekend festivities,
gay advocate groups publicly admonished him, and the story
of Amaechi had another month of air time.

So, to review: ESPN produces a book, reports on the book,
asks everyone what they think of the book, peeks under every
possible rock to find someone who doesn't like the book, finds
the person, reports on the person not liking the book, reminds
you where you can buy the book, looks for another book to
start the cycle again. Ta-da! Insta story! A "controversy," created out of thin air. Free money.

Stephen A. Smith

For years, Stephen A. Smith had been a moderately respected NBA writer for the *Philadelphia Inquirer*. He was known mostly for befriending athletes—he famously attended almost every party Allen Iverson ever threw . . . or at least the ones he told Stephen A. about—but was hardly considered a rising star in the world of sports journalism.

One thing he did excel at, however, as ESPN quickly learned, was screaming on television. Watching Stephen A. Smith on the air is like walking into a bar, striking up a conversation with a fellow sports fan, and quickly realizing that you have stumbled onto a madman whom you cannot leave. Smith's modus operandi on TV is to LET YOU KNOW EXACTLY WHAT THE TRUTH IS AND THAT'S JUST THE WAY THAT IT IS SO YOU BETTER LISTEN UP. It doesn't help that he stares so intently at the camera; it's impossible not to fear that he's going to reach through the set, grab you by the lapels, and shake you until you understand. Whenever I see Stephen A. on ESPN, I find myself instinctively ducking. It doesn't matter what he's saying; the majority of his rants are uninformed, but he could be talking about knitting, taxidermy, or a particularly well produced high school rendition of *Guys and Dolls*. The volume and intensity drown out everything but the creeping feeling that your ears have burst into flames.

These are strong reactions, and the key to ESPN's "coverage" of sports is that you Have a Reaction. Smith, therefore, became a network star, signed to a long-term lucrative contract and given his own show, *Quite Frankly with Stephen A. Smith*, which was launched to fanfare across—of course—all of ESPN's platform. (He was even profiled in a long, confused *Sports Illustrated* piece, which struggled to find a human angle on Smith that did not exist.) It simply did not matter that Smith made viewers want to cut off their ears.

Much to the network's chagrin, the show did not catch on; its ratings on ESPN2 were actually lower than the billiards reruns that previously held the time slot. It was almost as if— lo!—viewers had little desire to watch a program that consisted entirely of an unlikable host screaming at them for an hour. Because of Smith's contract, ESPN kept tinkering with the format and eventually shifted it to 11 P.M. For all the promotion, Smith complained that the network wasn't supporting him enough. One particularly gruesome innovation involved *Quite Frankly: Behind the Scenes*, a half-hour backstage look at the show, which mostly featured Smith testing his microphone and checking out his suit in the mirror. (It didn't help that Smith was ill-suited for off-network self-promotion; on *Late Show with David Letterman* he referred to the great Dave as "Jay.")

Eventually, the show was canceled, and Smith popped up throughout the ESPN family of networks, filling in here or there, still screaming, still making me duck. The general principle behind his rise still exists at the network, though: A personality does not grow organically, but is created in a boardroom and programmed to cause a ruckus and demand your attention. Smith was technically talking about sports, but what he was really doing was aggressively talking about himself. If you have a strong reaction—even if that reaction is to run out of the room—he has done his job. The show may be gone, but Smith isn't, and neither are his marching orders.

Harold Reynolds

Imagine, for a moment, that the Tampa Bay Devil Rays, without warning, fired their general manager. No press conference, no reason given, no official corporate statement: just a spokesperson saying, Chuck Le Mar is no longer the general manager of the Tampa Bay Devil Rays and that's it.

How do you think the journalists at ESPN would react to this statement? Fake press conferences aside, they have enough professional pride and basic investigative fervor to demand an answer, an explanation for why Le Mar was fired. It is in the public interest, they'd argue, and you can't just release someone who stood as one of the faces of your team without giving any reason. They would hound the Devil Rays organization until someone said something, on-record or off, and they had a full report.

Now, witness what happened with the dismissal of longtime ESPN baseball analyst Harold Reynolds, one of the more respected ESPN personalities, serving for years as one of their more prominent community-outreach people, broadcasting the Little League World Series every year and hosting a series of baseball instructional videos branded under the ESPN name. He had just signed a six-year contract with the network when, in May 2006, he was suddenly fired.

ESPN neither released a statement about Reynolds's dismissal nor gave a public reason for the firing; according to Reynolds—and his recent lawsuit against the network—they didn't even tell him. When journalists who *don't* work for ESPN asked them why Reynolds was fired, they simply refused to give a reason, claiming it was an internal personnel issue, as if they were a mom-and-pop store around the corner, just trying to mind their own business.

ESPN isn't just another player in this sports game; they're *the* player. The standard to which they hold everyone else in the sports world is not the one they hold themselves to in any way. They considered themselves above the usual business of hirings and firings that they make such a big deal about when it comes to the organizations they cover; they acted as if they were above the law. And the sad thing is: They were. Because they control so many avenues of distribution, they absolutely got away with it. Reynolds is still looking for a job in the world of baseball broadcasting—he does occasional Web reports for MLB.com—and ESPN just filled his spot and moved on, no questions asked.

There never has been an official explanation for Reynolds's dismissal—off-record sources claim it was for sexual harassment issues, and Reynolds has acknowledged this, though he has neither admitted to nor been told what the particular incidents were—and ESPN simply has no impetus to give one. If you press them on this . . . well, be ready to show up on their blacklist.

The reason, of course: ESPN will only send out messages it benefits from. If you don't like it . . . well, where else you gonna go?

Patrick Patterson

ESPN gets you hooked young. Patrick Patterson was a seventeen-year-old high school senior who was heavily recruited by many of the major Division I-A basketball schools. (He ended up going to Kentucky.) When he was close to announcing his university choice, ESPN approached him with a deal: They would broadcast his announcement live on ESPNU if he allowed them the "scoop" regarding his decision, shown on the bottom-of-screen crawl as an ESPN "exclusive." Patterson, wanting to keep the decision private and "within the family," declined, which, knowing ESPN, will surely cost him in the future. (He can probably count on showing up on "Not Top 10" anytime he misses a dunk or dribbles off his foot for the next decade or so.)

This is a minor (and more annoying and sinister, considering we're talking about what amounts to a bribe) example of what ESPN has become famous for in journalistic circles. They take scoops from newspaper reporters, reconfirm the stories, and slap them with their own "exclusive" label. Because ESPN is omnipotent, anytime they unveil any piece of "news," it's likely to be the first time the average sports fan has heard about it. So ESPN goes ahead and calls it an "exclusive" and assumes no one will challenge them, lest the reporter who lost his own scoop offend one of the few places left for him to peddle his wares.

Back in December 2006, the chattering classes of sports were all atwitter about where Allen Iverson would be traded; for years, the superstar had waited for the opportunity to play for a championship contender. Every NBA reporter in the country was desperate to find out where he was headed. The first to report that he was being shipped to the Denver Nuggets was David Aldridge, a reporter for the *Philadelphia Inquirer.* (He's also a former ESPN employee who got shoved aside when the network decided they would rather their NBA reporters scream at the camera than, you know, report news.) He posted the story of Iverson's trade to the *Inquirer*'s Web site . . . and within fifteen minutes, ESPN had suddenly "broken" the news and claimed it as its own "exclusive."

Aldridge, furious, wrote to sports media Web site The Big Lead:

> The Philadelphia Inquirer broke the story about [Tuesday's] trade. I should know, because I wrote it. It was on our site about 10 minutes before ESPN "broke" it. I don't expect everyone to read every website every minute of the day, and the Four-Letter is ubiquitous, so people almost always see it first. But in this case, they weren't first. We were.

Ask almost any reporter not affiliated with ESPN, and they will have a tale about one of their scoops getting swiped by ESPN. And all will shrug their shoulders and sigh. "Hey, it's ESPN. What can you do?"

The Scripps Howard National Spelling Bee

Like anyone who saw the movie *Spellbound,* I fell in love with the national spelling bee. I found it a perfect parable of, and for, America. Hard work, mixed with natural intelligence, splashed with geographic circumstance, will bring you to the top of your field. We see parents, who sometimes push their kids too hard and sometimes don't understand them at all. We see their friends, who can only dream of being so single-minded. We see hometowns, which range from the most flush suburb to the most hardscrabble inner city. And then, after we've learned to love them all, the kids come together and wipe each other out. It was a riveting film, human drama in its most pure form.

The folks at ESPN recognized this and decided, in the way that only they can, to destroy its charms through corporate synergy and self-promotion. Rather than keep the spelling expert broadcasters—whatever the heck classifies one as an "expert" in spelling bees—ESPN assigned morning radio boobs Mike Greenberg and Mike Golic as the official telecasters. Mike and Mike, as they are known, make their living off standard morning radio gimmicks, a dopey odd-couple pair who deliver schticky jokes about Greenberg being a metrosexual and Golic, uh, being fat and liking to eat. When ESPN bought the Arena Football League, they dispatched Mike and Mike to bring their signature brand of groaning humor to the booth, making it that much easier to promote the league all morning, whether we desired it or not. The spelling bee had been an unassuming oasis of cuteness; opportunistic ESPN wasted no time turning it into one more episode of the Mike and Mike traveling roadshow. One's girly! One's a slob! Now, sit there and look gawky, spelling kid!

John Kruk's Dictation

Baseball Tonight was once one of the more sublime pleasures of ESPN. For those of us who believe the NFL exists to satisfy our bloodlust instincts—and have no qualms with enjoying that to the fullest, of course—but deep down feel that baseball speaks to the pretentious poet in all of us, *Baseball Tonight* was a calm, wonky rundown of every nerdy aspect of the sport. It was just a bunch of dweebs like Peter Gammons, Tim Kurkjian, and Harold Reynolds, wallowing in the minutiae of a day's worth of baseball. We loved it.

It was only a matter of time, though, until ESPN, adhering to its dictum of "the Louder, the Better," turned the show upside down. Gone were Reynolds—for his own reasons, of course—and Jayson Stark, and in came *The Best Damn Sports Show*'s John Kruk, who slobbed the show up with his trademark belching and flatulence. But the real problem of the show went beyond Kruk; it was the producers' insistence that, instead of real debate, the "analysts" shoehorn in forced and stilted "controversies." You know, like they've done on every other show. (This can be called the "Baylessing" of ESPN.) After a while, no viewer could believe anything any analyst said anymore; their job seemed to be to disagree with whomever they were talking to rather than to offer actual analysis or reasoned arguments.

Never was this more evident than in a confession Kruk gave to a Milwaukee radio station. A week after Kruk claimed, on *Baseball Tonight*, that he believed the Pittsburgh Pirates would win the National League Central, the radio station—with their hometown Brewers nearly ten games up in the standings—asked Kruk how he could conceivably make such a proclamation. Kruk, chastened yet laughing, admitted that he really believed the Brewers would win the division. So why did he say the Pirates? Because the producers told him he was supposed to say that the Yankees—far behind the Red Sox in the American League East at the time—would be leading the American League East in a month. Kruk, ever a beacon of journalistic integrity, said no, so they compromised by having him make the "outrageous" pick of the Pirates.

And Kruk admitted this! But hey, why not: When you're playing the role of analyst, why argue that much with the script? If he wouldn't have gone blabbing to a radio station, no one would have ever found out. And we'd all be that much the dumber. You know, just a typical night on *Baseball Tonight*.

Woody Paige Ate Dog Food on Live Television

The longtime *Denver Post* reporter was famous for his off-kilter and willfully irrelevant columns before signing on for *Around the Horn* and *Cold Pizza*. And one morning in September 2005, as a logical extension of every other clownish gimmick he'd pulled out of his hat for the network, he ate a canister of dog food on live television. Whatever your thoughts on Paige, or any of the ESPN personalities, no one should ever be degraded to the point where they eat dog food on live television. Paige did this to himself, but he had help. Poor guy. Of course, later, he's being sued by a hairdresser on *Cold Pizza* for sexual harassment, with accusations that he grabbed her ass, "propelling her forward and into the air." Dirty dog.

This 1990s Poster

THE ESPN *CLOCKWORK ORANGE* EXPERIMENT

You know when parents catch their kid sneaking a cigarette, and as punishment they make him or her smoke a whole carton? Theoretically, the kid'll have so much of what he asked for that he'll never want to touch it again.

You can understand why I might try something like this myself. Like every other sports fan in America, I have come to watch ESPN regularly out of habit and inertia; if you like sports, you really don't have much of a choice. ESPN is a tough habit to break for a sports fan.

So I thought I'd venture into the land of the insane: I'd watch the ESPN family of networks—well, the only four channels out of the family my cable system has: ESPN, ESPN2, ESPNEWS and ESPN Classic—for twenty-four consecutive hours. Either the *Clockwork Orange*–like exposure would flush the network entirely out of my system, or it would bring me to some higher understanding. No matter what, I felt I would have to learn *something*.

Here's documentation of what could be called an experiment but more accurately described as a "gimmick." It must be said that I am not the first human being to come up with the idea of watching a television network for an extended period of time. Back in the '90s, writer Hugh Gallagher locked himself in a hotel room for a week and watched only MTV, and writer Chuck Klosterman appropriated the idea for *Spin* in 2003, with VH1 Classic. I'm appropriating it from both of them. Come with me, if you dare.

8 A.M.

I am greeted by the smiling Stan Verrett and Richard Flores, a black man and a Latino man who sound suspiciously like Scott Van Pelt. I remember reading how all television broadcasters are trained to use "an Ohio accent"; that is, they are meant to have as flat a tone as possible. Verrett and Flores sound like the same exact person. I look forward to watching this *exact same telecast* for the next five hours. Wonderful way to start this off.

First, it's highlights from an A's–Red Sox game. Verrett, while describing an outfielder throwing a man out at the plate, says, "Like Tony Soprano, he's got himself a gun." Ugh. Only twenty minutes in, and I'm already exhausted.

Over on ESPN2, it's the simulcast of *Mike and Mike in the Morning,* the "wacky" talk radio team. A year ago, this time slot was held by *Cold Pizza,* ESPN's attempt at a *Today* show type thing. The show's ratings were so poor that it was replaced by live video of two men talking in a studio. The "morning show" is now called *ESPN First Take,* which starts at 10 A.M. ET, which is a bit late for a "first take."

Seriously: It's just two men at a desk talking to each other. Occasionally, Mike Greenberg will take a sip of water. And you know what? This *is* more entertaining than *Cold Pizza* was.

9 A.M.

SportsCenter runs (again) its "Diamond Cutters" segment, which is sponsored by Chevrolet. In case you didn't notice that it was sponsored by Chevrolet, the Chevrolet logo takes up half the screen as Flores talks to Steve Phillips, who is talking (of course) about Roger Clemens. He actually uses the phrase, "Baseball, hot dogs, apple pie, Steve Phillips, and Chevrolet." I have now vowed to never, ever own a Chevrolet. I must hate America.

Over on ESPN Classic, it's PBA Bowling, the 1999 Brunswick World Tournament of Champions in Overland Park, Kansas. I don't want to overstep my bounds here, but I can't fathom the mind-set behind showing eight-year-old bowling at 9 A.M. It would make me extremely happy to learn that there is a cabal of late-'90s bowling enthusiasts gathering at Irish pubs across the country to watch classic matches like this one. It's so hard to watch this now, knowing that just two years later, our country would suffer through the tragic events of September 11. These bowlers seem so innocent; how little they knew. It warms my heart to remember a time when we could enjoy the simple pleasures of bowling without fear of global terror. It seems like only yesterday.

Mike and Mike is now replaying an interview I saw an hour ago; I just started watching at 8 A.M., so it's possible the time I saw it was a rerun too.

10 A.M.

All right! It's time for *ESPN First Take,* the morning talk show that starts at 10 A.M. (I suppose it would be odd to just call it *Brunch.*) Skip Bayless—who, sadly, has cut his mullet—is debating the world of sports with two brothers of the last name Stewart, who apparently host something called *Two Live Stews,* which I have never heard of. As tends to be the case on ESPN, everybody's yelling at each other. It's fun to hear Skip Bayless start calling random black players "thugs" in front of two black men who you just know would love to excrete down his neck.

One of the key aspects of *First Take* occurs at around 10:30 with the "While You Were Sleeping" segment, in which they show highlights of last night's West Coast games that, presumably, you were asleep for. The obvious problem with this is that the show airs at 10 A.M.; just doing the math on sleep here, it has to be difficult to find someone who *wasn't* up late enough to find West Coast scores that's just now getting ready for work. How much sleep does a sports fan need? You could make the argument that, to those on the West Coast, it *is* the morning. Of course, those people either stayed up and watched the games—because it wasn't that late, after all—or, you know, they watch *SportsCenter,* like a normal person. Which I'd be doing, if I hadn't seen the flipping thing three times already. I am now reciting the dopey catchphrases along with the anchors, which makes me want to pull out my tongue and smash it with a polo mallet. And we're only two and a half hours in.

11 A.M.

The NBA Finals are starting in two days, and Jalen Rose is the official "expert" of the ABC/ESPN conglomerate of networks for the next week. I will tread carefully here, but I think it's fair to say that Jalen Rose is the Eric Dickerson of NBA analysts. It's nice that ESPN asked him to shop at the Gap for his appearance; I think he's wearing the same thing my ten-year-old cousin wore to Thanksgiving last year. That said, my cousin wasn't wearing earrings, though his goatee is more fully formed than Jalen's.

The ratings for *ESPN First Take,* as one would expect from a show that's on live at 10 A.M., have been wretched from the get-go, but still, the show seems to haul in reasonable big-name guests. It's mostly because publicity agents can slip their clients on the program—speak to one thousand people at 11:15 on a Tuesday!—and tell their bosses they successfully put some clients on ESPN. So what if no one's watching? I congratulate, however, the national Rock, Paper, Scissors champion for his appearance today. That's a skill made for morning television if there ever was one.

On ESPN Classic we've got the 1998 NHRA Pennzoil Nationals in drag racing. I wonder, when they initially held this race, if they thought that in the year 2007 their cars would have jet packs and fly.

Noon

On *NBA Fastbreak,* they're previewing those NBA Finals, and Allan Houston is wearing a tie that is almost the exact same color as his tongue. I wonder if it was designed that way. Meanwhile, Tim Legler is all paisley, all the time. Neither of them has the sartorial panache of Jalen Rose, but what do I know? Four-plus hours into this, I'm wearing a sleeveless Nirvana T-shirt and a pair of cutoff jeans. I look like a fellow whose car is in the front yard on cinder blocks and whose television is sitting on a milk crate. I can't fathom what's gonna happen come 3 A.M.

On ESPN2, there are live sports: the French Open, the tournament that formed when, for whatever reason, someone decided it would be great to play tennis on clay. Currently, it's someone named Jankovic vs. someone named Vaidisova. You know, you can say what you will about athletes being dumb, but no sport has dumber participants than tennis. These are people who were tagged as "potential professional athletes" at the age of, oh, nine, and they've been homeschooled for years. And by "homeschool" I mean "an hour of math problems until it's time to hit the court again." You'll find that the vast majority of professional tennis players can barely write their names in the ground with a stick. Should I continue to watch this? Live sporting events aren't particularly compelling to write about six months later, which is when you'll read this.

I just switched back to ESPN, and John Clayton's toupee fell down over his eyes.

1 P.M.

Here's a nice touch: On ESPN at 1 P.M., they're showing a highlight film of a San Antonio Spurs title. You know, a *classic* season. On ESPN Classic, they're showing *2006 Madden Nation,* a "reality" show that features a series of stoner idiots riding on a bus across the country together competing in the video game Madden '07. That's right: It's a television show where you watch people play video games against each other.

But oh, if that were all! We're ten minutes into the show, and we haven't even seen a second of actual video game playing. Instead, it's been the bearded guy in the Titans jersey talking about the subtleties of his video game abilities, while the black guy in the Arizona Cardinals jersey speaks of his unique skills. Once we finally get to the "games," we are treated to a close-up of their faces as they manipulate video game controllers. I can't believe this show didn't catch on. My favorite part is that they've come up with the concept of the bus; if you lose, you're kicked off the bus. The bus has to be there because, well, because you can't just set an entire television show on a couch.

It is, however, incredibly entertaining to watch the white guys try to trash-talk the black guys. They all have that "wait, is that okay to say? I'm doing this the right way, right? You're not offended, are you?" look on their face. White people are hilarious.

2 P.M.

Oh, good—ESPN is now playing *The Best of Mike and Mike*, which is a highlight show featuring two men sitting in a studio talking to each other while drinking coffee. Considering that, this morning, ESPN2 replayed the same segment of the "unabridged" *Mike and Mike* three times, the fact that they're showing it again right now means I've seen it four times in the last six hours. I repeat: This is a *highlight show of two men talking to each other.* Because it's 2:45 in the afternoon and only stoned college students, bloggers, and old people are watching this, they just showed the "I've Fallen and I Can't Get Up" commercial. I totally understand how that lady feels.

3 P.M.

As we enter our eighth hour, ESPN is showing . . . "First and Ten." What's "First and Ten," you ask? Why, it's the exact same "debate" segment among Skip Bayless and those two guys I was hoping would excrete down his neck this morning. (This is what you get for asking.) Klosterman had a similar problem when he did his VH1 Classic experiment; sixteen hours in, they just started repeating the same videos he'd started watching in the first place. This forced him to write about the same topics he'd covered sixteen hours before, but he had to come up with all new jokes. This is an unreasonable request of a writer. Of course, Klosterman had sixteen hours until this happened, and he was dealing with a station that runs a perpetual video rotation; it was reasonable to believe it would repeat at some point. I'm only in my eighth hour, and I've seen the same *SportsCenter* four times, *Mike and Mike* yammering about Lou Piniella four times, and Skip Bayless claiming that LeBron James once strangled a small puppy twice. It's quite a party here in Brooklyn.

All right, fine, what else is on . . . well, on ESPN2, there's a tennis match from twelve hours ago, and on ESPN Classic, a damned football game from eighteen years ago. I head to check out ESPNEWS. Tim Kurkjian is talking about Roger Clemens. Are we *sure* this isn't VH1 Classic?

At 3:30, *ESPN Outside the Lines: First Report* comes on. *Outside the Lines* was once a casual, Sunday-morning investigative treat, a whole program devoted to exploring sensitive subjects with nuance. (Host Bob Ley, who just *has* to cut himself every time he sees what his beloved network has become, has the serious countenance yet gentle charm that a show like that requires; think of him as Charles Kuralt minus the soothing accent.) Now, though, the "investigation" involved three clips from a New England Patriots press conference and then Michael Smith and John Clayton debating . . . something. I am curious how this show is different from a blog.

4 P.M.

I'm learning a bit about how these ESPN bookings work; Troy Aikman, who works for FOX, after all, was on *Mike and Mike* this morning talking about his charitable foundation. This afternoon, he's on ESPNEWS. He must have a good agent, though; he was able to avoid the *ESPN First Take* gauntlet. Watching him now, he is talking about *the exact same topics* he talked about on *Mike and Mike;* not coincidentally, they're the same topics *NFL Live* and *Outside the Lines* were discussing as well: Tank Johnson's suspension, Michael Vick's dogfighting, and the Patriots' opening minicamp with Randy Moss. These are also the top stories on ESPN.com's NFL page. I've got a few more hours until this particular news cycle ends, and I'm expecting to hear four or five other white people talking about those same three stories. We're an hour from *Around the Horn.* Oh goody.

Jim Rome is on! I've never quite understood Rome's schtick. It is possible that I just don't speak enough smack and can't appreciate the subtleties of The Jungle. I guess I find it difficult to trust a man who dyes his goatee.

5 P.M.

Quite an all-star crew on *Around the Horn* today: Tim Cowlishaw, Jay Mariotti, Bill Plaschke, and Woody Paige. They've brought out the big guns for this Tuesday afternoon. Let's track their Wacky Gimmicks During Introduction.

> *Paige:* As usual, he has a "slogan" written on a chalk-
> board behind him: "Procrastinators Unite Tomorrow!"
> It is promising to see he is taking jokes from T-shirts you
> can buy on the Boardwalk in Atlantic City.
> *Cowlishaw:* Pretends to do a Jager bomb from a minia-
> ture Stanley Cup.
> *Plaschke:* "Jokes" about the physical attractiveness of the
> Phillie Phanatic.
> *Mariotti:* Holding a box of popcorn, for some reason.

Everyone's yelling at me. *Why are they yelling at me?* The funny part about *Around the Horn* is that, because the "competition" is "scored," they seem to legitimately care about whether or not they "win." Also, two of them have goatees.

Honestly, this show is going to send me into an epileptic fit. Everything's beeping, people are screaming, I'm getting an extreme close-up of Woody Paige's head . . . if I had HD television, I would have shoved sporks in my eyes ten minutes in. In the name of self-preservation, I haven't watched *Around the Horn* in a few months. I was wondering why the cerebral hemorrhaging had stopped. Now I know.

During the commercial break, Paige changed his sign to I USED TO BE INDECISIVE, BUT NOW I'M NOT SURE. Christ. We've clearly come across the most grueling part of this journey. *Pardon the Interruption*, a more tolerable show, is on next, but I'm not sure I'll be able to see through all the blood.

6 P.M.

All right, we've made it far enough into the day that we finally have a new *SportsCenter*. Well, calling it "new" would be generous. As predicted, the top stories are: Tank Johnson's suspension, Michael Vick's dogfighting, and the Patriots' opening minicamp with Randy Moss. Though I've always made fun of ESPN a little bit, I've always admired their ability to fill twenty-four hours of air time on six different channels. I no longer admire it so much. This is also the fifth different show I've seen John Clayton on today. I have no idea how he could possibly have time to work as a reporter; he's literally showed up on my television every hour and a half. He must just be there because of his pretty face.

Flipping around, I find some show called *NASCAR Now* on ESPN2 and, on ESPNEWS . . . CHRIST IT'S *AROUND THE HORN* AGAIN! Somebody stick a wallet in my mouth, fast! Back to *NASCAR Now:* Oh, you have to be kidding . . . Troy Aikman is on *this* show too. He's in front of the same fake city backdrop he's been in front of all day too. He's probably moved around today as much as I have.

7 P.M.

Now we're talking. On ESPN Classic, it's *American Gladiators.* It is impossible to overstate how much *American Gladiators* I watched during my formative puberty years. Tonight's episode is hosted by Mike Adamle—who was on the show throughout its entire seven-year run; it probably seemed like an excellent career move at the time, but now he's broadcasting MAC football games on ESPN Plus—and former Dolphins running back Larry Csonka, who took over for Joe Theismann. (Yep.) I'd like to take a moment to list the names of tonight's

Gladiators: Gemini, Lace, Nitro, Gold, Laser, Blaze, Thunder, Ice, Turbo, Diamond. I think these were the themes of the last ten Mattoon High School proms. I flip over to *SportsCenter,* still playing on ESPN . . . and Troy Aikman and John Clayton are discussing NFL concussions. I think I'm gonna stick with the Gladiators for a while. Running old *American Gladiators* episodes is clearly the best decision Bristol has made since . . . well . . . since taking Joe Theismann off *Monday Night Football.*

Tonight's sponsors for Billiards on ESPN2: oZone Billiards ("Your online source for billiard supplies"), Simonis Cloth ("Since 1680, the Cloth of Champions"), and Viejas Casino and Outlet Center ("Voted San Diego's Best Casino and Second-Best Outlet Center, Seven Years Running"). They're not playing billiards at an arena; they're at the "Dreamcatcher Showroom." The top player is Xiaoting Pan. The analyst informs us that Ms. Pan has been nicknamed by the Asian press as "The Nine Ball Pool Queen." Imaginative folks, that Asian press.

Because *SportsCenter* is just showing the same highlights I've been watching all day—hmm, I wonder how Tom Brady is gonna mesh with Randy Moss this year!—I'm still hanging around with the Gladiators. It's rather impressive how the show doesn't feel dated. Other than, uh, the hair. Every white Gladiator looks like a muscular Kip Winger.

8 P.M.

We're really just halfway through here? Fortunately, we've got the College World Series of Softball on ESPN2. It's the only live sporting event the networks are showing tonight, unless you're counting the WNBA game later tonight. Include it if you wish.

Which brings me to what ESPN is showing right now: the ESPN Poker Championships. No reasonable person can consider poker a sport, but that's not really the issue. ESPN would show a Clue tournament if they thought it would spike ratings. The problem is that—mercifully, for those of us who think that people who use the word "flop" in casual conversation are help-less dorks—the poker craze that blitzkrieged our sports planet for a couple of years has clearly crested. The reason for this is that there are no stars. When poker was still a niche event, the game had true, recognizable stars like Howard Lederer, Doyle Brunson, Jesus Ferguson. If you weren't a poker fan, you didn't know them, but if you were, they were the kings of the game, the LeBron, the Tom Brady, the Albert Pujols. When they won, or when they lost, it *meant* something. But now everybody wants to play poker.

The beauty of the game is that anyone can win; sure, there's skill involved, but on any given day, it's feasible that someone with a modicum of poker understanding could beat the greatest player in the world. This democracy might work well for the layman, but it doesn't make for inherent television drama. Anytime you turn on a poker event, the odds that you're not going to know a single player, even if you're a poker fan, are high. This is not a sustainable business model for television. After a while, you're just watching a bunch of anonymous dorks biting their nails and groaning. And you can get your fill of that just hanging around the office.

Also, they wear visors, and visors are fucking lame. Oh, and if you wear sunglasses indoors, you deserve to be punched.

Point is, I'm heading back to the softball. No visors, and they have breasts.

9 P.M.

Another hour of poker. I find it incredible that, on the largest sports media entity the planet has ever known, on prime time on a Tuesday night, I'm looking up the nostrils of a commodities clerk from New Jersey. If I were of the sneaky sort, this would be when I take a nap, before *Baseball Tonight* comes on at 10. No: If I'm gonna do this, I have to follow it through. That's pretty easy to say just thirteen hours in, though. Wait until John Kruk comes out of my television and tries to steal my socks around 4:30.

Nice: I just flipped over to the softball game, and all the players were running out on the field, slapping hands, jumping up and down, laughing, cheering, all that. I thought someone had just hit a grand slam to win the game or something, but it turned out . . . they'd just gotten the last out of the inning. That was all that happened. Softball players are so much more supportive of one another than baseball players.

10 P.M.

Hey, the WNBA game has begun. It's delayed because the softball game is in extra innings—when played at the high level it's being played at now, it's almost always scoreless—so they're showing the MIN and PHX score in the top right-hand corner. I wonder if there are rabid WNBA fans screaming for this game to finish so they don't miss a single basket. Somehow I doubt it. And I bet it's still garnering better ratings than the NHL.

A friend came by to keep an eye on me, and she remarked on a game she came across during a late night in England. It was called Net Ball, and she says it's "basketball for slow, shitty people." I think that's also known as the Ivy League. Or, well, maybe the Big Ten.

11 P.M.

Perhaps I'm getting punchy: Leading off the late-night *SportsCenter*, I became absolutely convinced that anchor John Buccigross looked exactly like Max Headroom. I suddenly want a Diet Pepsi. Buccigross is absolutely the perfect ESPN anchor. He's blandly inoffensive, spouting neutered, vaguely pop-culture-centric catchphrases, a completely forgettable man cut from the *Brazil* cloth. I suspect he doesn't look a lick different in HD. He's like Keith Olbermann from the early '90s, but run through a washing machine for a few hours and then bleached. That's right: John Buccigross is whiter than Keith Olbermann. Such a creature exists.

On ESPN Classic . . . bull riding! A teaser before a commercial break promises *Xtreme Bulls*. I can only hope that means the bulls are on fire. That would be kind of awesome.

When I mentioned that I was undergoing this project earlier in the day on Deadspin, the always active commenters had much empathy for my plight. One just wrote me:

- *Steve McQueen bounced a ball off his cell door in* The Great Escape.
- *Sir Alec Guinness whistled a jaunty march in* The Bridge on the River Kwai.
- *Robert Strauss did unthinkable things to his Betty Grable poster in* Stalag 17.
- *Frank Sinatra banged Mia Farrow during the filming of* Von Ryan's Express. (*Frank was not a Method actor.*)
- *In eighth grade, I attempted to gnaw my own arm off to escape seeing* Escape from Sobibor. *I was both unsuccessful and solidified my own social pariah status.*

I wish you the best of luck tonight, but remember one thing: Your current captors do not have the same respect for the Geneva Convention that the Nazis did. Tread lightly and do not eye the motorcycle parked on the street too long; the exposed light in your kitchen has a knot in the cord for a reason.

And I am merely writing about watching ESPN for twenty-four hours; people are reacting to this endeavor as if I am pulling a David Blaine stunt. This means something, I think.

Midnight

It's probably because there are little horsies dancing around my head right now, playing Uno and snorting heroin, but I find myself enjoying this WNBA game. I've never related to the animosity to women's basketball. Sure, the quality of play isn't at the level of the NBA, or even the NCAA Tournament, but it's certainly more entertaining than that *Madden Nation* show. (The people on the television right now are actually *moving.* As an example.) I'm also surprised by the volume of the crowd. There are plenty of empty seats in Phoenix, but those in attendance are screeching, and it's louder than Madison Square Garden has been in a few years. (And the coach isn't calling anyone a bitch, either.) Though it's rather depressing to watch these women execute a jump ball; it's like watching kittens try to bat at a string just barely above their heads.

It's still more compelling than what's on ESPN right now: *NFL Live.* Again. With Troy Aikman and John Clayton. Again.

1 A.M.

Scott Van Pelt just leapt out of the television and tried to attack me. Some might say it's difficult to blame him. According to some of my ESPN sources, Van Pelt was furious when Deadspin linked to a funny, Jon Favreau–in–*Swingers*-esque cell phone call that he'd left for a girl he'd met at a bar. To quote the message:

> *Hey, it's Scott Van Pelt. We shared a brief but exceptionally meaningful relationship last Saturday, I'm sure you remember it. Or maybe you don't. Just wanted to touch base; I figured sending texts gets real old. It's tedious with the typing and whatnot. I figured I'd just call up and leave a rambling message, which I'm great at. Um . . . I enjoyed meeting you. I knew as soon as you left I'd never seen you again. From the experience of many Dewey Beach summers, you have your people, and you lose track of somebody when you go someplace else and you'll never see them again, and that's how that went. Understood. But for what it's worth, you did pass everything on my checklist. I have a very lengthy checklist. As if I have any business having a checklist. At this point, I should talk to any woman who doesn't have a club foot or an amputee. If you have four limbs and you don't have Bell's palsy, I probably better just*

be signing up. I do have a checklist, and as I recall, you were passing everything. With that in mind, if I don't catch up with you this weekend, and if you don't happen to make it back down, I would be happy to fly down there and take you out to dinner like a civilized human being. So just let me know. Hopefully we'll catch up again, but if not, it was a pleasure to meet you. Take care, pleasure to see you.

Now, I didn't steal somebody's cell phone and record this message; it was floating around the Internet already, and I just linked to it. But Van Pelt nevertheless was not pleased. Personally, I found his message rather humanizing . . . but then again, it wasn't me.

Regardless, I've been watching enough of this channel tonight to fear he's going to strangle me through the television. It's a shame, too: Van Pelt and his partner, Neil Everett, are probably the two most tolerable "personalities" on the network. Their *SportsCenter* appearances are smooth and quietly enjoyable. And that's all well and good, because I'm gonna be watching the same exact episode for the next six hours.

2 A.M.

When planning this masochistic enterprise—which clearly, I now understand, I set up because I wasn't hugged enough as a child (or maybe I was molested! Memo for tomorrow morning: *Ask Uncle Hal about this.*)—I had a vague fear that I would fall asleep around 2:30, brain-infested with poisonous nightmares. A full hour of *Arli$$*. How in the world did Robert Wuhl end up in *Batman* and *Bull Durham*? It's like watching third graders put on a production of *Jerry Maguire*. At this point, I'm fully expecting Troy Aikman and John Clayton to show up.

In an indication of poker's continued demise, the World Series of Poker, scheduled to be on ESPN2 right now, has been preempted by a replay of the WNBA game. Expect Versus to do this regularly with the NHL next year.

3 A.M.

Now this is tremendously disappointing: My cable guide listed arm wrestling—specifically, "Arm Wrestling: 220lb Weight Class. From Rising Sun, Ind."—as our featured attraction on ESPN2 at 3 A.M. But they're showing a replay of that softball game instead. All those people who set their Tivos for arm wrestling when they went to sleep last night are going to be in for quite a surprise when they wake up. Not to sound crass here, but I think it's possible that a few of these women could certainly hold their own, should they find themselves in the Rising Sun area.

It's a crying shame, because ESPN is showing the Scripps Howard National Spelling Bee from the previous week. As mentioned earlier, I'm obsessed with the spelling bee; it's my favorite non-sports-event sports event. I've always kind of considered the spelling bee a reasonable alternative to the NCAA Tournament: a bunch of kids devoting their lives to a cause that will end up with the obliteration of each other. The pathos—it's everything I love about sports. Plus, it's nice to see acne on ESPN that's not caused by steroids.

On ESPN Classic, it's rodeo. One rider is on a bull named Gotcha. If I were a bull rider, that name might make me nervous. I'm going to be disappointed if Troy Aikman doesn't make an appearance.

4 A.M.

All right, it's probably time to admit that I'm losing my mind. I don't mean that in some "Wow, his wacky stunt sure has ended in some wacky circumstances!" type of way. I mean that I'm losing my shit here. My shit is gone. Where is my shit? *I don't know.* A few minutes ago, starting to really sense the precipice, I headed to my restroom, stared into the mirror, and splashed some water on my face. *And I saw the ESPN crawl at the bottom of my sink.*

The message was not encouraging: *Leitch Nearing Record 22 Hours of the Worldwide Leader . . . Expected to Soon Urinate*

*on Himself... Is Scratching Imaginary Bugs Under His Eye-
lids... Has E-Mailed Every Ex-Girlfriend in Last Three Hours
to Apologize for "That Thing with the Duck"... Is Now Legitimately Soothed by the Cooler Side of the Pillow... Having
Sexual Fantasies About Karl Ravech... Is Having Nightmares
of Losing a Spelling Bee to Bill Simmons... Van Pelt: "If He
Dies, He Dies"...*

One of the spellers just said that "looking at sparkly things
makes me calm." I bow to your wisdom, young lass, and will
follow you into hell.

5 A.M.

Hey, look: *SportsCenter* is back. In the past, when anchors have
made mistakes on the 1 A.M. show, they've corrected them for
the early-morning editions. Van Pelt and Everett were fairly
clean, though, so I'm noticing little difference between this one
and the initial one. Though, to be fair, I'm not much in the
frame of mind to notice anything right now. Hell, it took me
twenty minutes to notice the Komodo dragon in the corner of
my apartment. I'm not sure how he got here, but, between you
and me, I wish he'd leave.

By the way, if the 5 A.M. commercials are to be believed, all
late-night *SportsCenter* viewers are bald SUV drivers with athlete's foot and erectile dysfunction. I do not doubt in the slightest that this is the case.

6 A.M.

Well, well, give a gander at who's back on the air. It's Mike and
Mike. So much has transpired since I saw these fine gentlemen
last. There was, uh, a softball game, and a WNBA game, and
there were some Gladiators, and I had a brief moment where I
thought I might see some arm wrestling.

Heavens, Mike and Mike, are you ever so *perky* this morning! Twenty-two hours ago, I found it refreshing and invigorat-
ing. (I did, didn't I?) Right now? Not so much. Mike and Mike

have a distinct advantage on me: They know what day it, in fact, is. *Da-da-da . . . da-da-da!*

7 A.M.

And we have reached the end of this sick freak show. I would like to say that I learned something, that I have uncovered some insight into ESPN's global dominance that had previously escaped me. Or I wish I could claim that ESPN had won me over, that immersing myself in Bristol Country gave me a newfound appreciation for the work that goes into the whole enterprise.

But mostly I experienced what ESPN always does—though usually on a mercifully smaller scale—on an everyday basis. They pounded me into submission through pure bulk, polish, and repetition. I can tell you just about every topic ESPN covered over the last twenty-four hours. I am not sure that this means I know any more about sports than I did when I started.

I do now realize, however, the products that are most effective at getting blood off a couch.

BEWARE THOSE WHO COME
BEARING THE TAG "EXPERTS"

One of my best friends, Matt, writes about fantasy football. I don't mean that he pens hard-nosed, investigative pieces about the effect fantasy football has on the business world for the *Wall Street Journal,* or that he writes long-winded, slightly personal, pun-laden essays about fantasy football, though a surprising number of the former exist (and you're about to muddle through one of the latter).

I mean that he is a fantasy football *expert.* His job is to write columns about which players should be your starters and which you should bench. He'll advise you on trades, compile player rankings, and make predictions based on the bizarre and inconsistent scoring rules of fantasy football.

Matt is an intelligent guy and treats his job with the utmost seriousness. He writes with a sure sense of purpose and always delivers strong opinions. His yearly fantasy football guide is full of analysis and player descriptions, taking into account past performance, playing time, opponent data, and his supporting cast.

It's not that David Carr *might* be a bad fantasy football quarterback; Matt makes entirely convincing arguments that drafting Carr is akin to setting fire to your league fee. (Oh, I forgot: Gambling is illegal in the United States, and therefore all leagues are for entertainment purposes only.) After reading Matt's capsule description on Carr, you'd be convinced too. Matt's so good that before doing any of my own fantasy football drafts, I always consult his charts and writeups. In fact, when I need advice about my own teams, I call Matt. One of the advantages of being friends with a fantasy football expert is that you don't actually have to shell out cash for his magazines; you just have to buy him a beer now and then. His advice is always trenchant and on-the-money.

The thing is, of course, *Matt has no idea what he's talking about.*

You wouldn't know this from reading him; this is what makes him good at his job. You see, Matt has exactly the same information you and I have. Matt is not spending his days plumbing John Fox at practice for information and watching how Carr picks up the blitz or perfects his three-step drop. It is altogether possible that Matt has never watched David Carr play a single regulation NFL game in its entirety. This is fine— you also have probably never done either of those, unless you're a Panthers fan, in which case you likely need Matt to tell you that you shouldn't draft players from your favorite team because it's impossible for you to separate your draft strategy from your heart. (This is why all my fantasy teams of the early 2000s crashed and burned with Jake Plummer under center.) And to be really objective, you probably shouldn't even have a favorite team; emotions always get in the way . . . but, hey, to each his own.

Matt is a fantasy football expert because he says he is, and he has a newspaper that agrees with him. We consider him an expert because an "established" media outlet has told us he is. But he's just a guy who writes about fantasy football; this fake game that revolves around statistics is his *only* beat. Any of us could decide whom we like and don't like in fantasy football, and then spill our opinions onto an unsuspecting populace. We would be working from the exact same pool of information that Matt does. Matt is merely giving his opinion; he just happens to have a style of writing that makes you believe he really knows what he's talking about. As noteworthy a skill as this is, it's a pretty far cry from being an "expert" in anything but persuasive essaying.

I do not begrudge him this. I actually envy him for his ability to write with such conviction. Matt's bullshitting you, and he's so good at it—he has such "bonafides"—that you believe him. I respect him (still, he'll yell at me when he reads this) and his ability to find someone to pay him for just having an opinion. But I'm not sure, generally speaking, this is a good state of affairs. And in the world of sports, it's the norm.

And, for the record, when I'm in a league with Matt, I usually beat his ass.

WE have a sports media culture that runs on the concept of "experts." Every newspaper in the country has sports columnists, usually with a mugshot that was taken about fifteen years and seventy-five pounds ago, who exist only to describe events that we have already witnessed. They bring with them the authority and presence that says, *"It is through our years of wisdom that you can interpret what this all means."*

ESPN has fostered a subculture of these people, and it's sad, because we probably have Tony Kornheiser and Michael Wilbon to blame. These two middle-aged columnists are polar opposites—Kornheiser is Jewish, cranky, contrarian, and has a few wisps of hair that vaguely resemble what's left on the table after a Brazilian wax; Wilbon is black, polite, cheerful, and shaves his head in a way that will probably always be cool for black guys—who have been playfully swatting at each other for a decade in the pages of the *Washington Post*. Finally, someone came up with the idea of pitting them against each other on television, *Siskel & Ebert*–like, under constrained time limits and an endless soundtrack of dinging noises. The show was called *Pardon the Interruption.* It was an instant success, and for good reason: The hosts were smart, funny, and not afraid to call each other an idiot. (This was the same reason *Siskel & Ebert* was a success; neither host looked like he was groomed from birth to be on television.) The two guys were *on* ESPN, but they weren't *of* ESPN, and their raw, we-can't-believe-they-put-us-on-television banter was a joy to watch. It felt like something new.

As always happens with something new, it got old very fast, particularly when the inevitable imitators showed up. Suddenly, "experts" were everywhere. Since ESPN is a big corporation, and the nature of a big corporation is to find something that works and then shove it down our throats until we hate everything we thought we enjoyed about it in the first place, we ended up with *Around the Horn* and *Cold Pizza* and Jay Mariotti and Skip Bayless and Tony Reali and sweet Christ stop me before I start crying. The television became populated with people screaming opinions into the camera until it was time for another topic, which meant more opinions and more screaming. It didn't matter what position the "expert" took on an issue; what mattered was that it was in opposition to the person they were "debating" with, that it was forceful, loud, and quick.

The nadir of this has to be Bayless, who was briefly ESPN's next big star simply because he had an uncanny ability to inspire anyone watching him to put a fist in his face. It is possible that, offscreen, Bayless is an intelligent man. Maybe he's writing a comprehensive history of urban planning in nineteenth-century Romania; maybe he is the human who finally calculated pi; maybe he's an accomplished juggler. This is all irrelevant to his television persona, which is to pick the most ridiculous contrarian viewpoint possible—"You might say Tiger Woods is an outstanding golfer, but I ask you, *Why isn't he able to fly?*"—and defend it to death. Because Skip Bayless can walk upright and at least appears capable of sentient thought, he can't conceivably believe the vast majority of what he's saying. And surely his bosses know this. But that's not the point; the point is that *he gets a reaction*. The argument is that because he invokes hatred—true, violent, feverish hatred—among those unfortunate enough to watch him, he is somehow "controversial." *You might say you hate him but at least you're talking about him.* This was the mind-set that put Rush Limbaugh on the NFL Game Day program. I have little doubt that if the network thought John Wayne Gacy would have tipped the ratings point up a tick, you'd see him discussing the Jets defense with John Clayton.

This is, of course, the point; it's not particularly difficult to become an "expert" anymore. It's all for show. Hell, now that I run a sports Web site, people have come to call *me* an expert, and I'm damned sure that I don't know anything. I've been on radio shows where the host—typically named something like Mad Dog Jim or Wild B.J. or, in one memorable instance, Crazy Joe Rosenblatt—will ask me who I think will win the next Big Game, or who I think should win the American League Cy Young or something. Does the fact that I write poop jokes and puns on "Chien-Ming Wang" really qualify me to answer these questions? Typically, I tell them I am just another idiot who happens to type fast, and that my opinion should not be considered even slightly more credible than that of the guy who drove your cab to the station. They laugh, and then say, "Yeah, so really, who do you like?" And then there's some sort of wacky sound effect, maybe a gong, or a donkey braying.

But this is what fans have been conditioned to do: listen to anyone who has a soapbox and a willingness to fire away.

This is obviously not limited to old print guys turning to television; at least they're able to speak in complete sentences (unless they're Stephen A. Smith). For whatever reason, the sports consumer is asked to believe that Michael Irvin is an "expert" on football because he had the (occasional) courage to run crossing patterns over the middle . . . and do cocaine. The ex-jock-as-analyst concept has always been a confusing one. It makes sense if the former jock is giving us information that only a former athlete would know, like how grown millionaires tolerate living in such close proximity to one another for six months out of a year without going all sailor-on-a-submarine on one another. Unfortunately, most former athletes take jobs on television not because they have something to contribute to the public discourse, but because they've just retired from the only activity they've done since they were eight years old and suddenly have no idea what the hell to do with the rest of their life. They are expected to have instant credibility because they *once played the game,* which makes them, uh, not particularly unique at all.

Ultimately, former jocks who become "experts" mainly espouse athlete-friendly platitudes—"You see, Tony, unless you've really suffered a pinkie hangnail contusion, you really can't talk about how difficult it is to get back on the field"—that only succeed in further distancing the average fan from the events transpiring. Just take a look at the recent failed *Monday Night Football* pairing of Kornheiser and former Redskins quarterback Joe Theismann. Basically, Kornheiser's job was to say what the average football fan—you know, the one *actually watching the game and spending the money that makes all this happen*—thinks of a certain player or team, and Theismann's job was to tell him (and, through the transitive property, that assumed idiotic average fan) that he doesn't understand what athletes go through, man.

An example: During a preseason game two years ago, Eagles running back Correll Buckhalter ran for three yards. Any fan of the Eagles—or anyone who has ever played fantasy football—can tell you that Buckhalter has been one of the more annoying players in recent memory because, no matter what the circumstances, he's always hurt. There could be perfectly legitimate reasons for this, but facts are facts: The guy could be great but never plays. Kornheiser, because he's the "funny" one, said something to the effect of "Hey, Buckhalter carried the ball, was tackled, and didn't hurt himself. Fantastic!" Theismann, showing a grasp of irony that former athletes have had throughout the centuries, sniffed, "Now, I'm just happy for Correll. Good for him." God, I miss Theismann.

Now, ignoring the analytical attributes of the phrase "I'm happy for Correll, good for him," this statement is intended for someone who is not the average football fan and who is supposed to benefit from Theismann's status as "expert." It is not just intended for Correll Buckhalter, but also for all the athletes whom Theismann presumably was hanging out with before the game, and will hang out with afterward. It is, after all, a club, and it's a club that is insistent that fans never become members, because we *just couldn't possibly understand.*

The club is exactly why fans grow so frustrated with this "expert" idea, and traditional sports media in the first place. It is exclusive; it is talking down to you, acting as if the world of sports is just too deep for you to possibly understand. If this illusion isn't sustained, there will be a lot of unemployed people. Heck, the only people working in sports would be, uh, bookies, I guess. And their cut is way too steep.

Which raises the question: What, in fact, *does* make an expert? You could say it's someone like ESPN's Ron Jaworski, who spends hours analyzing game film before he describes the surprisingly complicated world of football in easy-to-understand terms. Want to know why that guy was wide open? This guy missed an assignment and the safety didn't cover in time. A = B = C. It's analysis and description and insight. Unfortunately, nobody cares what actually happens during a football play anyway. We just see the quarterback throw it, we see the wide receiver catch it, and hey, touchdown! Was that guy on my fantasy team?

So if we don't care to know how the sausage is made, and we really don't need to have someone else's opinions hurled at us when we have our own . . . why do these people exist? Where is this fake credibility coming from? What do they *do* for a living? Hey, don't ask me: I'm no expert.

None of this is to imply that my friend Matt—who owns several attractive hats—does not provide a valuable public service. The discerning fan can decipher his own viewpoints on his particular fantasy football team through his agreement or disagreement with Matt. But I'm not sure this makes Matt an "expert." Of course, I've been drunk with the guy on several occasions, and if you've really been drunk with a guy, you know to be careful not to call him an "expert" about anything, save for "nachos."

But maybe that's the point. Because I know Matt, I find myself incapable of considering him an "expert." The whole notion of expertise is predicated on the assumption that the fan is ignorant. So let's just lay it out here, okay? Nobody knows anything. They're all just talking out of their ass, just like you, just like me, just like everybody else.

Of course, if people only talked about what they knew . . . well, it'd be pretty quiet out there, wouldn't it?

DISPATCH FROM A. J. DAULERIO: THE SUPER BOWL IS DECADENT AND DEPRAVED

In February 2007, I sent A. J. Daulerio, a fellow editor of the late The Black Table Web site and a close friend, to cover Super Bowl XLI in Miami. I felt more comfortable orchestrating our Super Bowl coverage from home but wanted someone to head to South Beach and document all the typical Super Bowl madness. Daulerio certainly came through; he left for Miami a humble Web writer and returned a Web legend. And he owed it all to a mustache.

I've asked A.J. to write a brief recap of his week in Miami, but words cannot quite do it justice.

The first thing to do was grow the mustache. A couple weeks before I headed down to Miami, I decided I needed something to differentiate me from the rest of the Super Bowl XLI attendants that week. A mustache seemed to be a good idea; its connotations of espionage and low-budget pornography were exactly the type of vibe I wanted to project amid the media maw.

Miami was not my first Super Bowl; the year before, I spent a few days in Detroit covering some of the media happenings with moderate success—thanks, in part, to the terrible idea to stay at a then-girlfriend's parents' house. Most of my reporting centered around lazy, unprofessional video footage that was unwatchable, a football made of salami that I'd picked up from a local butcher, a lost rental car, and halfhearted attempts to get into media-sponsored events. This was all pretty much on par with the whole Deadspin edict of being "without access, favor, or discretion." Response was tepid, but given the infancy of the site, the piece was solid enough. By 2007, Deadspin had emerged as a dominant sports Web site with a savvy fan base, and the Miami report would have to exceed Detroit's limited expectations twenty-fold to escape colossal failure. The mustache wouldn't be enough.

I'd also gotten a hotel room smack in the middle of South Beach, which left little room for an excuse of a lack of material. The first two days at Super Bowl week weren't exactly brimming with opportunity; a good portion of the celebrities and media throngs had yet to arrive. With no real agenda until that Thursday, I resorted to some of the stock ideas that had sort of worked last year: an attempt to get onto the luxurious blue carpet of Radio Row, a drunken night out on the town with locals, and bitching about my hotel accommodations. But such crap wasn't going to work this year. The always opinionated, crass, and sometimes cruel commenters who navigate the Deadspin message boards had responded to my first days of reportage with the online equivalent of a tomato tossing. I knew that it wasn't the most groundbreaking stuff I'd ever done, but I did expect people to be a little patient. But I also knew that *I* wanted more—I was in South Beach, for Christ's sake—and there had to be something that could at least sort of measure up to the hype.

On Tuesday night there was a welcoming party on the beach for some of the early-arrival media. My plan was to basically sit outside the action and wait for anyone recognizable to exit. I had no plan. Also, I had one of the esteemed Deadspin commenters with me—"Lt. Winslow"—who mentioned he'd be up for going out with me on some adventures. Winslow essentially was serving as my wingman and cameraman; plus, he was an attorney, giving me some peace of mind should anything get really out of control.

"Tonight we really have to get something good," I said to him over dinner. We'd staked out a spot by the beach where we could monitor the party from afar. At around 10 P.M., we walked up to the two bouncers on the beach and asked them if they'd seen "anybody good" so far. Neither of them offered any information. Also, bouncers at South Beach are used to seeing celebrities all the time, so to think that they would say something like "Bayless is here" or "Jay Mariotti is tanked" was highly unlikely. To make matters worse, the entire event was blocked off by mesh fencing and a five-foot wall. You could see some of the conga line–like activities, but mostly you could just see the twenty-foot-high lighting structures with all of the liquor sponsor banners and the intermittent fireworks displays. By 11 P.M., Lt. Winslow had ceased even pretending to be interested in what was going on beyond the fence. He just sat on a park bench checking his cell phone messages, to see if any of his friends were doing something better than loitering outside a lame beach party.

I, on the other hand, was panicking as I looked at my watch and was coming to the realization that I might not have anything to report the next day. I hastily phoned Will to prepare him for the worst and let him know that there was a strong chance that Wednesday's Super Bowl updates would most likely be horrible. "There's absolutely nothing going on here," I told him. I even volunteered to get a tattoo at Miami Ink the next day—an attempt to manufacture a story that would, at the very least, appear to be ballsy. By that point, though, I knew it would only be perceived for what it was—desperate.

However, instead of going home, Lt. Winslow suggested we check out the Clevelander, a touristy hotel and nightclub that was known to have its fair share of celebrity clientele. Emotionally deflated, I decided that it couldn't make the night any less productive. Plus, I really, really needed a drink. When we arrived, we immediately saw Michael Strahan and Chicago Bears defensive end Alex Brown milling around the outside of the club. Plenty of people were running up to them for autographs and photos. I immediately took some shots of Strahan as he was leaving the building, satisfied because Strahan was still in the news at the time, thanks to his very public divorce from his wife. I concocted the post in my head and then relaxed a bit, thankful that I'd acquired some semblance of material to post the next day. We sat at the bar and then a bartender informed us that Michael Irvin was in the upstairs bar and that we could go up there. Our eyes lit up; mine because Irvin is enough of an interesting character to satisfy the clamoring Deadspin readers who'd turned against me, and Winslow's because it just so happened that Michael Irvin was his favorite player.

As we made our way upstairs, we saw Stuart Scott yapping away on his cell phone. We went inside to find a very small white-walled bar that had about twenty people inside. Michael Irvin sat in one corner with his bodyguard. Sean Salisbury was at the bar. Alex Brown was doing shots. The night suddenly took a complete 180, and I'd somehow broken through to the other side and hit the motherlode: a private party with ESPN personalities basically getting drunk and being big swinging dicks with plenty of local ladies on hand.

Salisbury was particularly newsworthy—he was quite extremely paranoid about carousing that week due to some very unflattering press about him allegedly sending cell phone pictures of his penis to female coworkers (a practice unbecoming of a man who works for Disney). He has declined to comment on these reports. We did get a photo of him, which he obliged to given that we'd promise not to post it on the Internet. Of course, I broke that promise, and about a million other rules of the guy code, when I reported about all of the women around the various personalities. Most notably, I hijacked a text message Stu Scott was sending to someone at 12:30 at night by peeking over his shoulder. The woman he was sending it to was an extremely hot former NFL cheerleader (a message he would acknowledge that he sent in an interview with the *Washington Post,* stating that she was an old friend who'd just gotten engaged). This would probably be something Stu's wife would not appreciate him doing. Of course, I just reported the facts, leaving readers to draw their own conclusions about why (and how?) Mr. Booya was corresponding with this hot chick at such a late hour.

The next day, when I posted all of the stories about Tuesday night's antics, the week completely changed. I'd suddenly transformed from a loser with limited to no access to having blockbuster first-person accounts of some of ESPN's top talent (plus a member of the Chicago Bears) behaving badly in South Beach. By the time Thursday came around, the story had spread all across the sports media landscape, and rumors were circulating that I was a marked man by both Salisbury and Scott and anybody else who was loosely affiliated with ESPN. In fact, Will received an e-mail from one member of the SportsCenter crew who not-so-subtly suggested I might get "the mustache knocked off" my face if I continued with my antics.

By the end of the week, I shaved my mustache, which had become actual "news" on the site, solidifying the fact that I'd finally calmed the angry readers who were collectively telling me how much I sucked just three days ago.

At this point, though, I was just exhausted. On Friday, I was walking back to my hotel on Collins Avenue about 4 P.M., finally getting something other than toxic liquids into my stomach. The sidewalks were a little more crowded, but they suddenly opened up and there was one man walking toward me, checking his cell phone: Sean Salisbury. I had no camera on me and am ashamed to admit that I wasn't in any mood to make my presence known. Instead, I not so hastily made a quick right into another hotel's parking lot and hid behind an SUV until he walked by.

It was at that point, when I actually hid from Sean Salisbury,
that I realized what a success that year's Deadspin Super Bowl
week had been.

YOU CAN'T FIGHT TERRORISM WITH A SPREAD OFFENSIVE SET, AND YOU PROBABLY SHOULDN'T EVEN TRY

While waiting for Cathouse to come back on HBO recently, I stumbled across the documentary *Nine Innings from Ground Zero,* and I'll be honest with you: It might have been the biggest crock of crap I've ever seen. (Note: This is an overstatement.)

The premise was simple, yet vague enough to make it impossible to refute. Just more than a month after September 11, 2001, the New York Yankees played the Arizona Diamondbacks in the World Series. According to the documentary, the series—a great one, actually, the one that ended with the bloop single by Luis Gonzalez; Buster Olney's book *The Last Night of the Yankee Dynasty* covers it excellently—served as a balm that helped heal the scorched heart of a tortured city.

As the theory goes, the home runs by Tino Martinez and Derek Jeter—neither of whom lived in New York City in the off-season—took our minds off the tragedies and confusion surrounding us; similar mythology envelops a home run Mike Piazza hit in September for the Mets. (The blown saves Armando Benitez served up toward the end of the season, costing the Mets a playoff spot, presumably mean that Armando cared less about the victims. It makes sense.) The Diamondbacks went on to win the Series after Mariano Rivera blew a ninth-inning save in Arizona, proving that he too was part of the terrorist menace. Fortunately, Luis

Gonzalez loved America, unless he was fighting against New York by trying to win, in which case, he's a member of Al Qaeda. It's all very confusing. Let's just go with this: Those who hit home runs wearing pinstripes love America, and those wearing that nasty Diamondback color of turquoise hate America. And Tim McCarver is just a nihilist. That's the best I can figure out.

Anyone who was in New York City on September 11 has a story from that day (or anyone anywhere, actually), and you can usually tell how close the person was to the actual devastation downtown by their willingness to tell it. One friend, after much cajoling and alcohol, talked about being in law school at NYU, about three-quarters of a mile from the World Trade Center, and of entering a stunned classroom minutes after the second plane had hit. The professor and the students were in so much shock that they continued on with the hour-and-a-half lecture even while they could hear screaming and destruction outside the window. When the lecture ended, they entered what was left of the outside world; they didn't have class again for a week. My story is comparatively banal: working in a hospital on the Upper East Side of Manhattan, expecting a flood of injured people that never came, walking downtown to meet friends in Chinatown and feeling like the only idiot going the wrong direction.

Like everybody else I knew in the days/weeks/months after September 11, I dealt with the planet shift in the most appropriate way possible: I drank. Many New York businesses suffered in the wake of September 11, but bars had to have made out rather well; that's where a good 20 percent of the income of most everyone I knew went. We were not drinking as distraction, or as a way to cope. We drank because that was what we had done before, and somehow, returning to the familiar drunkenness reminded us of something that resembled stablility. Quieter, perhaps, with a few more crying jags than usual, but collectively centralizing.

I didn't realize it then, but one thing we weren't doing was watching sports. This was a considerable change. The first sporting event I watched after September 11 was the same one that most people watched—the ESPN telecast of my beloved St. Louis Cardinals playing at Busch Stadium. Most people recall the game for a speech by the late Cardinals broadcaster Jack Buck, stricken with the final stages of the Parkinson's that would kill him less than a year later; he read a poem he had written in the aftermath of the attacks. His body racked with spasms, Buck spoke.

> *We've been challenged by a*
> *Cowardly foe who strikes and then*
> *Hides from our view.*
>   *With one voice we say there's no*
> *Choice today, there is only one*
> *Thing to do.*
>   *Everyone is saying the same thing*
> *And praying that we end these*
> *Senseless moments we are living.*
>   *As our fathers did before, we shall*
> *Win this unwanted war.*
>   *As our children will enjoy the*
> *Future, we'll be giving.*

Now, I confess that I'm no expert in the field of poetry, but . . . well . . . this is a pretty stupid poem. ("praying that we end these / Senseless moments we are living"? Does that mean we have to die? As an eight-year-old I stayed up until midnight for West Coast games and snuck a radio under my pillow to listen to Jack Buck, so it gives me no joy to say this, but: What the hell can a baseball broadcaster possibly tell me about September 11? As I watched the game with a friend, our reaction was not inspiration or fortitude in the face of an unprecedented calamity. We shut off the television and went to a bar. "Do you think they would give out Jack Buck bobblehead dolls?" my friend wondered, and that was the extent of our baseball conversation for the evening.

The rest of that baseball season, I'm sad to say, is a blur in my memory, and apparently I missed a lot. (I remain convinced that the real reason the reaction to Barry Bonds's seventy-three homers that year was more muted than the reaction to Mark McGwire's record run three years earlier was not racism or Bonds's unlikability; it's because we had better things to worry about than fucking *baseball*.)

Sure, if you could enter the right mind-set, sports could distract you from the horror around you; that is the point of sports after all, to *distract*. But as the years go on, somehow Buck's poem—along with that Yankees-Diamondbacks series and the Mets' discovery that wearing FDNY hats helped people forget that they were all millionaires who got the hell out of the city within hours of season's end—has grown in stature, entering that set of transcendent moments when Sports Mattered, when it Helped Us Cope.

This is human nature; being a sports fan means investing a ludicrous amount of time and mental energy into something that, by definition, bears no relevance to real life. It is normal to attempt to justify one's fandom by attaching significance to sporting events. We rewrite history to fit what we wished would have happened rather than what actually did. Reporters tired of discussing the lack of bite on Barry Zito's curveball are eager to pump up their word counts and internal gravitas by waxing column-inchy on What This All Means. They get to pretend to be, you know, *real* reporters. It helps them compartmentalize all those times they had to pretend to care about that mid-August Orioles-Tigers game. And it can rationalize the free buffets and late-night strip club nights in Tampa.

It's not just a game; it must Mean Something. Thing is, your average sportswriters are incapable of stretching past the sedentary limits of their job description. By overextending their perspective, they insult everyone, even the players they're supposedly deifying.

This tendency to overextend led to some pretty awful stories that only come to sound worse over time. Here are some of my favorites:

Woody Paige, *Denver Post:* "Miss Liberty bowed her head. From on high and nigh, she witnessed the horrifying cataclysm. There were tears in her eyes. And the nation cries with her. Denver was not torched, but it has been touched." (Four years later, Paige, while wearing a dunce cap and wacky glasses, would eat dog food on live television.)

Jay Mariotti, *Chicago Sun-Times:* "Our local baseball managers have addressed the idea of a white-flag mentality and suggested players might not be inspired to resume the season, a folly when you consider firefighters and rescue teams are working around the clock and risking their lives."

The best was Skip Bayless, whom we have discussed before. He has a terribly difficult time shaking his combative schtick. His column, titled "Athletes Failed in Duty to Provide Us Escape," in the *San Jose Mercury News* read like satire. "To my disgust, I spent Wednesday and Thursday hearing outrageously paid athletes tell us how irrelevant sports are and how they just didn't feel like playing. Will these eight-figure whiners tell us how 'truly unimportant' sports are before the next work stoppage? Do they think any of us felt like going to work Wednesday? Many in this country needed baseball and football to be played as soon as possible—baseball by Thursday or Friday, college football by Saturday, the NFL by today. This was the least sports could have done for us after all we've done for them."

I do understand that Overpaid Athletes and the Fat-Cat Owners Who Enable and Pamper Them are as essential to the sportswriter canon as the Somebody Fire That Manager! and Why Are All These Readers Sending Me Hate Mail? columns, but there is a time and place. Alex Rodriguez could have been making $110 million a swing or $1 a year, and on September 16, I could not have cared less. No reasonable human could. It's kind of frightening, actually, that it bothered Bayless so much. But it was not a good month for perspective, from any angle.

But when you write about sports in a vacuum, spending all of your time with other sportswriters, and trying to control those who do or play the sports themselves, you lose touch with how the rest of the planet works. It's a fundamental concept: Sports *do not matter.* The average fan understands this—despite pretty much every sports commercial, which portrays fans as some sort of unwieldy, testosterone-laden, beer-shotgunning mob of delinquents—and that is why we put sports in its proper place: as something we partake in and enjoy because we want to escape from our jobs, our bills, our responsibilities, our *lives.* The world is a terrifying place, with grays and complexities and confusion at every turn. Sports afford us none of this: If our team wins, we are happy; if they lose, we are sad. It doesn't have to be more than that. That simplicity is enough. It's plenty.

Yet at every turn, someone's trying to convince us that sports are something *more* than sports. But just because Lance Armstrong overcame cancer and we wear his bracelets doesn't mean sports *mean* anything. Life is hard. Sports are where we go to hide.

PETER KING WANTS YOU TO SEE PICTURES OF HIS DRUNKEN DAUGHTER

Five years ago, Peter King was the top NFL reporter at *Sports Illustrated,* which is one of the choice gigs in sports journalism. He was at the top of his field, highly respected, and tapped into every front office in the league. If you wanted to know what was going on in the NFL, King's *SI* work was the place to start.

Problem was, though, nobody knew King's face, and few outside the industry probably even noticed his byline. He was an anonymous reporter, nobly detailing the world of the NFL in the distanced, dispassionate fashion that journalism schools teach you. (When I studied journalism at the University of Illinois, one professor argued that no newspaper or magazine stories should have bylines, which was easy for him to say—he already had a job.)

Almost on a whim, SI.com—then partnered with CNN—asked King to write a weekly column uninventively called "Monday Morning Quarterback." It was a way to expand his weekly notes columns from the magazine, allowing him to add in all the tidbits he wasn't able to fit in the issue. Because King was so dialed in, it instantly became required reading for NFL fans. Not only was it a one-stop source for NFL info, it allowed a rare glimpse into the life of an NFL beat reporter. It didn't appear particularly glamorous; mostly, King just detailed an endless parade of delayed flights, Starbucks grabs, and a life spent mostly on the phone in airline terminals. King is a talented writer, though, and he emerged as a likable fellow who was fully aware that he had a job most fans would envy.

King embraced the medium like most print journalists embrace the Internet when they are first exposed to it: He started providing readers with every detail of his life, no matter how superfluous or inane. King wrote about sitting next to a flatulent man on the plane, what he had for breakfast, what television shows he was watching—"You know what's gripping television? *House!*"—and whatever else might happen to come across his brain. The column was a huge success, at least among other journalists; King's profile skyrocketed, and he went from an anonymous behind-the-scenes guy to an on-camera presence for CNN and, later, HBO and NBC. He became one of the most recognizable sports presences outside of ESPN, and it is not a stretch to say his online column served as the catalyzing event. Peter King was no longer a byline; he was a brand.

These little nuggets of personal information, in the end, distributed diminishing returns. After a while, the details of King's day-to-day life began to drag on rather than enlighten. Two incidents turned the tide of sports fan public opinion against him. First, King gave a rather gruesome description of his colonoscopy. He might have intended this as a Katie Couric-esque attempt to educate the public on the dangers of whatever his potential affliction was, but in a column that people read for details on the Jets' backup running back situation, it was a bit much. The second incident was even shakier. King began to greatly enjoy writing about his daughter Mary Beth's field hockey team at her Montclair, New Jersey, high school. These updates often went on for a thousand words and served only to make King popular at his daughter's practices. When she left for college, he continued the Mary Beth updates, at one point even mentioning the dorm she lived in. King volunteered this information. Had he never written about his daughter, no one would have ever known, or cared.

Enter the mostly anonymous bloggers of Kissing Suzy Kolber, an acerbic (and quite hilarious) NFL blog started by a group of guys who initially met as commenters on Deadspin. One day, as a half joke, they posted a rant about King's pointless personal information, noting that anyone who wanted legitimate NFL news had to wade through pages and pages of dumb biographical info on the King family. To drive their point home, they threatened to post pictures Mary Beth King had posted to her Facebook page, pictures that featured her in various stages of public drunkenness. They set a noon deadline for King to renounce his extraneous info ways and get back to football. I thought they were joking. They weren't.

After what I would find out later were rather intense ethical debates within Kissing Suzy Kolber, they went ahead and posted the pictures. They weren't particularly inflammatory—just a drunk college girl doing what drunk college girls do—but a shitstorm erupted immediately. It was not difficult to understand the uproar over the (supposedly) private pictures of a journalist's family member, posted only because of a petty beef with the content of a free column. Simple, right?

Maybe. Kissing Suzy Kolber did ultimately take down the photos, admitting they were "assholes" and apologizing. But an argument could be made that King got exactly what he deserved.

First off, this was publicly available information; it's not like someone sneaked into King's daughter's dorm room and snapped the pictures of her when she wasn't looking. She was the one who made the decision to post them; she obviously wanted someone to see them. But more to the point: *This is the way the Web works.* Peter King made his career—the new career, the one in which he's on television all the time and making considerably more money—because of his presence on the Internet. You can't just take the good of the Web and ignore the bad. The Web does not exist just so King can make a good career move.

When you tell your readers what college your daughter attends—*what dorm she lives in*—you can't act all surprised when some weirdos find drunken pictures of her and post them elsewhere on the Web. She wasn't a public figure until her father made her a public figure. Whether what Kissing Suzy Kolber did was "right" or "wrong" is beside the point; the point is that *someone* was going to do it. King drew them a road map.

Listen, I am not endorsing the publication of pictures of ESPN personalities' teenage daughters. (People have actually sent some to me, thinking I would. I won't.) But the Internet is not just this well of replenishing goodness. When you write about your life on the Internet, there is a presumption that you have opened yourself up, and made your private matters fair game for public use. This is the law of the jungle. Let's just say that if you, as a media guy or an athlete, give out personal family information, shit is going to happen. It doesn't make it right. It just makes it the truth.

So perhaps it would behoove those who write about their families and friends and private lives to look before they leap, or at least be prepared for the consequences. I can speak to this first-hand. Not only do I have my share of drunken pictures on the Web, there's actually a Web site out there with pictures of my mother and comments on how "hot" she is. The only reason people can pass judgment on the hotness of my mother is because I posted her picture. (With her permission.) As much as this site might turn my stomach, I really have no business complaining.

And Mom's not complaining either; she's actually quite flattered. My father, on the other hand . . .

TEN MOST LOATHSOME ESPN PERSONALITIES AND THEIR WORST MOMENTS

10. **Colin Cowherd.** On his radio show, Cowherd—known as "Schrutebag" in the blog world—encouraged his listeners to shut down the independent Web site thebiglead.com by unleashing a Denial of Service attack. (This involves overloading a site with fictional hits using a script written to wreak havoc.) The site went down for two days. Cowherd is most renowned for using material from blogs without credit.

9. **Joe Morgan.** Notorious for being a baseball flat-earther, Morgan—the keeper of the traditionalist Baseball Man flame—repeatedly insisted that A's general manager Billy Beane *wrote* the bestseller *Moneyball*, rather than being its subject.

8. **Jay Mariotti.** One of the talking head dopes on *Around the Horn*, Mariotti once petitioned Wikipedia to take down all negative references to him.

7. **Skip Bayless.** The pathological contrarian once accused former Illinois basketball star Eddie Johnson of being a child molester, when, in fact, it was a different Eddie Johnson. He was named in a lawsuit filed by the former Johnson, which was settled out of court.

6. **Joe Theismann.** So many to choose from here, but Theismann's most embarrassing moment must have been interviewing Christian Slater for ten minutes during a Seahawks *Monday Night Football* game.

5. **Dick Vitale.** High-volume even while whispering, Vitale once appeared in a Hooters commercial sporting a creepy leer.

4. **Stephen A. Smith.** The oft-shifted personality who signed an ill-fated (for ESPN, anyway) four-year contract right before his *Quite Frankly* show tanked. Denies that he told one of his interns to encourage guests via e-mail to boo Cubs manager (and guest) Dusty Baker. (He even blamed me!) His show was canceled less than a month later.

3. **Sean Salisbury.** This blustery, mentally deformed NFL analyst reportedly took a picture of his penis and sent it out to female colleagues.

2. **Chris Berman.** Mostly just general fatigue here, but anyone who has ever heard him broadcast the All-Star Game home run derby—with its endless bombast of "Back back back back back back back BACK!"'s—has to wonder what they did to deserve this.

1. **Stuart Scott.** ESPN's resident white-boy bro dawg who, while hosting ESPN's New Year's Eve bash (which is its own story), chastised fans for booing professional athletes: "When you go to the sporting events and you're watching the athletes compete as hard as they can, stop booing, okay? There's no point in booing these athletes. They've all worked hard. They've all trained hard, and let's see you get out there and do it, all right?"

FIVE PEOPLE WHO OFFENDED THE ALMIGHTY ESPN AND PAID THE PRICE

1. **Mike Freeman.** Wrote a book called *ESPN: The Uncensored History,* which painted the network's Bristol campus as a big frat house gone awry. It detailed Mike Tirico's addiction to "sexual" banter, evidenced by his tendency to tell female staffers, "I want to fuck you, but you can't tell my wife." Once word of the book got out, Freeman's publishers were spooked, and it was ultimately published by a tiny university press. Freeman, who once worked for the *New York Times,* has bounced around the industry and, needless to say, has never been on *The Sports Reporters.*

2. **T. J. Simers.** Irascible *Los Angeles Times* columnist who would appear on the deadly *Around the Horn* show until, a week after his last appearance, he wrote a column criticizing the show. He was immediately contacted by ESPN brass, who told him to knock it off or he'd be kicked off the program. He refused to stop, and he was canceled from the show and now hosts a radio show in L.A. He never appeared on ESPN again.

3. **Jason Whitlock.** Longtime *Sports Reporters* panelist and writer for ESPN's *Page 2* who, when interviewed on the

Web site The Big Lead, called colleague Scoop Jackson "a clown." He was promptly fired by the network.

4. **Keith Olbermann.** Self-involved but obviously talented personality who rode the *SportsCenter* celebrity wave before freaking out and heading to NBC, then FOX, then MSNBC. Was blasted for cooperating with Freeman's book and general grousing attitude. Said Bristol was "the most boring city in America."

5. **Gregg Easterbrook.** "Serious" journalist whose "Tuesday Morning Quarterback" column was notable for its references to NASA and creepy-old-man cheerleading ogling. Was fired after mentioning "the Jews who run Disney." This did not go over well; he was immediately not only fired but also erased from ESPN.com, archives included.

These last two are notable because, as tends to be the case with anyone who wants to keep one foot in the "respectable" world and one foot in the sports world, they ultimately came crawling back to ESPN. Olbermann made appearances on Dan Patrick's radio show, and Easterbrook took a yearlong sojourn to NFL .com before returning and never, ever writing anything about religion. Wisely.

GLOSSARY

Albert, Marv. Famed NBA broadcaster most noted for his odd sexual peccadillos. In 1997, pled guilty to misdemeanor assault charges for biting a girlfriend on the back fifteen times (she also accused him of forcing anal sex). Reportedly has been involved in several threesomes and enjoys wearing women's underwear. YES!

Andrews, Erin. Attractive sideline reporter for ESPN college basketball, usually assigned to linger around Big Ten student sections and pose for pictures, which are later Photoshopped into various sexual scenarios. Responsible for 35 percent of masturbation fantasies in the states of Iowa, Michigan, and Wisconsin.

Bayless, Skip. Longtime columnist turned ESPN personality, considered the personification of a car alarm that won't stop blaring. Renowned for ridiculous contrarian views designed only to sound "controversial."

Berman, Chris. Living legend at ESPN, famous for his grating player nicknames and tendency to quote songs no one under the age of forty has ever heard. Friends with Huey Lewis, which somehow makes the "Power of Love" singer *more* lame. Perhaps most renowned in this decade for his sexual exploits, exemplified in the famous "You're with Me, Leather" story, in which Berman successfully picked up a woman wearing a leather jacket at a bar with that exact line. Since then, the phrase has been slyly quoted in various media outlets, and less subtly screamed at Berman anytime he's in public.

Bernstein, Bonnie. Sideline reporter once accused of sleeping with Patriots coach Bill Belichick, a rumor later debunked. Noted for lacking a sense of humor and for his ability to coax Roy Williams into saying, "I could give a shit about North Carolina right now," on live television, just months before he returned to his alma mater to coach the Tar Heels.

Bilas, Jay. Former Duke basketball player, accomplished lawyer, and Bill Raftery impersonator. Played Good Alien in the 1990 Dolph Lundgren film *I Come in Peace*. Bears uncanny resemblance to GOB from *Arrested Development*.

Bradshaw, Terry. Bald, warbling yokel analyst for FOX Sports who somehow turned his "wacky" appearances on FOX NFL Sunday into a pseudo-acting career. His major film role was in *Failure to Launch* (starring Matthew McConaughey), appearing nude next to Kathy Bates.

Brown, Hubie. Skilled NBA analyst renowned for extensive soliloquies in the second person singular.

Brown, James. Harvard graduate who toggled between FOX and CBS, bringing a jolly black-man blandness that led to a side career hosting *America's Funniest Home Videos*.

Buck, Joe. Son of late famed St. Louis Cardinals broadcaster Jack Buck. He's ubiquitous on FOX, calling both baseball and football. Seems to find himself hip, somehow, and has spoken of his desire to have his own sitcom, à la Bob Uecker on *Mr. Belvedere*. Famously lambasted Vikings receiver Randy Moss for mock-mooning Green Bay Packers fans after scoring a touchdown, screaming, "That is a disgusting act!" Asked Mark McGwire to give him a hug after he hit his sixty-second home run, and, according to several old Cardinals beat reporters, gave then-Cardinal Todd Zeile foot massages on the team plane. Is not in fact black.

Clayton, John. Tweedy ESPN NFL reporter with unusually large cranium and a countenance that often resembles the guy in *RoboCop* after he falls into the toxic waste just before he's squished by the oncoming car. Spends most of his time trying not to be stuffed in lockers by his ESPN colleagues.

Cohn, Linda. Longtime ESPN news anchor, seemingly pregnant every six months.

Collinsworth, Cris. Talented HBO and NBC broadcaster whose sense of humor, no-holds-barred approach, and legitimate understanding of the game often put him at odds with fellow broadcasters. Looks like Sideshow Bob if Sideshow Bob got a haircut.

Cook, Beano. Elderly college football analyst, born in 1832. Once claimed Notre Dame quarterback would win four Heisman Trophies. Real name is "Carroll."

Corso, Lee. Gimmicky college football analyst for ESPN whose trick is to wear mascot masks on his head while making predictions. For whatever reason, has inspired fans at *College GameDay* live locations to wave LEE CORSO IS A PENIS signs behind his head. Strangely, promotes making crayons out of soybeans and has a day job producing No. 2 pencils.

Cossack, Roger. ESPN legal analyst made famous during the O. J. Simpson trial. Delivers sober-faced legalese from outside the endless string of athlete trials.

Costas, Bob. Omnipresent elfish broadcaster known for smugness and tiny stature. Fancies himself a Renaissance man not pinned down by the brutish world of sports. Pees sitting down.

Cowherd, Colin. ESPN radio host often criticized for stealing stories from Web sites without accreditation. Schrutebag.

Dickerson, Eric. Former Rams running back who spent one ill-fated year as a sideline reporter for *Monday Night Football* despite his difficulties with the English language. Often compacted sentences with fifteen or sixteen syllables into one glorious Cuisinarted mash-up.

Eisen, Rich. Former ESPN anchor who is now the linchpin of the NFL Network. Has natural smugness that serves him well during guest appearances on *I Love the '80s*. The last person that friends, family, and sport fans ever expected to receive bikini self-portraits from a Philadelphia television news reporter.

Everett, Neil. ESPN anchor suspended by the network for referencing the Berman "You're with Me, Leather" line on the air. From Hawaii.

Fowler, Chris. Indie-rock-loving host of *College GameDay*. He is married to Jennifer Dempster, the former host of *BodyShaping*, an old ESPN workout program used for dormitory masturbation in the late '80s and early '90s.

Gammons, Peter. Legendary baseball reporter known for his love of Boston, man crush on Tom Petty, and resemblance to former president Andrew Jackson.

Golic, Mike. ESPN morning radio host. The fat one.

Gomez, Peter. Once-respected reporter destroyed by ESPN's assignment to follow Barry Bonds around for two years. At the end of his tour of duty, Gomez was released to the wild, and never quite looked the same, as if he had spent the last twenty-four months in the Hanoi Hilton.

Gottlieb, Doug. Former college hoops star turned ESPN analyst. While at Notre Dame, Gottlieb fraudulently used his roommate's credit cards and was kicked off the team. He also was accused of draft dodging by the Israeli military.

Gray, Jim. Twerpy sideline reporter who seems to believe his job is one that requires ability in journalism. Sidles up to famous athletes like Kobe Bryant and Mike Tyson in order to garner athlete-friendly "exclusive" interviews. In his most famous moment, he questioned Pete Rose about whether he was "ready to apologize" for betting on baseball. Although he received considerable criticism for asking, it's probably the only worthwhile moment Jim Gray ever produced.

Greenberg, Mike. ESPN morning radio host. The gay one.

Gumbel, Bryant. Former *Today* show host whose sports fandom led him to be host of *Real Sports with Bryant Gumbel*, a worthwhile HBO journalism program almost completely derailed by Gumbel's fatuousness and "banana-in-the-tailpipe" vocal inflections. Wins points for being an enemy of Willard Scott.

Gumbel, Greg. Bryant's bushy-haired brother who somehow manages to be more boring and white than his sibling.

Irvin, Michael. Hall of Fame wide receiver who parlayed his beaten-and-confused-by-cocaine-and-hookers personality into a gig as one of ESPN's top NFL analysts. Incoherent and visibly paranoid, he consistently talks his colleagues into a stupor and has a tendency to get busted for having drugs on his person every two years or so. Once said Cowboys quarterback Tony Romo was so quick that he must have had a black slave ancestor. "His great-great-great-great-grandma must have pulled one of them studs up outta the barn [and said], 'Come here for a second,'" went the quote. He later "apologized." Eventually was fired by the network.

Jackson, Tom. ESPN analyst who offered intelligent analysis until the network required him to start yelling like everybody else. Is intensely disliked by Patriots coach Bill Belichick, in one of the more boring feuds in American entertainment.

Jaworski, Ron. Noted film room addict and *MNF* host owns an Arena Football team with Jon Bon Jovi.

Kay, Michael. New York Yankees broadcaster who alternates between Orwellian pro-Steinbrenner propaganda and unhinged outbursts on the air. The most famous of these was when he compared a caller on his radio show talking about a perfect game to "those who say the Holocaust and slavery didn't make sense."

Kellerman, Max. Wunderkind boxing analyst formerly of ESPN whose obsession with the sport allowed him his own show before he turned thirty. Brother Sam was killed by a boxer he had been attempting to train. Generally considered far more intelligent than he comes across on television.

Kilborn, Craig. Former *SportsCenter* anchor who left the program in 1996 to host *The Daily Show* on Comedy Central. Left the show in 1999 to host *The Late Late Show with Craig Kilborn*, which he (once again) left in 2004 to pursue a career in movies. Has never been heard from again.

King, Peter. Longtime respected NFL reporter for *Sports Illustrated* whose career took off when he began writing a weekly "Monday Morning Quarterback" column for SI.com, which, in addition to NFL news and notes, featured endless references to his daughters, Montclair; New Jersey; and his own prostate exams. Ended up in the "expert reporter" role on HBO's *Inside the NFL* and NBC's *Football Night in America*. Even though his career was launched by the Internet, has become an anti-Web advocate because he believes it infringes too much on people's privacy, an odd stance coming from a man who insists on blogging each and every one of his personal coffee choices.

Kiper, Mel. Hair-helmeted NFL draft "expert" who is unseen for eleven months of the year before finally emerging from an underground lair to talk about the physical attributes of underwear-clad, muscular young men.

Kolber, Suzy. Workmanlike NFL sideline reporter whose legend was cemented when a drunken Joe Namath told her on air, during a Jets game, that he wanted to kiss her. Handled the situation gracefully and is now known as the only woman who has never known Namath in the biblical sense.

Kornheiser, Tony. Longtime *Washington Post* reporter whose show *Pardon the Interruption* rocketed him into a multimedia career, including a wretched short-lived CBS sitcom called *Listen Up*, which featured the comedic star pairing of Jason Alexander and Malcolm-Jamal Warner. Eventually became the would-be Howard Cosell on *Monday Night Football,* though his job mostly consists of making "jokes" about fantasy football, awkwardly "interviewing" in-booth celebrities, and generally disappointing his many media friends who were all rooting for him to succeed. Bald.

Kruk, John. Oafish former Philadelphia Phillie whose arrival on the *Baseball Tonight* set secured the program's descent into irrelevance and flatulence. Has one testicle.

Ley, Bob. ESPN's Serious Journalist. Somehow successful at coming across as above the network's mania while still saying things like "We now take you to Stuart Scott and the season premiere of *Dream Job*." Reportedly brings a scorebook to baseball games, increasing his general likability.

Long, Howie. Square-necked FOX football analyst whose appearance in a series of Radio Shack commercials with sag-headed actress Teri Hatcher sparked off a short-lived, mostly embarrassing acting career, highlighted by the 1998 film *Firestorm*, in which Scott Glenn did his best to avoid looking depressed that he was second-billed behind Howie Long.

Lupica, Mike. Snotty New York *Daily News* columnist known for his self-classification as a Serious Writer. Trashes supposed steroid cheats today for their evil nature, but made serious coin on a book he wrote about the Mark McGwire/Sammy Sosa home run chase in 1998. After failing as a Serious Writer, now writes young-adult sports novels, which, ahem, there is nothing wrong with whatsoever.

Madden, John. ACE hardware pitchman at the forefront of the video game revolution. Famously afraid to fly after losing a friend in a plane crash when he was younger. Surprises many by pointing out that he was once a serious football coach. Surreally, spent September 11, 2001, on his famous Madden Bus with figure skater Peggy Fleming.

Marino, Dan. Former Dolphins quarterback whose playing career is remembered mostly for his inability to win a Super Bowl. Marino is constantly needled for this deficiency and unable to disguise his rabid disgust—which makes for compelling CBS television, where he's an analyst.

Mariotti, Jay. *Chicago Sun-Times* columnist known for his cowardly bombast. Rarely attends the games he writes about, drawing the ire of any athlete or coach confused enough to take him seriously. Called a "fag" by White Sox manager Ozzie Guillen, an unfortunate term, but not unfortunate enough to prevent almost every media member, most of whom famously hate Mariotti, from taking Guillen's side. Once e-mailed Wikipedia to complain about his own profile.

Mayne, Kenny. "Wacky" ESPN anchor who appeared on *Dancing with the Stars* and various silly commercials. Considered a relic of an earlier ESPN era, when the channel was so hip that it appeared in Hootie and the Blowfish videos.

McCarver, Tim. FOX baseball analyst despised by most viewers, mostly for his tendency to express the most obvious point and then marvel at himself as if he had just discovered cold fusion. Rumored to be having an affair with "Scooter," the animated talking baseball on FOX broadcasts.

Mees, Tom. Late original ESPN broadcaster who drowned while trying to save his daughter in their swimming pool in 1996. Was renowned for his inexplicable obsessions with both ice hockey and the Republican Party.

Michaels, Al. *Miracle on Ice* broadcaster who has become the leathery-faced personification of Los Angeles. Was "traded" by ABC to NBC for cartoon character Oswald the Lucky Rabbit.

Miller, Jon. Rotund and bald ESPN and San Francisco Giants broadcaster charged with defending two indefensibles: Barry Bonds and Joe Morgan.

Morgan, Joe. ESPN baseball analyst and dean of aging, out-of-touch baseball fraternity. Notoriously suspicious of statistics and people who are not Baseball Men. Believes Billy Beane "wrote" *Moneyball.* His ESPN chats are famous for their "earth-is-flat" proclamations.

Musburger, Brent. Longtime broadcaster, first famous for Kevin Nealon's impersonation of him on *Inside the NFL,* now famous for ogling Erin Andrews during Big Ten ESPN broadcasts. Was once ticketed for driving away after a football game with an open beer in his car.

Nantz, Jim. CBS broadcaster who somehow is more white than Joe Buck. Is the perfect golf announcer because he has the personality of a fairway. Friends with George W. Bush.

O'Brien, Dave. ESPN baseball broadcaster assigned to call World Cup games in 2006 despite his total ignorance regarding soccer. Thankfully, resisted any "Why can't they use their hands?" comments.

Olbermann, Keith. Former ESPN anchor whose considerable talents ultimately outweigh his erratic personality, forcing him to switch jobs every few years. Now hosts *Countdown with Keith Olbermann* on MSNBC, which feeds Olbermann's ego enough because it's not about something as frivolous as sports. Was once victimized by an anonymous blog that spun yarns of Olbermann's sexual prowess—site proved to be a source of news that America was unaware it wanted.

Olney, Buster. Talented former *New York Times* reporter whose move to ESPN gave him more money and more exposure, but also required him to ask fake questions at fake press conferences on bewildering *SportsCenter* features. Runs an excellent baseball blog on ESPN's site.

Packer, Billy. Lead CBS college basketball analyst known for his ACC bias, grouchy, Dick-Cheney-esque personality, and occasional lapses into racial insensitivity. Looks like a Muppet.

Paige, Woody. *Denver Post* columnist who left his longtime job in the Rockies for a move to New York City to appear regularly on *Around the Horn* and *Cold Pizza.* Once respected, ultimately became network clown who wears frizzy wigs and eats dog food live on the air. Was sued for sexual harassment after a makeup person accused him of pinching her so hard that she was "propelled forward, and into the air."

Paolantonio, Sal. ESPN Philadelphia-based reporter who wrote a storied column on ESPN.com accusing *The Sopranos* of being racially insensitive to Philadelphia Italians like himself. Reported to be a bit of a jerk.

Patrick, Dan. Longtime ESPN anchor known for his on-location ability to pick up women, dry wit, and T.G.I. Friday's commercials in which he is covered in barbecue sauce. Not the originator of the Olbermann blog, contrary to popular belief. Left the network in 2007.

Rashad, Ahmad. Famous hanger-on to famous athletes, most notably Michael Jordan, for whom he likely provides neck massages. Married to Claire Huxtable. Despite his name, is perhaps the least militant black man on earth.

Reali, Tony. Former intern at *Pardon the Interruption* who now hosts *Around the Horn,* contributing to the daily lobotomy the program administers. Seems like the type of guy who would take rec league softball *way* too seriously.

Reynolds, Harold. Former *Baseball Tonight* analyst fired by ESPN for "improper contact with an intern." Supposedly this "contact" involved an "inappropriate hug" at a Boston Market, the most sexual thing to ever happen at a Boston Market. Suing the network over his dismissal.

Sager, Craig. TNT NBA sideline reporter known for his terrifyingly loud suits and ties. Married to a former Chicago Bulls dancer.

Salisbury, Sean. Unsuccessful NFL backup quarterback who somehow parlayed his ineffectual quarterbacking into a spot as an NFL analyst. A career that began on *BattleBots* led to ESPN, where he had two major incidents in the span of a month. The lesser of the incidents involved an accidental slip of the tongue, saying the word "Jew" when he meant to say . . . well, something else, presumably. The other was more serious and insane; was suspended by the network for allegedly taking pictures of his penis (or "Lil Sean") and sending it around to female staffers. Has never publicly denied the incident, and the photos have never shown up online, presumably for the sake of national security.

Sargent, Danyelle. Little-known former ESPNEWS anchor who was let go after screaming "What the FUCK was that?" on live air. Now works for Fox Sports Net.

Scott, Stuart. Lazy-eyed ESPN bro dawg, noted for his annoying attempts to introduce his particular form of slang to an unwilling audience. Completely ruined the otherwise pleasant experience of flipping one's pillow to enjoy the side that is cooler than the other. A road trip lady warrior, experienced his career nadir by hosting not only ESPN's New Year's Eve special—in which he berated fans for "booing athletes"—but also a prime-time David Blaine special in which the magician, sadly, did not drown. Let him know.

Simmons, Bill. ESPN.com columnist the Sports Guy. Has a great sense of humor about himself. Friends with Jimmy Kimmel, if you haven't heard.

Simpson, O. J. Former Heisman Trophy winner.

Smith, Stephen A. Former *Philadelphia Inquirer* columnist who achieved considerable stardom on ESPN for his screaming antics and love of Cheez Doodles. Appeared in every possible sports medium to promote his ESPN2 show *Quite Frankly with Stephen A. Smith*. When poor ratings proved that viewers enjoyed programs hosted by someone who didn't make them want to run under their couch and hide, he blamed the network for a poor promotional campaign. Stayed on the network after his show was inevitably canceled.

Summerall, Pat. Elderly, bourbon-infused NFL broadcaster who has been dead since 1994.

Sutcliffe, Rick. ESPN baseball analyst suspended for a week after he appeared unannounced on an Arizona Diamondbacks broadcast. He had been out drinking all evening with, of all people, Bill Murray, and declared that George Clooney was "over there" in the Middle East "tryin' to solve that thing."

Theismann, Joe. Former *Monday Night Football* broadcaster. Mensa member and Rhodes scholar. Ask him about the time Lawrence Taylor broke his leg. He loves that.

Tirico, Mike. *Monday Night Football* play-by-play man, as well as NBA lead gabber. Competent and boring, which makes his past sexual harassment exploits that much more shocking. In his book *ESPN: The Untold Story*, author Mike Freeman recounts: "In another story, one female producer—who had been to dinner with Tirico and his fiancée—was startled to receive an e-mail from him saying that he wanted to sleep with her. Later, when the staff went to a bar after a late night covering the NCAA tournament, Tirico approached her and said, 'I wish I was single. If I were, I'd throw you on the table right here and fuck your brains out.'" Is said to have finally received treatment for his "problem."

Van Pelt, Scott. Competent *SportsCenter* anchor who received Internet notoriety in 2006 when audio of a drunken phone call he made to a woman he had tried (and failed) to pick up hit the Web. In the audio, he sounds charming, befuddled, and self-deprecating, much like Jon Favreau in *Swingers*, not like an assertive TV anchor. Was reportedly furious at the leaking of the audio.

Vitale, Dick. Modest chronicler of bright young men planning for their future while they display the beauties of the great game of basketball.

Walton, Bill. ESPN NBA analyst, known for bombastic rhetoric and regular acid flashbacks. Single-handed proof that the Grateful Dead are responsible for 64 percent of the world's tragedies, including Al Qaeda.

Ward, Pam. Excellent college football broadcaster. Oh, and . . . a woman! Whoa!

Wilbon, Michael. Kornheiser's cohort from the *Washington Post* and *Pardon the Interruption*. He's an accomplished journalist who is mostly able to avoid the tomfoolery of ESPN. In no way resembles Malcolm-Jamal Warner.

PART IV: FANS

In which your stoic purveyor of warmed-over whimsy cloaked as "satire":

WILLIE MCGEE: MY SISTER'S FIRST BLACK MAN

In 1983, when I was seven years old, my father took me to meet Willie McGee, Dave LaPoint, Tommy Herr, and manager Whitey Herzog. It was a part of the then-yearly Cardinals Caravan, in which, in order to maintain the team's fan base in central and southern Illinois, various Cardinals luminaries would hit such exotic locales as Effingham, Centralia, and Pocahontas. We hit the Effingham stop on the tour. My sister and I were decked out head-to-toe in Cardinals gear. I remember it was raining, and that was no problem; I had my Cardinals red slicker as well.

The player I was most eager to meet was McGee, the rookie center fielder who had become an instant fan favorite thanks to his speed, leaping grabs in the outfield, and a loping, sad-sack presence that made it seem as if his spine had been surgically removed. (His less-than-chiseled visage somehow helped too; his nickname at the time was "E.T.," which seems a bit more derogatory now than it did when I was seven.)

The Cardinals all sat at a table in a conference room at the Best Western Hotel, talking briefly and then taking questions from the crowd. I was not to be denied. This was my first press conference, really, and I shot my hand in the air. It's difficult to turn down a mop-topped seven-year-old, so the panel moderator called on me.

"Willie! Willie! Um, I think you're great! I loved when you made that catch over the wall in the World Series! That was really good! What was that like? Did you know you could do that?"

(Forgive me. I was not particularly incisive at seven. It might have been the first question I'd ever asked that didn't involve boogers.)

Willie smiled and laughed in that hangdog Willie way, and I have no idea how he answered. Afterward, attendees were ushered up to the players to ask for autographs and take pictures. Willie put his arm around me and smiled for my dad's camera, and the photograph is still, twenty-five years later, on the wall of our home in Mattoon.

It was a happy day. Well, for me, at least. As Dad escorted us up to McGee, my sister started screaming and crying, kicking her legs into Dad's chest as he carried her. She wouldn't settle down until after we'd hopped in the truck and drove home. My father couldn't figure out what her problem was, until we talked to my mom back at the house.

"Bryan," my mom said, "Jill says she was scared of Willie McGee."

"What?" Dad said. "Why?"

"Because he's black." My mom frowned. "She'd never met a black person before. She's three, Bryan. She was terrified."

She hadn't. And neither had I.

THE above story might speak specifically to the population characteristics of Mattoon, Illinois, more than anything else—a friend of mine in high school remembers opening the yearbook and exclaiming, "Wow, we have black students here?" I told him that yes, we did, and that they were specifically avoiding him (wisely, as it turns out)—but I think it's telling. As much as television programming and pop culture would like us to believe otherwise, we are not such a racially integrated society.

We're, frankly, not that close. Where else was a seven-year-old from central Illinois going to see a black man? On television, playing sports, of course.

This is hardly news to you. Stephen Colbert has brilliantly satirized the whole "my black friend" phenomenon, and whether you live in the suburbs, in farm country, or in the big city, you know how human beings, by nature, tend to socialize mainly with their own type. This is not a statement of approval or disapproval, just a fact; if you're white, the majority of your friends are white, if you're black, the majority of your friends are black, if you're an Eskimo, the majority of your friends are Eskimos (or penguins). In fact, if you're not like this, people of your own race tend to think there's something wrong with you.

Fact is, the most contact the majority of white sports fans have with black men, on a day-to-day basis, is through watching sports. The average white man will never understand what it means to be a black man in America, but he *can*—or at least thinks he can—get what it means to be an athlete.

You see this in its most striking way, as one sees most things in sports, through the interaction of athletes and the media. If you go to a postgame news conference, you'll note immediately that almost the only black men are the people being interviewed. Three or four black men taking questions from a room full of middle-aged white guys. This can lead to some particularly egregious double standards.

An illustrative story: Back in 2004, Denver Nuggets forward Carmelo Anthony took considerable heat for appearing in a Baltimore documentary called *Stop Fucking Snitching*. The video was meant as a goof, a way for a local "filmmaker" to document what life, was like in inner-city Baltimore. But the dominant theme of the video was how people in the community— not just criminals, but "civilians" as well—no longer considered the police their allies, but, rather, their opponents. This is what happens when 50 percent of black men are either in jail or on

parole in a particular community. While the director was cart-
ing his camera around, he came across Anthony, who was hanging out with some friends in his hometown neighborhood. He
made a few jokes, saying nothing about "snitching" whatsoever,
and probably never gave it another second's thought. But when
the video was released, Anthony was lambasted by a white media that surely never saw the video in the first place, let alone
understood what it meant (or Anthony's place in it). A few
years later, Anthony threw a punch during a brawl at Madison
Square Garden. Within hours, television personalities and
columnists were ripping him apart for—well, what, exactly?
Throwing a punch to defend a teammate? No: doing it on national television, in a way that embarrassed the league. Not
himself: *the league.* No one looked at Anthony's punch and
thought, "Man, he really is an asshole." They thought, "Oh, the
league isn't gonna like that." And the league didn't, suspending
him for a whopping fifteen games.

Every once in a while, a black athlete will make a comment
about how he feels like "a well-paid slave," and he will be evis-
cerated for it. But when a black player is arrested, or even does
something that's slightly different from what the official league
sponsors would prefer him to do, he's hammered for it at a far
more fervent rate than the crime warrants. The subtext is clear:
Look at the thug, messing up a family game. It seems so strange,
now, that Allen Iverson could have ever been thought of as
"controversial" simply for having a few tattoos (tattoos that
were airbrushed out for an official NBA magazine cover photo)
and some shady friends. And pity the rare black sports columnist. Any column they write about sports that isn't about the
role of black players is seen as somehow shirking the issue; any
column they do is accused of blatantly playing the race card.
And they get this from their fellow black columnists too!

People like to imagine sports as a great equalizer, a place
where nothing matters but performance. And while athletes
claim that this is true in the locker room—I have my doubts

about that, too—it's certainly not true in how our sports are covered, and how we perceive them. The corporate sponsors who make our leagues motor are primarily white; the players are predominantly black (or Latino). This is a dichotomy that's difficult to resolve. So we pretend that it doesn't matter, that we just root for our teams to win and don't care about anything else. Until something off-the-field happens, or someone does something that offends deep-held sensibilities. Then the player becomes a "problem." These codes are ingrained in our sports vernacular, and in our hearts, when we look close enough.

This goes the other way, too. I'm sorry, kids—and it pains me, as a Cardinals fan, to say this—but the only thing that separates David Eckstein and Ronnie Belliard is a few points of on-base percentage, some isolated power (both in Belliard's favor, by the way), and, of course, a few inches of height. Eckstein is white and looks like he's running hard and playing his heart out. Belliard has cornrows, keeps his jersey untucked, and wears his hat sideways, for some reason. Eckstein is gritty and feisty; Belliard is a slacker slob who couldn't find a contract in the off-season after he was an integral part of a St. Louis Cardinals World Series victory. Eckstein gets a bobblehead and World Series MVP award for a series in which he didn't have a hit until Game 3.

Every fan base likes to have its white hero. Okay. It's human nature to find the player you can identify with. But Major League Baseball, on the eve of the World Series, ran a poll on its Web site encouraging fans to pick their "all-hustle" player," the "role players who sacrifice for their team in often unrecognized effort." Eckstein was on the list, as were Ty Wigginton and Wes Helms. You know what was notable about the list? *Every single player was white.* (You could make an exception for Jose Valentin, though his thick mustache identifies him pretty much as a white guy.) Freaking John Mabry was on that list! (The only "role" John Mabry plays on a baseball team is "old.") But it was indicative of how we really perceive the players: Blacks are athletic, and whites hustle.

This would not be a huge deal—everybody has their own racial prejudices; personally, I can't stand the people who live in the southeast quadrant of the Northwest Territories—but the fact is, race is out there in every aspect of our sporting lives and, often, white people's major reference point for other cultures is through sports. You could say the only colors you notice are the ones on the uniforms, but you'd be fooling yourself.

Though, all told, I *am* tired of the media's rampant anti-white-quarterback bias. Like Rush Limbaugh said, it's like they only notice the *bad* stuff Rex Grossman does!

I feel obliged to point out, by the way, that my sister, now fully grown, is not racist in any way. Hell, she lives in San Francisco. I'm told there are black people there.

WHY I CHEER FOR THE BUZZSAW THAT IS THE ARIZONA CARDINALS

As anyone who has ever had the misfortune to date me knows, I'm a quivering ball of weirdness. Here's a quick checklist:

- Terrified by chewing gum.
- Obsessed with Meat Loaf and REO Speedwagon in a way that is not even the slightest bit ironic.
- Completely lacking in body hair. I am barely a mammal.
- No ability to smell. (I had scarlet fever as a child. And you thought that only happened on the Oregon Trail.)
- Tendency to call everyone I meet "sir" and "ma'am."
- When in a crowded bar and forced to sit while someone standing has their derriere in my face, I pretend to order food out of the offender's ass, as if I'm sitting at a drive-through window. (This is actually quite fun; I recommend it.)

But of all my quirks, the one that stands out among my fellow sports fans, is my unabashed love of the Arizona Cardinals.

You might have heard of them—maybe. The franchise routinely ranks among the worst in all of sports. They've had one winning season in the last twenty-three years, and have an owner who wears bow ties and seems determined to run a made-to-order moneymaker into the ground. The organization named its home field "The University of Phoenix Stadium." Yeah, that one. The train wreck.

Come football season, I live and die with the Arizona Cardinals. I've been through all of it. The gruesome Gene Stallings years, the hyper but empty Dave McGinnis era, the Joe Bugel four-year stretch, the Denny Green "crown their asses" speech, even—God, it hurts to think about this—the Buddy Ryan implosion. I watch every game, with the jersey of whoever's unfortunate enough to be the starting quarterback, at a sports bar in New York City, sitting in the back, watching the one television the sympathetic bartender has afforded me. It's usually black and white, and about the size of my iPod. There hasn't been an Arizona Cardinals game worth watching in the months of November and December in more than a decade. And still, I watch, in the back room, doomed and alone in my beaten-up Stump Mitchell jersey, the laughingstock of NFL society.

This is a terrible fate, one I never would have chosen if I had, you know, *a choice.*

Growing up a contrarian in central Illinois, I made the mistake of selecting the St. Louis football Cardinals—to let you know just how sad the franchise was, it wasn't even the most popular team *named the St. Louis Cardinals,* necessitating the "football" addendum. No one was saying "the St. Louis baseball Cardinals." This made perfect sense to my ten-year-old mind. I already cheered for the baseball team; why wouldn't I root for their football equivalent? So, while everyone else in Illinois was going mad for the Bears and the Super Bowl Shuffle, I was stuck watching the Big Red go 5-11 under Jim Hanifan. (They were actually shut out 16–0 by Tampa Bay, a team that went 2-14 that season.)

This did not discourage me. I'd lucked into enough bliss from the running, stealing, AstroTurf baseball Cardinals and felt, even at the age of ten, that watching a lousy team was my penance, even a character builder. Sure they stunk now, but when they inevitably came back around and rose to the top of the communist structure of the NFL, it would be only *I* who could claim to have followed them the whole way. I would mock the bandwagon jumpers, those who had not suffered through the lean times. I just had to hang in.

Since that 1985 season, the Arizona Cardinals have had exactly *one* winning season. This is difficult to do, even if you are trying. This is a team that started *Stan Gelbaugh* for a whole season, whoever the hell that is.

And yet I have stuck with them. I do not expect points for this, ass pats, *attaboys,* or even a stick of butter with which to floss. Once I made the decision to cheer for that team, the die was cast. Because a real fan never leaves his team . . . even if they leave him.

A friend of mine told me recently how difficult his life is as a Cleveland Browns fan. He had the usual fan complaints: They don't care enough about their fans, they don't have a concrete plan in place, and (of course, the most important) they'd never made it to a Super Bowl. (As fans, we have all kinds of different whines and empty threats about our team, but it ultimately just comes down to winning, like everything does.) My friend went on for a while about this, because that's what he does. At least I think it was my friend; he was wearing one of those Dawg Pound masks at the time, so I suppose it could have been anybody.

But I had no sympathy. If he were a real fan, he would have celebrated his first Super Bowl win seven years ago . . . with the Baltimore Ravens.

See, here's the thing: Being a fan is a year-round job. At the end of the season, you've got your free agency period and then the draft and then your salary cap cut date and next thing you know, it's training camp. So, when, exactly, was I supposed to switch loyalties? Was there one day that I cared about Vai Sikahema, and another when I was supposed to just stop? I read some piece of

information about my Cardinals every day of the year. I know the
fifty-three-man roster, I know the draft picks, I know the coaching staff, I know the name of the guy who plays the mascot. It's a
full-time position, rooting for a football team . . . so how am I just
supposed to say, "All right, yesterday I cared about these players,
but now I care about these"? If something as silly as geography
guides your rooting interests, isn't it wishy-washy to move your
loyalty around just because someone realized the franchise could
make more money in Boise rather than Topeka? Yes, it's a corporation you're cheering for, but they're *your* corporation. There's
nothing rational about it; being a sports fan never has anything to
do with being rational.

But what about the St. Louis Rams, you ask? Yeah, what
about them? The Rams came to St. Louis in 1995. I simply did
not understand why St. Louis fans transferred their loyalty. Sure,
owner Bill Bidwill had left St. Louis for what was presumed at
the time to be the greener pastures of Tempe. But how does that
change *my* life? Sure, a sports team can offer civic value to a city,
but not just out of nowhere. The reason the St. Louis Cardinals
are a fixture in the city is because families like mine have patterned their entire social structures around them for decades.
How can a team just show up and suddenly have devoted fans?

And as for "abandoning" a city . . . please. On the whole,
NFL teams and their fans live in the same city about, oh,
twenty-seven days a year. A team and its fans have as much in
common as your hand and that vending machine. It's all senti-
ment. And I don't get to be angry about Bidwill and company
leaving St. Louis; hell, *I* don't live there anymore either.

So the only way to be honest with oneself is to pick a team
and stick with them. Sure, I wish I had picked a better team, but
true fans stay around, no matter what; people from Houston
should root for the Titans, people from Charlotte should root
for the Hornets, and people from Minnesota should root for the
Dallas Stars. Otherwise, you're the one who's disloyal. You're
just following whomever it is convenient to follow.

I looked at my friend and just shook my head. I didn't want to hear it; if he were a real fan, he'd have had his Super Bowl. Eight years ago, over the New York Giants. Ray Lewis was the MVP. You can look it up.

So, yeah: This is my long-winded rationalization of why I continue to put up with the Arizona Cardinals despite their desperate attempts to push me away. I'm a battered spouse who follows his team no matter how far she tries to run. My team can be in Arizona, and I can be in New York, and thanks to the satellites, I don't have to miss a game. Which is encouraging, considering I've never even *been* to Arizona. You wanna crown my ass, crown my ass.

BUY A JERSEY OF YOUR FAVORITE ROBOTIC STAT PRODUCER

In 1993, my freshman year of college at the University of Illinois Urbana-Champaign, a friend of mine named Pat, a sophomore at the university and a fellow resident of my hometown of Mattoon, called me and asked if I'd be interested in joining a "keeper" fantasy football league with some other Illini Mattoonians. I was a rabid sports fan, but I was yet to enter the world of fantasy sports. It didn't seem too difficult, though; I'd just choose players I know are good, toss in a guy or two from my favorite team, receive stat updates at the end of the week, see if I won. I told him I'd be honored to join. I didn't have many friends in Champaign yet, anyway.

On a Tuesday evening, as a couple of Pat's roommates played Super Tecmo Bowl in the background—the Phoenix Cardinals and running back Johnny Johnson were strangely fantastic, though Timm Rosenbach's passes tended to float—twelve of us gathered in Urbana for my first fantasy football draft. The league had already been running for a couple of years, and I was the new guy, a year younger, being indoctrinated into this world. I hadn't done much research; it was football, and man, I knew football. This would be easy.

My first three picks in this 1993 league: Cowboys quarterback Troy Aikman, Steelers running back Barry Foster, and the

Buddy Ryan–led Arizona Cardinals defense. I felt dominant, ignoring the titters around me.

You know what happened: Aikman only played four more unproductive years, Foster was quickly usurped by Jerome Bettis, and the Arizona Cardinals have made the playoffs once in the last thirteen years, with a team that didn't have a particularly good defense. My team was instantly toast, and because this was a keeper league, my team stayed toasted for a solid eight years. (I eventually figured out what was going on and took the Seth Joyner poster off my wall.) Not that I was ever able to know my standing while the games were going on; our stat collection technique involved Pat poring through Monday's *USA Today* and scribbling on the back of a bar napkin in pencil. None of us had e-mail addresses yet, and as far as I knew, the computer was something used primarily for Minesweeper.

Even though my team sucked, I was, like most of you, instantly hooked. A *Daily Illini* fantasy baseball league, dubbed the Ernie Broglio Memorial League (we were evenly split among Cardinals and Cubs fans), began two years later, and we went high-tech this time, hiring a stat service that would fax us stats from two weeks earlier every Monday.

Needless to say, it was all over for me at that point; by my senior year, I was playing fantasy *hockey*, using statistical categories that I didn't even understand. When in doubt, I just figured it was wise to pick the Russian guy with the fewest number of vowels. These days I am involved in four fantasy baseball leagues, six fantasy football leagues, and one fantasy basketball league. And I'm moderate; one friend is in double digits in all three categories. (If they had a fantasy league for players of fantasy sports, he'd be my first-round pick every year. Remarkably consistent, particularly with his inability to find a feasible way to start a conversation with a woman.) I have to limit my fantasy leagues, because if I'm not careful they will take over my life the way they've taken over the lives of so many of my friends.

The league I concentrate the most on is the one I started, a fantasy football gathering called We Are Searching for Bliss. It began when I worked at *The Sporting News* in 1998 and now, with friends from all over the country, constitutes the closest thing to a constant family atmosphere I have. I write a weekly newsletter for the league that I devote more energy to than I have to most of my jobs. It's a good way to keep in touch with old friends and update them on the goings-on. During the hardest times in my life, I have always written my league's weekly newsletter, checking in with old pals and screaming about the inability of Willis McGahee to resist the siren song of the fumble.

Fantasy football has more presence in my life than actual football; I obsess over it more, analyze it more, and talk about it more. When there's a conversational lull with any friend of mine, we don't talk about politics, or the weather, or our love lives. We also don't talk about Terrell Owens or LeBron James. We talk about our fantasy teams.

This is a perfectly natural evolution of the way fans interact with sports. Who needs actual human athletes to follow when we have their stats, stats that we control? Why bother with reality sports, you know?

FANTASY sports, thanks to the instant gratification and tinkering allowed by the Internet, have revolutionized sports, and in the best possible way: in 100 percent favor of the average fan.

Because fantasy sports are driven so much by the passion of the fan, and not by a league edict or some market element, many sports leagues have been slow to embrace the concept. Only in the last couple of years, with their hands forced by the immense popularity (and therefore profit potential) of the games, have leagues started offering fantasy football on their official sites, and they're light-years behind Yahoo! and ESPN and other online offerings. (Major League Baseball went so far as to attempt to argue that they actually *owned* the statistics produced from their games, which is akin to President Bush claiming that he owns any discussion of employment figures or the Gross Domestic Product. Every court has swiftly struck down any and all of MLB's claims.) Other than a few women who dislike football in general and therefore find the concept of fantasy football akin to one of those five-hour games of Risk they'd stumble across in the college dorms, no one considers fantasy football players statistical nerds anymore. It's too huge, and it's only getting bigger.

(A note on this: My friend Aileen, no fan of football, absolutely cannot understand fantasy football. I think she's getting caught up on the word "fantasy." Whenever she hears us talking about our fantasy football teams, she will interject, "Hey, did you just score a touchdown? Because that's how this works, right? Will, you'll say, 'Hey, I have a touchdown,' and then A.J., you'll go, 'Well, I have a field goal!' and then you just go back and forth like that. Or are there dice?" It provides us great fun to walk up to Aileen and just yell, "Touchdown! I just scored one right now!" And then I high-five her. She never gets tired of this. Really, she doesn't.)

The reason anyone even discusses the notion of fantasy sports being "nerdy" is because so many of the people who bring it up on our airwaves are former athletes, who are understandably bewildered that millions of people are enraptured by whether or not their bodies fell past the thick white line. (If they had fantasy sports for any of our regular everyday jobs, I'm convinced we'd all be paralyzed in fear. Imagine thousands of people checking for mislabeled e-mails or successful Power-Point presentations, and making money off whether or not you clocked more billable hours than Chuck down the hall. This would terrify me too.) It's becoming less and less common for athletes to betray their fear of fans who practice fantasy sports. Athletes tend to think of fans as unwashed, face-painting scream machines, which, when you consider what they tend to see in the stands every night, is understandable. When an athlete does admit to being in fantasy leagues, like Washington Redskins tight end Chris Cooley did (he went so far as to claim he sometimes rooted for opposing players because he had them on his team), he is accused of not caring enough about The Team.

But we don't need The Team anymore. We have our own teams, and they're teams that we control and are therefore closer to. It's difficult sometimes not to feel ignored by your favorite team. They can raise ticket prices, build a new stadium, bring in a slothful superstar, start playing "Cotton-Eyed Joe" during the seventh-inning stretch, sacrifice babies at midfield . . . there's all kinds of terrible things they can do. And there really isn't much you can do. You will keep giving them your money because you are a fan, and the fundamental concept of a fan is someone who will shell out money for pretty much whatever. (Imagine if you chose your shoes based entirely on what kind of shoes your father bought growing up. I hope you enjoy your Buster Browns.) But with a fantasy team, you are in charge. The emotional ties are yours and yours only; you can pick and choose whom you are attached to, whom you want around, and whom you just don't want to look at anymore. It's the next generation of fan; sports is becoming a Choose Your Own Adventure. Pissed that the Cubs signed Mark DeRosa? No worries: You don't have to have him on *your* team.

In Sam Walker's wonderful book *Fantasyland,* which documents the explosion of fantasy baseball over the last decade, he tells the story of Steve Moyer, founder of Baseball Info Solutions, a fantasy sports service. Moyer has no qualms—he doesn't care about any "teams" in a conventional sense. He only cares about his own. This doesn't make him less of a baseball fan, he argues; he loves baseball more than he loves just about anything else. He just doesn't see any particular need to tie himself to one franchise in what would be an irrational connection to what is really just a corporation that happens to have a singular color scheme. He takes this extremely far, to the point that he will purposely buy unpopular jerseys, like a Scott Rolen Phillies jersey, or a Vince Coleman Mets jersey, because they're cheaper and no one else wants them.

This makes absolute sense—even if it's a theory I can't necessarily subscribe to myself, if only due to emotional, geographic ties that are etched in my DNA; this is why I always find a way to draft Joe McEwing, who is, alternately, scrappy, gritty, gutty, and/or plucky—because it takes sentimentality out of the discussion, and any discussion of sports these days requires a surgical removal of sentimentality. If you like a jersey, you buy it. If you like a player, you draft him. If you don't like him, you cut him. It's the ultimate in fan empowerment.

This is easier contemplated than accomplished, of course. All fantasy players have faced the awful experience of having one of their pitchers face their favorite boyhood team. As usual, what I believe in theory—that it's all just laundry, that rooting for the Cardinals is just like rooting for Nike or Barnes and Noble—tends to take a backseat once emotions get involved. When I own Tom Glavine, and he's facing the Cardinals, I tend to bench him. It removes the whole dilemma from the equation. It's all about making it easier on myself, I think.

I have some friends who consider themselves purists, who believe fantasy sports devalue the games, with fans looking no deeper than statistics. *It's not about whether that wide receiver scored today,* exclaim the purists, *it's about whether or not the left tackle was taking care of the outside blitzer.* These are the type of fans who are often surrounded by game charts, and they are the types of fans who are often sitting at the bar alone. Of *course* fantasy sports don't accurately reflect the games on the fields. If we wanted that, we'd put on some tight pants and become a coach. (I've always wanted to own a whistle, now that you mention it.) The simplicity of fantasy sports is what makes them great; remember, we have enough going on in our lives.

Life is complicated; the beauty of sports is in its blacks, whites, and agate text. Who *cares* how my team won? All that matters is that they did. Fantasy sports speak to this splendidly. I have the satisfaction of a victory or the frustration of a defeat, and it was all directly attributable to my own choices. What more can you ask for from any life endeavor, really?

Therefore, actual athletes and participants become what, frankly, they have been all along: robotic producers of statistics. This is not a terrible thing. This is being realistic in the face of the soft-focus human-interest stories shown during any network telecast. It much more accurately reflects the connection we have with athletes.

Remember when Terrell Owens may or may not have attempted to kill himself in September 2006? With all that talk about the ability of organized sports to diagnose and treat mental illness within its ranks (and the still-unanswered question of why Owens would hire such an incompetent publicist), the average fan had one major unspoken question: Is he going to be able to play Sunday, or not? Whether or not we said it, we were thinking it. Why wouldn't we?

Immediately after the Owens topic came up on Deadspin, many commenters and observers found it crass that we would be more concerned about our fantasy teams than the fragile mind of Terrell Owens. But, honestly, why *should* we care about Owens's mental state? Nothing in his twisted brain affects our lives in even the slightest way . . . except for whether or not we have him on our fantasy team. He's a player; is he playing or not?

This is the place that athletes hold in our lives. They provide entertainment. Cincinnati Reds utility man Ryan Freel might have an imaginary friend named Farney—whom he blames for all the times he runs recklessly into walls—but if he's not stealing bases and scoring runs, what do we care about that? Fantasy sports distill the athletic process to the core and treat athletes with the reverence that they deserve—none. They *are* robotic stat producers, and no matter how much they might scream and carry on, that's all the use we really have for them. If they did not produce statistics and/or victories, they would be just another one of the billions of human beings we don't take into account. They can run fast and jump and hit things; our only concern is whether or not they will be doing that the next time we watch.

Outside of the production of stats, athletes are pointless. Fantasy sports are honest—cold, but honest—about the relationship between the games and their fans, and for that, they should be celebrated.

That said . . . there's one major drawback to investing all your sports capital into fantasy sports. When your team stinks, there's no one to boo but yourself. And this is not a recommended activity. Bad for the soul.

WHAT ATHLETES ARE TALKING ABOUT WHEN THEY'RE TALKING ABOUT GOD

The surprise winner of the 2007 Masters was Zach Johnson, a quiet, unassuming Iowan who had never so much as finished in the top 15 of any previous major. (In his eleven majors up to that point, he had only made the cut four times.) His win was shocking—he held off Tiger Woods, after all—and one of those rare underdog moments in sports that we claim inspires us, even while we keep buying any product with Tiger's name on it. After he sank his final putt on the eighteenth hole, a gaggle of golf reporters surrounded him, notebooks in hand, ready to document his initial reaction to this breathtaking event. This was the first time most reporters had ever spoken to Johnson; what would he say after such a groundbreaking achievement? Reporters, along with millions of viewers watching at home, stood waiting to hear the plucky new champ wax rhapsodic on his victory.

CBS stuck the microphone in Johnson's face. He took a deep breath and spoke.

"I was not alone out there. Jesus was with me every step of the way." He then started to cry.

The reaction was immediate. Jim Nantz audibly sighed—you could almost *hear* his microphone droop—and the swarm of reporters, as recounted by the *Washington Post*'s Sally Jenkins, "lifted our pens up from our notebooks and waited for him to say something we could write about."

Indianapolis Colts coach Tony Dungy inspired a similar reaction when he thanked Jesus after his team won the Super Bowl last year. Fans don't like it when an athlete starts quoting God or thanking Jesus for his success, and, occasionally, with good reason. It's difficult not to be irked when you notice that the winning team tends to thank the Good Lord at a disproportionately higher rate than the losing team does. Why, we wonder, does Jesus care about a stupid sporting event played by a bunch of rich people? Did the Bears lose because Jesus just liked the Colts more? Are the Colts morally superior to the Bears? (If so, Bears fans can unite and blame Tank Johnson, though Brian Urlacher also didn't do himself any celestial favors by sleeping with Paris Hilton.) It is reasonable to ask Johnson, in the wake of his comment, what he thinks Tiger Woods did to piss Jesus off to the point that He made him lose the tournament.

It is worth noting, however, that the fans who most often complain about athletes quoting God tend not to be Christians themselves, and therefore resent the world of religion and its invasion of the otherwise secular sporting world. No Christian would be confused by Johnson's shout-out to the Lord. While we see someone acting as if he won because Jesus Christ decided he deserved to win more than the other guy—as if Jesus said, "Hey, Johnson's a nice guy, let's move his ball closer to the cup on that drive"—a Christian sees it as something else entirely—that is, a humble acknowledgment that nothing any person does can ever be attributable to themselves. It's a guard against pride.

Witness what Christian blog Redeeming Prufrock wrote about Johnson's comments right after his win:

> It seemed that Johnson diverted the glory for his victory towards Jesus because it never crossed his mind not to. In the

midst of great personal accomplishment, of years of work ethic paying off, of the achievement of the American dream, Johnson refused to feed his pride because he knew of his own inadequacy. But what's more, he also knew of the perfect sufficiency of the one he called Lord.

What's more, living this life of relationship with Christ meant that Zach could not help but share the Gospel with the watching world. On Sunday, he told the truth, that the strength for his victory came from the presence of his Jesus. Certainly this ruffled some feathers. Yet for Zach, no other way seemed possible. He answered the question honestly, and in doing so, tactfully told the world about the goodness of God in his life. If you will permit me another dirty word often deserving of a technical foul, he evangelized.

Consider the mind-set of athletes like Johnson, or Dungy, or Kurt Warner. Their Christianity isn't some peripheral aspect to their life; it *is* their life. We might not agree, but as they see it, everything they do, from showing up at church on Sunday, to buying meat, to scoring a touchdown, is done for the glory of Christ. They don't thank Jesus for helping them win a game; they thank Jesus for *everything*. What sound like mealy-mouthed platitudes to us are heartfelt beliefs for them. And from Johnson's perspective, that moment of victory is likely to be his major moment on a national stage. One of the founding principles of Christianity is to spread the gospel of Christ. This was Johnson's big opportunity. While the reporters were sighing and waiting for him to say something they could *use*, millions of Christians at home were awed by Johnson's humility in the name of Christ. Why this bothers us more than, say, LeBron James flashing his Nike logo every time he talks to Jim Gray is bewildering.

I'm not coming from a Christian perspective here; a brief flirtation with youth ministry back in the early '90s was derailed by the emergence of breasts everywhere I looked. (Until marriage? *Really?* The math didn't work out well for me there, not at all.) And I certainly don't mean to imply that there isn't a handful of mock Christians out there in the sports world, hypocrites who praise Jesus when they win, blame the refs when they lose, and hope their corporate sponsors don't find out about all the seeds they've spread across this great land. (My favorite story about sports life on the road came from a female friend of mine who was briefly dating an assistant coach. She said that when she went to visit him at a hotel, an official representative of the team was handing out room assignments to a line full of hopeful groupies. "You're here to see Smith? Room 139. Who's here to see Johnson? You? 252." That team employee deserves a raise.)

I understand how frustrating this is; the hypocrites who genuinely believe that Christ actually cares about the result of a sporting event (and, in fact, helped a team win)—as opposed to the legitimate Christians who believe their victories are simply for the glory of God—tend to spoil the brew on this issue. But there is a difference between those guys and Zack Johnson. Whether you agree with the Zach Johnsons or not, though, God is their life's major focus. Just because they believe Jesus was with them while they won, that doesn't mean they believe Jesus was *only* with them.

We recoil when we hear athletes talk about God, but most really believe. *You* don't need to believe Jesus knows what the Vegas betting odds are to make some sense out of all this.

FANTANKING IS BAD FOR THE HEART

Neal Pollack once wrote an excellent essay for *Slate* about "The Cult of the General Manager." The premise was that, in the era of celebrity general managers like Theo Epstein and Billy Beane, the average fan spends more time thinking about roster construction than he or she does about the players themselves. "Sports commercials used to encourage people to drink beer to 'bring out your best' on the amateur football field, or implied that the right deodorant would get you laid as often as Joe Namath," he wrote. "But the interface between consumer and sports has changed. When sports-loving kids stare wistfully into the distance now, they're not daydreaming about being like Mike or coming to the plate in the bottom of the ninth with the bases loaded. No, they're dreaming about pulling off a deadline trade or finding a 'sleeper' in the low rounds of the draft." This is an overstatement—my eight-year-old cousin is impersonating Albert Pujols's batting stance, not Billy Beane's worried stare in the Oakland Coliseum skybox—but the principle holds true. In a world in which we obsess about our fantasy teams, it's only natural that we'd start obsessing about salary caps and franchise tags. Look at Theo Epstein; he looks like about ten guys I went to college with. Who's to say he can be a general manager and I can't?

The problem is that the cult of the celebrity manager has led to a serious plague on the world of sports fandom, and it's called "Fantanking." The term, coined by Bill Simmons as he lamented the collapse of his Boston Celtics, involves rooting for your team to lose when you know they have no chance at a championship. The idea is that the more your team loses, the better a draft pick they will have the next season, and the greater opportunity they'll have for success down the line. It's exchanging the present for the future. Who cares about a meaningless game in April if it means drafting the next hot star?

There's no question that teams, when the season is lost, take tiny measures to minimize the opportunity for victory. It's not the players who do it; they're programmed to try to win from birth. (It's not like they're purposely missing dunks or striking out.) It's the coaches and the front offices. They'll deactivate players who might contribute to late-season wins, or, more often, put lineups on the court that guarantee failure. A four-guard lineup, for example, or an undersized power forward playing center, that kind of thing. They're trying to save their jobs here, and nothing helps more to save a job than drafting a superstar.

But that doesn't mean we have to fall prey to the same temptations. Believe me, I *understand.* I'm a fan of the Arizona Cardinals, a team that has played maybe four meaningful games in December over the last twenty years. There's a little voice in the back of my head, every season, that tells me I should be happy that Arizona keeps losing late, that each loss pushes them up another spot in the next year's draft, that I'm just *planning for the future.*

And then I sit down to watch a game, and I just can't bring myself to do it. The Arizona Cardinals play sixteen days out of the year; if I'm rooting against them for five (or more) of those days, how can I possibly call myself a fan of that team? Not much is required of me as a fan. The only requirement, really, is hoping that my team wins. It is the fundamental aspect of being a fan. It's not reasonable to root for losses; it's *sadistic.*

Never mind the fact that fantanking rarely works. It sounds great in theory, but if your team is in a position where it could possibly have the top draft pick the next season, the odds are good that the management of your team is not of a very high caliber. Fantanking is bargaining what is certain for what is uncertain; it's turning real sports into fantasy sports. And it certainly didn't help the Celtics.

It also takes so much joy out of the process. I don't care how much you think it's for your team's ultimate good, if you actually are *pleased* when you sit down and watch an entire game of your team losing . . . I seriously question whether you can legitimately be called a fan.

Four years ago, my Cardinals played the Minnesota Vikings on the last weekend of the season. The Vikings were playing for a playoff spot; the Cardinals were one loss away from the No. 1 overall pick. As time ran out, Arizona quarterback Josh McCown hit Nate Poole in the end zone for a game-winning touchdown. In the long-term fantanking sense, this was a devastating defeat for me; the touchdown and subsequent win cost Arizona two spots in the draft (ultimately missing out on . . . Eli Manning!). Arizona had absolutely nothing to gain from that victory; it was, essentially, against the team's better interests.

None of this dawned on me, though, as I ran through the sports bar, screaming and high-fiving anyone I could find. My team had won. I was happy. It was as basic and pure and real as anything. Remember the basic rule of sports fandom: If your team wins, you are happy, and if they lose, you are sad. It's black and white. There's no need to inject gray where there isn't any. Go team.

RULES FOR FANS: HOW NOT TO BE A JERK AT A BASEBALL GAME

1. *Don't get in people's way.* In most hockey arenas, ushers won't allow you to find your seat until a break in play. Baseball ushers have no such directive, so you're on your own. Ideally, wait until the end of a half-inning, or at least until a visit from the pitching coach. If you can't do that, at least wait until an at-bat is over, and haul ass. Oh, and we don't live in England, so stay on the right side of the aisle, whether you're moving up or down. If an at-bat starts while you're en route, crouch down so the people behind you can see, and don't ask everyone in the row to stand up until the at-bat is completed.

2. *Don't kill the child behind you.* As much as you might like to, you can't slap the child kicking your chair behind you. He's a kid, so you're gonna have to ignore the first couple of taps, but once it becomes unbearable, slowly turn your head in a nonthreatening, friendly matter and see if you can make light eye contact with a parent. If the parent is a good-hearted person, he or she will shrug his or her shoulders apologetically and gently admonish the child. If the parent is coldhearted, you might have to take matters into your own hands. Without being rude, engage the child with a joke or a

"Who's your favorite player?" line. (Also acceptable: giving the child something to distract him, like a program or a blunt object.) If the parent continues to ignore you both, and the child won't move, find another seat. No matter how annoying he is, if you confront him, you're the bad guy.

3. *Be nice to the people who sneaked into your nicer seats because you were late.* Hey, we've all moved to better seats before, so please don't be a smug classist about it and start huffing and puffing. Just because you have more money than you used to doesn't give you the right to be an asshole. I tend to take the "hey, we're all friends here" approach. Even though you haven't done anything wrong, go ahead and be nice, ticket stub in hand, and gently point out that you think these might be yours. Never show up with the "get out, buddy, I paid for these" demeanor; they know they're in the wrong seats and will probably gracefully bow out. They will move, because the world is a good place full of people with pure hearts and warm souls.

4. *Be smart about moving to better seats yourself.* Unless it's an afternoon game that has suffered through a two-hour rain delay to thin out the crowd, don't move down to better seats before the fifth inning. When you're convinced the ticket holders aren't showing up, make sure the usher who is theoretically in charge of keeping you from the field level is occupied. Then just sneak by with your ticket in hand so it looks like you know what you're doing. If you plan on being drunk and obnoxious, that's fine, but don't sit next to a family, who will have every right to report you. Once you're in your newly adopted seats, stay there; if you keep moving every ten minutes, you will arouse suspicion, and you'll miss the game. Oh, and only take better seats if they're open *on the aisle.* Don't be an annoying faker who makes people move out of the way to

get to seats you don't own. And, without question, always, *always*, when confronted by an usher, make sure you take out your ticket, eye it closely, and look completely confused and flummoxed that, jeez, you must have taken a wrong turn, because you were *sure* these were your seats. The usher will be on to your act, but this Kabuki theater is necessary in order to preserve the natural order of things.

5. *Careful when ordering that beer from the middle of the aisle.* To attract the attention of a vendor, don't start waving your arms wildly and acting all frustrated; he wants to sell those beers as badly as you want to drink them. The key to passing your money down the aisle is to make it a one-way transaction; if at all possible, have exact change (plus tip) the first time so the ten people between you and the vendor don't have to pass the money back as well as forward. Never, ever make the guy four seats down pass you small change.

6. *Know whom you're knocking over for the foul ball.* Whom can you push out of the way for a pop fly in the stands? A helpful guide:

   Kids: No.
   The elderly: No.
   The disabled: No.
   Everyone else: Yes.
   Any grown man wearing a glove: Oh, God, yes.

7. *You might have to let it go with the loud guy in your section.* Don't try to be a hero: The screaming man wants attention, and trying to engage him is only going to make matters worse. Give him an inning to shout himself out; if he doesn't start to quiet down, try to make eye contact with other people in your section to put together a coalition of the

willing. (You don't want to be the one person tugging on the usher's sleeve.) Once enough fellow fans have had enough, subtly flag down an usher. Ushers have enough to worry about and will be happy to shush the fellow to get him out of their hair. All told, it's best to just *be* the loud person.

8. *Heckle the right way.* First off, the odds are that your seats are far away enough that the only people who will be able to hear you are the people in your section, so keep that in mind. Any racial/homophobic epithets are out of bounds, unless you are heckling Alex Rodriguez. It will be impossible to yell anything particularly clever, so don't try. Stick to the basics: This player makes too much money, this player chokes in the clutch, this player was once arrested. If you can, sneak in information that only a true fan would know.

9. *Never leave too early.* My rule is never to leave early, ever; I'll sit through a four-hour rain delay with my team down by six runs. (And this has happened.) But I recognize that not everyone feels this way. In a practical sense, sometimes it can be tough to sit through those last couple of innings of a blowout when you've got an 8 A.M. meeting the next day. Good rule of thumb is, if your team is down by more than five runs in the eighth inning, you can safely exit. No one in your section will judge you. If the game is close, *particularly* if your team is a run or two behind, it is unacceptable to leave; if people pelt you with food items, you have to accept it and display the appropriate shame.

10. *Don't bring a sign.* Seriously. If you have a sign that spells out the name of the network showing the game, you are a douchebag. I hate to be the one to tell you this, but, please, don't kill the messenger. It's just federal law.

WHY A CRAPPY FLATIRON YUPPIE BAR IS NOW THE CLOSEST THING I HAVE TO A HOME

During Game 6 of the 2006 National League Champion-ship Series between the New York Mets and my beloved St. Louis Cardinals, I sat in the upper tier of Shea Stadium, wear-ing a blue Cardinals hat, carrying my scorebook, and feeling absolutely miserable.

It wasn't just that the Cardinals were about to lose, though obviously that was the precipitating event. At the beginning of the night, I had attempted to reach a state of agreeable Zen. It was only Game 6, and the Cards were up 3–2. If they lost, they'd still have tomorrow. But if they *won* . . . well, I would be there to see the Cardinals clinch a trip to the World Series. That was impossible to turn down.

But as I sat there, surrounded by Mets fans, most of whom were tossing peanut shells at my Cardinals hat—I'd stupidly thought wearing a blue one would help me blend in—watching my Birds' limp ninth-inning rally peter out . . . well, at that moment, Shea Stadium seemed like the last place on earth I wanted to be. It was bad enough that I had chosen to *live* in this city, away from my screaming red-sweater masses in St. Louis. What the hell was I doing here, in the belly of the beast?

Game 7 was the next night. My friend, who had procured

the tickets for us, said she could probably snag a couple more for the deciding game. To my surprise, I shook my head.

"I'm sorry," I said, "but I need to be among my own people."

BEING a fan of a specific franchise is a tricky business, as we've discussed elsewhere. And it's particularly tricky if you no longer live in your team's city. When I moved to New York in 2000, the first question—well, it wasn't exactly a *question*—my father had for me was, "If you get out there and become a god-damned Yankees fan, don't bother coming home for Christmas."

It's easier now to cheer for an out-of-town team, thanks to digital cable and the Web and free long-distance calling plans. If you can stay devoted to a franchise, it's not too difficult to keep abreast with what's going on. And for the first six years of my life in New York, I hadn't encountered any serious problems. I was happy in my solitary Cardinals life. When the stressful madness of postseason baseball came around, I spent my time wearing holes into my apartment floor, yelling at the television, throwing soft objects across the room, and generally feeling sane only because no one else could see me. (Every year I watch the Cardinals in the postseason, and the sleepless nights, the sunken disposition, the knuckle bruises from punching anything that won't punch back, it all makes me wonder why I put myself through this. *This is supposed to be fun? This is "rec-reation"?*) Being a Cardinals fan in New York City was something that made me different, unique, special; it was a part of my persona as much as having floppy hair and smelling vaguely of ether.

But this series was another animal entirely. This was a land-mark season for the Mets, and suddenly their fans were every-where. I made the mistake of wearing a Cardinals T-shirt while jogging through Queens; people actually yelled up at me from the Brooklyn-Queens Expressway *while I was jogging on an overpass.* Trusted friends whose Mets fandom had never stood in our way before were refusing to return my phone calls. Every day that I picked up a newspaper, some balding middle-aged man was telling me why Albert Pujols was an asshole and how all Cardinals fans were rubes and used leaves as toilet paper. The city that I loved, that I had claimed as my home, was violently rejecting all that I held dear. I was suddenly a pariah.

A couple of non-Mets friends of mine had asked if I wanted to watch Game 7 with them. But a game this important—not just to the Cardinals, but to *me,* to my jarring referendum on New York City that had been thrust in my face—could not be viewed while putting up with social chitchat. I had to find some Cardinals fans. But who? I didn't know any Cardinals fans in the city; the Cardinals are so personal and so religious to me that I had claimed them entirely to myself and deemed casual "the Cardinals are my favorite team in the *National* League!" fans unworthy. I needed to connect; I needed someone who cared as much as I did.

I remembered an e-mail someone had sent a few weeks earlier, at the start of the playoffs, a New York resident who read Deadspin and had been wondering if there were any places Cardinals fans congregated for the playoffs. I had written her back then and told her that I didn't know and that I wasn't all that interested anyway; the vital Cardinals games, I'd felt, were best witnessed alone. But alone was the last thing I wanted to be at this point. I shot her an e-mail and asked if she'd ever found a place. She wrote me back immediately: "A few of us have been going to Dewey's in the Flatiron District. There aren't many of us, but we've been growing as the series has gone on. We could use you. We need to drown out the Mets fans. They're a lot meaner than Cardinals fans."

I knew nothing about any of these people except that they were Cardinals fans. That was enough. I put on my Rick Ankiel jersey, grabbed my cap, and hopped on the subway. I'd like to say that it was vital to me at the time to find out which home was my *real* home and which place I was just visiting, to discover whether I could keep my roots in this suddenly terrifying city . . . but mostly, I was just worried about whether or not Jeff Suppan could keep the ball down against Carlos Delgado.

Knowing my nerves needed alcohol fast, I showed up at the bar an hour before first pitch and saddled up to the bar. A woman bartender wearing a Yankees hat smiled at me.

"There's more of you Cardinals fans here every game."

"It's a big game tonight." (I have no idea if this is was an appropriate response. They were the only five words in my brain at the time.)

"Well, everyone's been very well behaved."

"We're nice people."

I sipped a Bud Light—and by "sipped" I mean "finished in three swigs"—and ordered another. A man sat down next to me. I noticed he was wearing a Cardinals hat.

"Hey, I'm Will."

"I'm Mike."

"You ready for this tonight?"

"No, man. Not at all."

And just like that, Mike and I were best friends. We talked nonstop for the next forty-five minutes about every aspect of the game we were about to see. Then we veered into Cardinals history, our favorite players, the games we were there to see in person, the heartbreakers, Willie McGee, everything. We both talked fast, like we had been waiting to talk to someone about this for a while, like we were too nervous to do anything but just yammer to ease some of the stress on the synapses. We looked up at the television; first pitch was in ten minutes. Then we looked behind us.

The bar was packed with people wearing glorious red. Living in NYC, away from other Cardinals fans, I have this urge, every time I see someone on the street wearing a Cardinals hat or shirt, to give them a wave and yell "Go Birds!" Most of the time, they look at me like I'm crazy; people don't think about what they're wearing when they're wearing it, and I like to think they remember a few blocks down the street, and smile.

But this was overstimulating. I wanted to high-five everyone, to plunge myself into the crowd like the lead singer at a rock concert. Suddenly, in New York City, I was surrounded by my own people, vagabonds, people adrift and desperate for a common bond. A man down the bar, wearing a Mets hat, noticed the group. "Jesus, where did *these* people come from?" He felt like a minority in his own city. I understood how he felt, and had no sympathy.

By first pitch, our group had turned into a collective cube of angst. I was grabbing the shoulders and hands of strangers. I've been to bars just outside Busch Stadium, where everyone is a Cardinals fan, but this had a different feel, as if we were all on some secluded island where only we could survive. There was no joy, not yet; just people who had gone through a week of anguish and dislocation, leaning on one another.

I'm not sure how well you remember Game 7 of the NLCS, but it was not one of those games in which you have much opportunity for relaxation or, you know, *breathing*. The score was tied at 1 almost throughout, with Suppan and Oliver Perez taking turns rifling through the order. It was raining, I remember that, and every time we'd sneak out for a cigarette break—you never smoke a cigarette quicker than when you can't possibly miss a single playoff pitch—we couldn't believe they were playing a baseball game of this much importance just a few miles away. The game might as well have been beamed to us from the moon, or from our hometown driveways. We had no perspective anymore.

To make this playoff historically relevant, it would need a signature moment, a play that would never leave the memory of even casual fans. This game had four.

Endy Chavez's catch of Scott Rolen's near home run. When this happened, it was as if someone had rolled a giant bowling ball into the bar and decapacitated all of us. I fell to the floor and dropped my face into a mysterious liquid for about ten seconds. When I looked up, there were at least ten other Cardinals fans down there with me.

Jeff Suppan pitching out of a bases-loaded jam. After Rolen made an I-can't-believe-I-missed-that-homer throwing error, Suppan was forced to strike out Jose Valentin and get Endy Chavez to fly out to keep the game tied. At this point, the game was no longer fun, just a series of feats of strength. I would like to say that, while all this was going on, this gathering of people became lifelong companions. But this didn't happen, yet. Mostly, we were just holding on to each other as tight as we could.

Yadier Molina's home run. Molina hit his fly ball to the same part of the field Rolen had hit his, and we knew better than to cheer too early. We gritted our teeth and stared silently. When the ball went over the wall, the room exploded. *Release.* Everyone hugged everyone, and, with little concept of what was happening, we all ended up on the floor again, screaming.

And then . . . *the bottom of the ninth.* Between innings, I called my father in Mattoon.

"Jesus Christ."

"Jesus Christ."

"Where are you, anyway? It's loud there."

"It's unbelievable. I'm at a bar with nothing but Cardinals fans. It's like Woodstock here, except if everyone took Bud Light instead of acid."

"Wait, you mean you're at a bar in New York and it's all Cardinals fans? I didn't know New York had those."

"Me neither, Dad . . . I'll call you if they pull this off."

As you probably remember, the Mets ended up loading the bases for Carlos Beltran, facing rookie closer Adam Wainwright. Then, on three pitches, including the last one, in which Beltran just watched one of the most amazing curveballs I've ever seen pass by him—a Deadspin commenter would point out that, because of his motionlessness, Beltran was in no danger of being attacked by a Tyrannosaurus Rex—a strikeout, and then jubilation, and a biblical unleashing of pent-up humanity. The room was suddenly set on fire.

Suddenly, the bar wheeled out cheap champagne—had we seen it earlier, we would have rejected it, out of fear of a jinx—and we grabbed at it like infants to a mother's breast. (Except we had teeth, and we were using them.) I shook up two bottles and sprayed anybody in sight, then poured a bottle over my own head. Then I grabbed two more and repeated the process.

The madness continued for about two hours, full of requisite interjections of "YAHHHHHHH!!!!!!" and "AGGGGGGH-HHHH!!!!" and "WOOOOOOOO!!!!" Everyone in the bar was immediately bonded for life at that point, and we busted out digital cameras and Kodaks and anything to help us record what was happening. I kissed a woman I had never seen and might have been standing next to her husband, who just smiled and danced.

The night wore on, and nobody stopped screaming until about 3 A.M. (Somewhere, out there on the Internet, there is a video of me dancing in the rain after this game. In any other context, this would be embarrassing, but I think anyone who has witnessed their team clinch a World Series trip can understand.) Around 3, people weren't calmed down as much as they were wistful. The night began to take on the feel of the last night of summer camp, when a bunch of people who'd been thrown into a universe so different from the one they normally lived in eventually understand they'll have to head back to the real world soon, and just really don't want to let go. I had already booked tickets to go home to Illinois for the World Series—it would have been a miserable week had the Mets won—because I knew if I was going to watch this game with stand-ins from home, for the World Series I would need the real thing.

As we accepted that it was time to leave—we had to go to *work* the next day!—everyone made plans to meet again for

Game 1 of the World Series, an outing I knew I'd miss. But mostly, everyone just hung on, not wanting to go back to our New York lives. For one night, we lived in the Midwest Embassy, the Cardinals Fan Oasis, where everyone understood one another (even if we didn't know each other's names). We all hugged again, and yelled out one more "Let's Go Cardinals!" cheer. For that night, we were at home.

AS you might have heard, the Cardinals ended up winning the World Series. I was at the clinching Game 5, and after all *that* screaming was done, I did, actually, think of my friends at the Cardinals bar, how much fun they must have been having. While actually home, I was thinking of my virtual home . . . and thinking about how much I couldn't wait to go back to it.

Last April, the 2007 baseball season began on a Sunday night, in Busch Stadium, against the New York Mets. This became, of course, a reunion for all of us. We all met up an hour before first pitch. It was a celebration of the Cardinals' championship, but mostly, it was a way to try to relive that night. I hadn't seen or corresponded with any of them since. I was afraid something would spoil.

I walked in, alone, wearing my Ankiel jersey and blue Cards cap. I immediately came across my old pal Mike, who smiled, walked up to me, and shook my hand.

"Good to see, you, man."

"You too."

(Awkward silence.)

"How are things?"

"Good, good. Cardinals won the World Series, you know."

"I know. That was good."

Everyone became reacquainted, but it was all stilted, strange, confused. It didn't help that the Cardinals fell behind early and never recovered. Around the fifth inning, after more difficult conversations, Mike walked up to me.

"So, you know, it's weird. I'm here tonight, and I'm shaking people's hands and making small talk like I always do, and it feels entirely wrong."

"I know. Why do you think that is?"

"Why? Well, Jesus, it's kind of odd to be all formal again with people when I look at them and just think, 'Christ, I've been to third base with every single one of you people.'"

I laughed, long and hard, and suggested we do a shot. We did, and then our group did, and then we were back again, inside of our synthetic bubble of a home. The Cardinals lost, and we didn't care; the game didn't matter anymore. What mattered was that we had found something that would be here to remind us who we are and where we came from. We could live our regular lives outside of the Cardinals bar, and we would do all the regular things that life requires of us, but we knew that we could always come back to our home. The Midwest Embassy.

We now hit the place up every month, no matter how the Cardinals are playing. A couple of the group members are dating each other. The Cardinals are our secret handshake. No longer are we alone out here. You can be a fan of any team, anywhere, but the bonds that connect us sometimes need to be experienced with others. We can leave St. Louis, but the Cardinals can never leave us . . . and now, we're all stuck with each other. None of us would have it any other way.

That's what happens when you go to third base, I guess. Go Birds.

BARBARO: THE HORSE THAT CURED CANCER

I don't understand horse racing. Specifically, I don't understand why horse racing is considered a sport. The only thing that makes it a sport is that you can gamble on it, and I'm not sure that's enough; it's basically poker with oats and mounting. I'm not a gambler—watching sports is stressful enough. I don't need my livelihood to hinge on whether or not Bonzi Wells hits a late free throw—so I don't give much attention to horse racing.

That said, thanks to history and convention, we pretend that we care and end up considering the Kentucky Derby a sporting event, as if there aren't enough actual sports going on at the beginning of May. At Deadspin, I figured I'd toss in an occasional mention of the horsies, mostly to make cheap jokes about the last-place horse being fed to the first-place horse.

But in 2006, Barbaro hit.

What can I tell you about Barbaro? I ask in all seriousness: *What can I possibly tell you about Barbaro?* Barbaro, like thousands of horses before him, is a genetically blended, processed animal. It is fed, bred, and whipped to run fast, and that's pretty much it. Because we are so programmed to find some meaning behind our sporting events, we attach human qualities to horses like Barbaro, claiming that they have courage or some sort of "winning instinct." I love animals, but, you know, horses lack sentient thought. Their primary motivation is to eat, have sex, and stop the tiny man on top of them from hitting their ass. Well, come to think of it, that sometimes sums up the human experience as well.

Anyway, when Barbaro won the Kentucky Derby in 2006, the sports world, as it always does, began sniffing around for a Triple Crown winner. I don't understand why we think a horse even comprehends what it means to win the three most popular races, let alone cares, but whatever. We'll take our uplifting stories where we can find them. The real explosion of forced emotion happened when Barbaro, at the Preakness Stakes, snapped his leg and was unable to complete the race.

Typically when this happens in horse racing, especially in low-profile races, the horse is promptly euthanized for his own well-being; a horse that cannot stand or walk doesn't have much chance of survival. (After all, there are many natural predators of racehorses, like, say, the dogs of professional athletes.) But this was the Preakness, and this was Barbaro, the horse that had won the Kentucky Derby. So we turned Barbaro into a human being in a desperate battle for life.

Barbaro was treated at the University of Pennsylvania and—in a nod to the crazy Internet—a message board was put together by the staff so well-wishers could send their hopes and prayers. You can probably guess the type of person prone to doing this: mid-fifties, female, alone, surrounded by cats.

Here are some of my favorites:

> Whoa B! Aside from being soooo photogenic, you actually LOOK right into the camera, at the person taking your photo. Yup. In almost all your photos. The other horses do not! It is that something inside you that knows. WOW! XO Ronnie Veronica; Tewksbury, MA
>
> My one & only Bobby: So I heard that you had a special visitor, Edgar, & that you are back to nipping—you naughty

boy! I'm so proud of you—you just keeping munching on the apples & grass. Everyone loves you—we'd like to be nipped, too!—J Bell, 53; Pulaski, VA

How ya HOOFING? I sent a message this A.M. but don't see it. I just want to say my prayers are with you and all involved with your care. Get well. Warm weather is coming. JAN; SOUTHINGTON, CT

Angel Barbaro and Dr. R. loving companions. Angels On Earth. Who are love. Who are very beautiful. God gave you, Dr. R. a dear friend . . . Barbar. Affirmed. My Love, Dee Mirich.—Dee Mirich, 40; Merrillville, IN, U.S.A. posted on 2007–01–17 09:57:56

As tends to happen, the Deadspin commenters grabbed onto this as an infinite source of mockery and flooded the Pennsylvania board with comments, at one point nearly shutting it down. I found it rather amazing that lonely people would be so desperate for contact and meaning to the point that they would send *e-mails to a horse,* but I was clearly in the minority. Barbaro was a nominee for Sportsman of the Year—he won Deadspin's version of the award, though perhaps for different reasons—and NBC did a feature-length documentary on the "heroic" horse who "touched so many lives."

When Barbaro died, I was sad, because it's sad when a living thing dies. (It is. Honest.) But it was a horse. We are so starved for heroes that we look for them in the face of a *horse.* Rest in peace, Barbaro; we will never see another like you, except for every single day at the race track, when we see all the other animals. You'll be missed, I *guess.*

GLOSSARY

Baseball

Angels, Los Angeles of Anaheim. Geographically confused. Typically younger than your Dodgers fan; thinks Vin Scully died fifteen years ago, and very well might be correct. If the person is a real fan, he insists on using the full name at all times.

Astros, Houston. Still coping with the ill-fated "Enron Field" years, a name the stadium should be forced to use for the next thirty years. Loves Craig Biggio above all others, and thinks that Roger Clemens's kid has real potential. Absolutely loves it when Barbara Bush makes out with her husband behind home plate.

Athletics, Oakland. Convinced that the publication of *Moneyball* makes up for the fact that no one ever goes to their games and refuses to admit that the Giants could field a lineup of ferrets and still draw more fans. Probably spends *a lot* of time on the computer and has a dart board with a picture of Joe Morgan.

Blue Jays, Toronto. Is hated by teenage son for naming him "Cito." Secretly hopes to talk the wife into having sex in that hotel atop the SkyDome. Absolutely hates it when people think they speak French.

Braves, Atlanta. Stopped paying attention to the team around the sixth consecutive division title, and now wonders why Martin Prado is wearing Jeff Gordon's number. Has threatened on several occasions to murder Skip Carey, but is envious of Don Sutton's hair.

Brewers, Milwaukee. Drunk. Wears matching sweater with best friend, with the first letter of his first name stitched on the lapel. In a mountain of gambling debt thanks to the continued resilience of the bratwurst in the sausage race.

Cardinals, St. Louis. Drunk, but with a mullet and a tattoo of Whitey Herzog on his back. Thinks David Eckstein is scrappy and "plays the game the right way," while blasting Juan Encarnacion for being "lazy." Unaware that nine of his ten favorite players are white, and one is Albert Pujols. Believes Joe Buck is hilarious but still can't hold a candle to his old man. Has a shrine to Glenn Brummer.

Cubs, Chicago. In the dark of night, when all alone, can't help but admit to being secretly happier that the Cubs haven't won a World Series in one hundred years because young postcollegiate women love the whole "loser" thing. Would beat Steve Bartman's ass if given the opportunity. Currently doing a keg stand.

Devil Rays, Tampa Bay. Bewildered why, on a gorgeous and clear seventy-degree night, they have to go *inside* for a baseball game. Admits to enjoying Yankees spring training games considerably more than lounging with three thousand other bored souls at the Trop.

Diamondbacks, Arizona. Still proudly shows off that World Championship pennant but doesn't volunteer the whole "we did it because of Curt Schilling and Randy Johnson" thing. Hates the fans sitting in the hot tub behind the center field wall, only because he wishes he were there.

Dodgers, Los Angeles. Awfully tired of the whole "doesn't arrive until the fourth inning and leaves in the seventh" business, clearly a myth that ignores traffic on the 405. Mostly just pissed that the guy in the office down the hall has the Lakers tickets and he's stuck inhaling Dodger dogs in the Upper Deck. Has never quite understood what "Think Blue" is supposed to mean.

Giants, San Francisco. Loves saving the environment, hates President Bush, drives a Hybrid, marches in pro-choice rallies, owns *An Inconvenient Truth* on DVD, has lots of gay friends, and is against testing drugs on animals (unless it's for stem cell research). Thinks Barry Bonds is a persecuted American hero, and simply cannot understand why anyone might find that strange.

Indians, Cleveland. Feels frustrated that everyone thinks Bob Uecker broadcasts the games and that the slugger sacrifices chickens in the locker room. Doesn't understand why people appreciate the Cubs and Red Sox "curses" but still no one gets behind the equally doomed Indians. Can't figure out what might possibly be wrong with the smiling, cartoonish Chief Wahoo on the hats.

Mariners, Seattle. Still convinced that the team is better off with Ichiro than the Griffey/A-Rod/Unit/Piniella combo. Knows Felix Hernandez is going to blow his arm out and already prepared for it. Thinks the Japanese are smarter and cooler than we are.

Marlins, Florida. Has lots of friends who are Cubs fans and never, ever points out the two World Championships. Not quite sure where the stadium is, actually.

Mets, New York. Could win three championships in a row and will still have that daddy complex with the Yankees. Has thrown up in four different aresas of Shea Stadium; ironically, none of the incidents involved alcohol. Secretly wishes to grow Keith Hernandez's mustache. Loving Willie Randolph right now.

Nationals, Washington. Orioles fan, in fact. Keeping an open mind until the new stadium, though. Scared of Dmitri Young. Pretends Montreal never happened.

Orioles, Baltimore. Openly despises Peter Angelos but knows he's the first guy they'd hire if someone sideswiped them in a Lexus. Worships Cal Ripken, but wishes Billy Ripken would stop calling to borrow money.

Padres, San Diego. Looks like Tony Gwynn. Uses only PETCO products. Thinks it's completely awesome when team wears those camouflage uniforms. Wishes all players were named "Bip."

Phillies, Philadelphia. Hates everything about the team, including the fans. Does everything possible to make sure playing for the Phillies is a miserable experience, and then excoriates anyone who might deign to play for a franchise and fan base that makes baseball fun. Like the guy who is so mean to his girlfriend that he forces her to break up with him, then calls her a bitch for leaving him.

Pirates, Pittsburgh. Never wants to hear the name Barry Bonds again. Knows how beautiful that stadium is, yet can't quite manage to visit it. Owns Andy Van Slyke jersey, but isn't proud of it.

Rangers, Texas. Can't figure out why Roger Clemens never signed with them. Liked the younger, skinnier Sammy Sosa better. Confused how that whole "fire Buck Showalter, enjoy World Series title" strategy didn't work. Loves Chuck Norris and would like him to be the mascot.

Red Sox, Boston. The only ones on earth who still consider the Red Sox "underdogs." Owns four pink Red Sox hats left by BC coeds whose names they can't remember. Still can't figure out how to handle the whole Johnny Damon thing and deeply regrets October 2004 Halloween costume. Secretly loves *Fever Pitch*.

Reds, Cincinnati. Thinks Pete Rose should manage the team every year for the rest of his life. Didn't really mind Marge Schott's whole Nazi thing. Enjoys ignoring the class struggle. Like former mayor Jerry Springer, has paid prostitutes with a check.

Rockies, Colorado. Finally were repaid in 2007 for their years of watching Dante Bichette. Still wish Rick Reilly would stop calling them and asking if they've heard any stories about sports that made them cry.

Royals, Kansas City. Stat-obsessed, but with teams other than the Royals. Considers baseball a link to youth rather than something entirely relevant to life today. Masturbates to a picture of Bill James.

Tigers, Detroit. Pleased by the team's resurgence, if just because that means no longer having to rewatch *Tiger Town* every Christmas. Has about ten family members who look like Jim Leyland (and also smoke). Still feels stomach pain every time someone hits the ball back to a Tigers pitcher.

Twins, Minnesota. Can't understand why everyone keeps insisting Minneapolis is so *cold*. Doesn't like it when you bring up Kirby Puckett's postbaseball life. Owns at least forty Homer Hankies. Thinks he could be best friends with Joe Mauer, if only someone in the Twins front office would just give the catcher the message.

White Sox, Chicago. Knows that they'll always be the second franchise in town in an ugly stadium in a lousy neighborhood, but after that World Series, doesn't really care much anymore. Feels Ozzie Guillen thinks pretty straight, for a Mexican.

Yankees, New York. A supernatural being that has generally been described as a malevolent spirit; in Christian terms is generally understood as an angel not following God. A Yankees fan is frequently depicted as a force that may be conjured up and shakily controlled. The "good" Yankees fan, in recent use, is largely a literary device, though references to good Yankees fans can be found in Hesiod and Shakespeare. In common language, to "Yankeeize" a person means to characterize him as evil, or as the source of evil. (Paraphrased from Wikipedia.)

Basketball
Bobcats, Charlotte. Briefly thought it was cool that Michael Jordan was going to be running the team before realizing his

work as "president" would consist of chasing down women in Vegas and hanging out on the golf course looking for Nicole Brown Simpson's real killers. Also, very much regrets that Adam Morrison pick and thinks maybe he should have suspected something was amiss after the whole crying business. Enjoys that you can smoke in the airport, though.

Bucks, Milwaukee. Can't remember which senator owns the team. Wishes the Brewers would lend over one of the sausages. Still can't figure out what went wrong with Glenn Robinson. Pleased all that purple is gone. Is rather creeped out that Charlie Villanueva has no body hair. Hates the Chinese guy.

Bulls, Chicago. His collection of old Jordan posters is in storage at suburban home, which was bought with a girl he met at a Cubs game ten years ago and is just down the street from parents' house. Stuck with the team during the Tim Floyd years but still gets drunk with college buddies and talks about the night they did shots with Dennis Rodman at Harry Caray's. Thinks he plays point guard like Scott Skiles.

Cavaliers, Cleveland. Know, deep down, that LeBron is going to leave them eventually and are already mentally preparing themselves to hate him when he's a Knick. Just used Craig Ehlo as real estate agent. All told, this fan doesn't consider himself a "witness."

Celtics, Boston. The Bird jersey is a given. Still coming to terms with the fact that he rooted for his beloved team to lose for an entire second half of a season. Loves all the new stars but really does wish one of them—just one—could have been white.

Clippers, Los Angeles. Secretly owns a Kobe Bryant jersey. Enjoys the "outsider" status at the Staples Center but actually enjoys being second-tier; it makes him "unique." Wishes team still played at the L.A. Sports Arena. Can't figure out why he can never find Clippers games on the radio.

Grizzlies, Memphis. Still not quite sure they have a team, or, if they do, why.

Hawks, Atlanta. For years, thought the old logo was Pac-Man and never understood why. Never got over Lon Kruger's unibrow. Thinks Michael Vick would make an outstanding swingman when he gets out of jail.

Heat, Miami. Has a feeling the next few years are going to be ugly and kinda wishes Dwyane Wade would party a little bit more. Would love to be arrested by Shaq. Often makes it rain.

Hornets, New Orleans. Still wondering, you know, when they're gonna be able to have a house again. Did enjoy when the Hornets alternated between New Orleans and Oklahoma City, allowing the team to conceivably be called NOOCH.

Jazz, Utah. Hates it when all sports fan friends from other cities think he has multiple wives; has enough trouble finding one. Freely admits that his favorite white basketball player is Karl Malone. Really would prefer it if there weren't so many tattoos.

Kings, Sacramento. Kind of pissed Will Ferrell stole the whole cowbell thing from them. Can't figure out why Ron Artest wasn't a stabilizing influence. Wishes Arnold came to more games.

Knicks, New York. Thinks Isiah Thomas is the devil's spawn but sort of likes his popcorn. Can't figure out how Woody Allen still has such good seats even though none of his movies have made money in two decades. Realizes every time he buys a beer at the Garden that a dollar of the purchase is still going to Allan Houston. Would like daughter to someday be a Knick City Dancer, even though he must confess he'd sleep with every one of them, should the opportunity present itself. Thinks he'd like to go in on a real estate deal with Isiah, but would be worried about the daughter.

Lakers, Los Angeles. Freaked out when Jack Nicholson shaved his head. Can't figure out why Phil Jackson is still hanging around. Hates the whole Staples franchise.

Magic, Orlando. Hey, just here for the tax breaks and the steady business that came with operating on Grant Hill.

Mavericks, Dallas. Can no longer rationalize that Mark Cuban is a positive influence. Still not over that loss to the Warriors, and probably never will be. Intrigued by Dirk Nowitzki's musical choices; once actually bought a David Hasselhoff CD, and, man, it was fucking terrible.

Nets, New Jersey. Doesn't refer to the stadium as "The Meadowlands" but, instead, "Exit 120." Has nightmares about running into Jason Kidd's wife in a dark alley. Never liked Vince Carter.

Nuggets, Denver. Loves it when Kobe comes to town. Thinks Carmelo Anthony gets a bad rap, but wonders what Allen Iverson has under that arm sleeve thing. Calls his third child "Nene."

Pacers, Indiana. Thinks Peyton Manning should play point guard. Is quite pleased to have those troublemakers like Ron Artest and Stephen Jackson out of town, replaced by nice, untalented white guys like Mike Dunleavy Jr. Still incredibly depressed and confused how life led to a point that Indianapolis is home.

Pistons, Detroit. Never imagined loving Rasheed Wallace as much as this. Prefers it when the Pistons get in fights, and secretly dreams of a Red Wings–Pistons battle royale. In disbelief, roots heartily for a team led by a man named Chauncey.

Raptors, Toronto. Quite pleased, actually, that Vince Carter pulled that stunt because it opened up an outlet to release anger, in a polite Canadian way, of course. Desperate for someone to realize it's not the early '90s anymore and change that dumbass nickname.

Rockets, Houston. Proud to have Yao Ming, if just because it provides something to talk to those people who do the dry cleaning about. ("We're so worldly!") Also, enjoys the spaceship logo, which looks like some image from a '50s instructional video on what to do in case of a nuclear holocaust.

76ers, Philadelphia. Hates everything about the team, including the fans. Does everything possible to make sure playing for the 76ers is a miserable experience, and then excoriates any-one who might deign to play for a franchise and fan base that makes basketball fun. Like the guy who is so mean to his girl-friend that he forces her to break up with him, then calls her a bitch for leaving him.

Sonics, Seattle. Wondering how much flights to Oklahoma City cost. Thinks Kevin Durant could have been happy here.

Spurs, San Antonio. Enjoys milk, vanilla ice cream, *According to Jim,* the music of Garth Brooks, films starring Meg Ryan, the dulcet tones of Dr. Phil, and the V-chip. Please, no Tabasco.

Suns, Phoenix. Thinks Steve Nash might be an anti-American commie pinko, but doesn't really mind. Has at-tempted to grow Mike D'Antoni's mustache, with wildly fluctuating levels of success. Still waiting in line to audition to be the amazing trampolining Phoenix Gorilla.

Timberwolves, Minnesota. Still holding out hope that Kevin McHale is a genius. Wouldn't mind having Latrell Sprewell back, truth be told.

Trail Blazers, Portland. Endlessly frustrated that, despite Greg Oden and an exciting young team, everyone *still* calls team the "Jail Blazers."

Warriors, Golden State. Ghost riding like crazy in Oak-land, and pleased not to be associated with the tofu-chomping Deadheads of San Francisco. Stand out as the most exciting, raw fan base left in the NBA, which success will inevitably spoil. Expect the Bubble Yum Court at Wells Fargo Arena to open in the next five years, with the skyboxes actually located at center court.

Wizards, Washington. Blessed with the wonder that is Gil-bert Arenas, the type of athlete who reminds you why you be-came a sports fan in the first place. To their credit, Wizards fans understand and appreciate the gift that has been bestowed upon them, which will make it that much more tragic when Arenas inevitably signs with another team.

Football

Bears, Chicago. Ditka-themed Underoos aside, they've mostly made their peace these days with the 1985 team, focusing instead on Brian Urlacher, a monster made even more frightening by the fact that he once dated Paris Hilton (and was involved in a paternity suit with . . . Michael Flatley!). Have had just about enough of Rex Grossman's shit, though.

Bengals, Cincinnati. With the old Bengals Headed to Jail stories in their rearview mirror, now can bring the focus back to worshipping Anthony Munoz and Cris Collinsworth and inhaling chili. Would still rather see the Reds do well, though.

Bills, Buffalo. Still shell-shocked from those four Super Bowl losses, now happy to just have the team hanging around to make living in Buffalo at least slightly interesting. That is, until the team leaves for San Antonio or Los Angeles. Thinks O.J. is innocent.

Broncos, Denver. Glad to be rid of that politically mouthy Jake Plummer, a man so devoted to his cause that he slept with a team cheerleader. Hates it when you refer to the team as "the Horsies."

Browns, Cleveland. Inevitably the guy at the bar who won't stop barking in your ear. Alternately terrifying and pathetic. Imagine if this team were halfway decent. To show the level of insane fandom involved with this franchise, witness James Filiaggi, a man who was convicted in 1994 of killing his wife and was put to death in Ohio in early 2007. These were his last words: "When the Browns are in the Super Bowl in the next five years, you'll know I'm up there doing my magic." If the Browns *do* end up winning the Super Bowl in the next five years, it is suggested that you not leave your house for a while.

Buccaneers, Tampa Bay. Still giddy after the Super Bowl win a few years ago, ably erasing memories of teal and pewter. Regardless, would rather watch NASCAR.

Cardinals, Arizona. No one in their right mind becomes an Arizona Cardinals fan.

Chargers, San Diego. Will never admit it, but bought a Ryan Leaf jersey when he was drafted and it still hangs in the closet. If they're feisty, it was a blue lightning-bolt jersey. Still get fired up for games, but it's a San Diego type of fired up and typically involves a nap.

Chiefs, Kansas City. If you've ever been to Arrowhead Stadium, you know it's like being in the middle of four or five violent weather events all at once. Considering the mild-mannered denizens of Kansas City, this is the one place to unleash all rage. It would be unwise to deny them this.

Colts, Indianapolis. Like the 2006 St. Louis Cardinals, earned their championship through the foibles of others, an odd experience but one that helps them get through those cold, industrial park nights of Indianapolis. Fans often make musical selections based on what Peyton Manning has on his iPod. Silently prefer Tom Brady anyway.

Cowboys, Dallas. Has "How 'bout them Cowboys?" as cell phone ringtone. Can't figure out why they could never talk Bill Parcells into wearing the ten-gallon hat. Spends every Friday night screaming obscenities at fifteen-year-old boys for missing blocks.

Dolphins, Miami. Truly embarrassed to count Hootie as a fellow fan. When the final undefeated team loses, opens a wine cooler in honor of 1972 heroes. Only wears Isotoners.

Eagles, Philadelphia. Hates everything about the team, including the fans. Does everything possible to make sure playing for the Eagles is a miserable experience, and then excoriates anyone who might deign to play for a franchise and fan base that makes football fun. Like the guy who is so mean to his girlfriend that he forces her to break up with him, then calls her a bitch for leaving him.

Falcons, Atlanta. Silently petting their dogs, wondering what the heck happened.

49ers, San Francisco. Loves that Mike Nolan sometimes wears a tie to games. (As do I.) Religious watcher of *Dancing* *with the Stars.* Still trying to figure out how to properly rhyme a "Let's Go Prospectin'" chant.

Giants, New York. In complete denial about Eli Manning and under the misguided Yankees-inspired notion that their team should win the Super Bowl every year. Absolutely refuses to admit that they play all their games in freaking *New Jersey.*

Jaguars, Jacksonville. Astounded, to this day, that Jacksonville has a professional sports franchise.

Jets, New York. Quite proud of his ability to spell the team name.

Lions, Detroit. Convinced Matt Millen could keep a temp job for ten years. Doomed to a string of miserable Thanksgivings until the end of time.

Packers, Green Bay. Seventy-five percent of all articles of clothing are Packers-related even though extreme waiting lists ensure the impossibility of ever actually attending a game. Often learns a bit too late that it's not a smart idea to construct those cheesehead hats out of actual cheese.

Panthers, Carolina. Thinks Rae Carruth was innocent and that the Super Bowl against the Patriots was a tragic accident. Will never get truly excited until Dean Smith takes over coaching duties.

Patriots, New England. Proof that, no matter how beleaguered and inept your franchise, if you start winning on a consistent basis, you will turn into an insufferable asshole.

Raiders, Oakland. Many believe that Raiders fans wear skull and bones skeleton masks to intimidate opposing teams. In fact, they're just silently honoring owner Al Davis.

Rams, St. Louis. Pleased by the Greatest Show on Turf years. That is, until the Cardinals won the World Series; then went back to forgetting that the team exists.

Ravens, Baltimore. As I've argued before, old-time Browns fans should be ecstatic that their team finally won a Super Bowl a few years ago, though I doubt they see it that way. This team has the largest scoreboard in existence and has a defensive unit that has watched *The Wire* a few too many times. The fans lack the appropriate madness.

Redskins, Washington. You know, one would think a fan base that wears pig masks and grandmother dresses would be more sensitive about the inappropriate team name. Actually, one wouldn't.

Saints, New Orleans. Is Reggie Bush enough to make up for, you know, the whole "lack of a home" thing? As long as the French Quarter is up, no one will really care. Sure does seem like a lot of white fans are at these games, though.

Seahawks, Seattle. One of the more nondescript fan bases, they crawled out slightly during the Super Bowl year but mostly seemed frightened of the Steelers fans. It is difficult to blame them.

Steelers, Pittsburgh. Rabid, terrifying fans who once climbed the Space Needle in Seattle simply to wave a Terrible Towel. In ten years, they'll all take turns whacking Ben Roethlisberger's head with things. You know, for fun. Seriously, do not taunt a Steelers fan.

Texans, Houston. Likely will never get over passing up Vince Young, who might be rather popular in the Texas area. Will someday hire Nolan Ryan as general manager.

Titans, Tennessee. With the "Flaming Thumbtack" logo design, they end up rooting for something you can buy at Staples. Jeff Fisher will likely coach the team until the end of time, which allows me to make my third mustache reference in this glossary.

Vikings, Minnesota. Great for boating trips; just don't let them steer. And take lots of pictures. If you see one of these guys wearing those annoying Viking horns, shoot him. No jury will ever convict you.

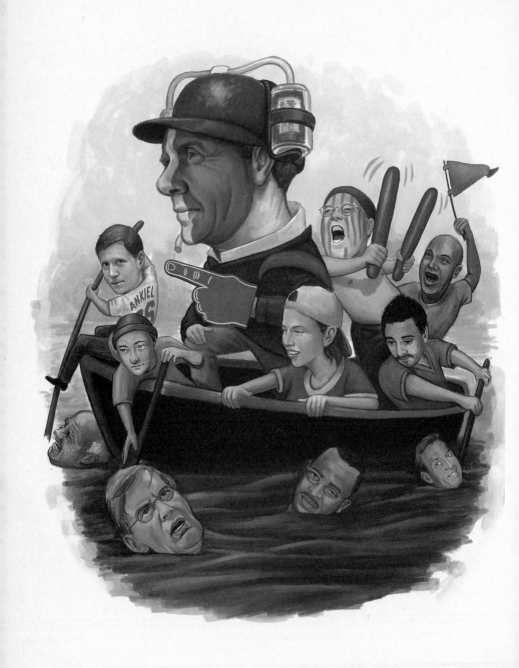

THERE IS HOPE FOR
YOU YET

In which your now defeated "author" finally cries uncle.

It is with considerable amusement that I hear the mainstays of sports journalism speak of blogs—the form of communication I use to earn a paycheck—as if they are predicting some impending apocalypse. According to them, bloggers are this rampaging band of orcs, oozing bile, and blood, banding together to take down all that we have held holy for decades. There's an element of truth to this; I have actually seen several bloggers excreting on Red Smith's grave. (I found this a bit over the top.)

What's strange about all this is that, of course, blogs are merely a medium. When Deadspin started to grow in popularity, "mainstream" types who admired the site but feared what it represented would ask me if I could be a check on smeller blogs with less sense of decorum than mine. (For example, I have a firm "no more than five fart jokes a day" rule, a maxim passed down through generations of the Leitch family. Other families are not so gauche.) I found this assumption, that somehow all sports blogs were in a kind of union and met, top secret, at some mountaintop resort. What is simultaneously compelling and terrifying about blogs is that they are only the voice of their author; there is no manifesto that all bloggers abide by. People have asked if bloggers are journalists; this question, by definition, is only answerable on a case-by-case basis. Blogs are just a way to release information. They're a fun, easy, efficient way to do it, which is why they're becoming more popular. The key to this is that everyone's a blogger; *anyone can do this.* This is not news to anyone, save for the world of sports journalism, which, traditionally, is a few years behind every other section of the paper. The sports equivalent of Watergate was the steroid scandal, and in the sports world, Deep Throat is blasted for not being devoted to his team and for trying to use the media to save his own skin. We don't really want citizen journalism in sports. It takes years for anything in the sports world to change, which, I think, is why Deadspin became popular so quickly—it signaled an actual change. (As always, I remind: Deadspin reaches about one one-hundredth of the people that ESPN does. I use the term "popular" loosely.) If it hadn't been me, it would have been somebody else. Fans were screaming out for something new.

It was little surprise, then, in October 2006, when my e-mail box received a little bundle of manna from the heavens. One of the nice things about writing about ESPN is realizing just how many nice, intelligent people work there. They're the ones with a sense of humor about themselves, the people who tend to enjoy the occasional tweaking I do. And, because you can never underestimate people's desire to bitch about their jobs, from time to time they'll send me funny, moderately embarrassing internal memos from Bristol. (I particularly enjoyed the one they sent out about half-price Diet Cokes in the ESPN cafeteria to celebrate record ratings for *Monday Night Football.*) The October 2006 memo, however, started all kinds of a ruckus. It was sent out by one of ESPN Radio's general managers, in response to a few hosts' mentioning Deadspin on the air.

Per ESPN editorial policy, the use of "underground" web sites as a source of credible information within any ESPN platform is strongly discouraged. Specifically speaking, the use of the

site "Deadspin.com" as a source of credible information is not
allowed under any circumstance. As always, any breaking hard
news story off of any site must be approved through the
proper channels.

    Please see me or another programming manager if you
have any questions or seek clarification on the web sites called
into question. Thank you.

As you could probably guess, this sent the Deadspin readers
into a tizzy. Suddenly, Deadspin readers were not a bunch of
disgruntled sports fans goofing off at work. They were Members of the Underground. As is typical of big media, the desire
to quash competition only served to stoke the flames. What
started as a way to avoid Excel spreadsheets somehow transformed into a revolution.

(For the record, I cannot grow a mustache.)

As much effect that blogs had on the sports world before, everything seemed a little different after that. More stories started showing up about how blogs were ruining everything, how they were the Wild West, how they were just—all together now—losers sitting around in their pajamas in their parents' basement. (My parents' basement has no Internet access, much to my annoyance.) It appeared that a war had indeed been declared; the ESPN "enemies list" was released, and you started hearing coaches, who had never much understood what this whole information superhighway thing was, closing practices because of "bloggers," as if they were this nebulous boogeyman lurking around every corner. (They're under your bed, Coach Weis!) Blogs became the bad guy.

More telling, though, you started seeing the larger sites— ESPN, SI, FOX Sports, Yahoo!—all starting up their *own* blogs, either buying up existing sites like True Hoop or hiring their own journalists to assume a "blog voice." This is perfectly natural, and this would have happened eventually anyway. But what matters is that they're recognizing a new way of going about this odd business of covering sports. They might be lumbering and lurching toward it, but they're trying. This is not all because of Deadspin, or the "underground." It's because of the growing influence of the everyday fan. We run these games, we make it all happen, we pay for all of it. No longer will we be so easily ignored.

The key to taking our games back rests not just with blogs— though it has been immeasurably exciting to watch talented people who never had a voice succeed just by starting up a free Blogspot site and showing off their stuff—but with recognizing our power. It's not a matter of organized fan boycotts, or somehow pretending that you don't care about sports as much as you actually do. It's about embracing the matters you *do* have control over, whether it's through blogs, or through demanding results on obvious antifan decisions like the existence of the Big

Ten Network, or just remembering the basic tenet of fandom: You are the one who decides what's important. You can ignore the Skip Baylesses, the Stephen A. Smiths, and *ESPN Baseball Sudoku*. If we prove to those who have power that we are smarter than they think we are, they will have no choice but to follow our orders. We're in charge. Let's make the rules.

Until then, though, we continue to watch our games and enjoy them for what they are: a welcome respite from the scary clawed things that we face in life every day. Because if you can't let yourself go and enjoy sports, you can't enjoy much of anything.

An open letter to John Walsh, Executive Editor, ESPN

John—
We received your resume, sir, and thank you! Currently, Deadspin is not looking for new contributors, but I appreciate your
"committement [sic] to new media" and your desire to "go to
a place where Chris Berman will stop putting his hand on my
leg." We will take your application under future account. If
you have any more questions, please have your assistant call
my parents, who will surely wake me up for your call. Unless
of course Mom's making waffles.

Will Leitch
Editor
Deadspin.com

ACKNOWLEDGMENTS

For my last book, I forgot to thank one of my closest friends, and she was mad at me for an entire calendar year. So I tell you in all seriousness: This is my least favorite section of this book to write. Oh, well, here goes: Let's see who gets pissed off this year.

First off, I must thank my agent, Kate Lee at ICM, who was with me back when I was terrified by blogs—OK, *more* terrified—and had faith in me when I couldn't even get my parents to read anything I was writing. But the reason you're holding this book is David Hirshey at HarperCollins, who saw this in me long, long before I did. So thank/blame him. Working with him, along with Kate Hamill, John Williams, and Josh Baldwin at HarperCollins, was far more fun than the editing process is ever supposed to be. Thanks also to Rachel Elinsky and Kevin Callahan for their publicity and marketing prowess, and to David Koral, senior production editor. Oh, and how about that Jim Cooke? His illustrations are the smartest, classiest, most imaginative parts of this book; I apologize for cluttering his work with all my damned words.

Before there was a Deadspin, there was a Black Table, the single most fulfilling creative undertaking I've ever, uh, undertook. (Sorry: *Undertucken*.) A. J. Daulerio, Aileen Gallagher, and Eric Gillin aren't just lifelong friends; their inspiration, talent, and hard work keep me going; make me push myself during those days I'd rather eat Bagel Bites and watch *Arrested Development* reruns.

The reason any of this has happened is because of Deadspin, of course, and there are two people primarily responsible for that. Greg Lindsay, a fellow Illini and as close a friend as I have, spoke up for me to Gawker Media when they probably had no idea who I was. He doesn't get enough credit for whatever Deadspin became, and he should. But the person who deserves the most blame for Deadspin's "success" is Lockhart Steele, my former boss at Gawker Media. I always joked that at the time Deadspin started, he was the only heterosexual non-Euro male in the company, but his support for my work far exceeded simple demographics. He was the site's lone champion from the get-go. He's also the best boss I've ever had, mainly because he left me alone and encouraged me to trust my instincts, something bosses never, ever do.

Also from the Gawker stable: Noah Robischon, Scott Kidder, Chris Batty, Richard Blakeley, Gaby Darbyshire, Meredith Katz, Tom Plunkett, and, of course, Nick Denton, not just for paying for all this, but, being a pretty excellent guy, actually.

Also, my collaborators at Deadspin deserve much love: The Mighty MJD, Matt Sussman, Unsilent Majority, J. E. Skeets, Rob Iracane, and, especially, Rick Chandler, who does more outstanding work than most will ever realize.

Now, for the long lists. I must thank the following people for getting me through the process of actually writing this thing without killing myself, or showing their support in one way or another: Amy Blair, Mike Bruno, Mike Cetera, Mandie DeVincentis, Sophie Donelson, Denny Dooley, Matt Dorfman, Jason Fry, Shari Goldhagen, Jen Hubley, Paulina Kubiak, Andy Kuhns, Chris Bergeron Linton, Matt Pitzer, Lindsay Robertson, Sue Rosenstock, Erin Schulte, Dan Shanoff, Nikki Summer. Particularly special mentions go to Tim Grierson (who has been an inspiration since junior high), Alexa Stevenson (who makes me very, very happy), and, of course, A. J. and Aileen, whom I seriously will never be able to thank enough.

The best part about writing about sports every day is that you get to meet amazing people, even if, uh, you never actually meet some of them. A huge, comprehensive list of people to thank for their support of the cause, whatever the heck the cause is:

Henry Abbott, Alex Balk, Bill Bastone, Andy Behrens, Neil Best, Carl Bialik, John Bolster, Larry Borowsky, Arie Bram, Bill Brink, Russell Brown, Mark Bryant, Jim Buzinski, Tim Cain, Will Carroll, Bryan Curtis, Jeff Daniel, Richard Deitsch, John DeVore, Brian Doolittle, Big Daddy Drew, Mary Duenwald, Stefen Fatsis, Christopher Goodman, Greg Gutfeld, Toby Harshaw, Jon Heyman, Rany Jazayerli, Sally Jenkins, George Kalogerakis, Jonah Keri, Chuck Klosterman, Dan Kois, Robert Kurson, Mark Lamster, Josh Levin, Andy Levy, Hugo Lindgren, Mark Lisanti, Michael Malice, Ben Mathis-Lilley, Herb Meeker, Brooks Melchior, Bernie Miklasz, Jamie Mottram, Keith Olbermann, Jesse Oxfeld, Jeff Passan, Whitney Pastorek, Jeff Pearlman, Mark Pesavento, Kristen Pettit, Andrea Reiher, Tom Rosinski, Josh Sabrowsky, Bill Schulz, David Shipley, Michael David Smith, Dan Steinberg, Orson Swindle, Wright Thompson, Karen Travers, Clay Travis, Matt Ufford, Sam Walker, Adrian Wojnarowski, Steve Wulf, Dave Zirin, Claire Zulkey.

And, of course, my family: My father, Bryan; my mother, Sally; and my sister, Jill. Even though I shamelessly offer up their private lives for public consumption, they still love me. And, as long as you promise not to tell them and embarrass all of us, I have to say I love them, too.